CONTENTS
SADRŽAJ

||||||||||||||||||||||||||||||||||||||

✂ P9-EAY-398

BOSNIAN-ENGLISH
ENGLISH-BOSNIAN
DICTIONARY

HIPPOCRENE CONCISE DICTIONARY

BOSNIAN-ENGLISH
ENGLISH-BOSNIAN
DICTIONARY

Nikolina S. Uzicanin

HIPPOCRENE BOOKS
New York

For information, address:
HIPPOCRENE BOOKS, INC.
171 Madison Avenue
New York, NY 10016

ISBN 0-7818-0276-8

Introduction

The Bosnian language is spoken by 4.5 million people: Muslims, Serbs and Croats living together for centuries in Bosnia and Herzegovina.

The Bosnian language is a symbiosis of the Serb and Croat Languages, which are Slavic tongues, with strong Turkish and German influences. Bosnian is written in two alphabets: Cyrillic and Roman. In either alphabet the spelling of Bosnian is more consistent phonetically than any other Slavic language. This is an orthographic language in which each sound is represented by its own letter, and each letter is pronounced consistently. Thus, words are pronounced exactly as they appear.

Bosnian vocabulary reflects the influence of Turkish and German languages. Although the Turkish influence is heavier among Muslims and Serbs, and German among Croats, some words are common to both languages, especially the names of everyday objects. For example, the Bosnian word for "neighborhood" is "komšiluk," which is Turkish; the word for "butter" is "puter," which is German.

This dictionary is primarily intended for Bosnian speakers who wish to improve their knowledge of the English language, but it is also valuable to the English speaker learning Bosnian. It has been designed to help Bosnians better comprehend American English in order to improve facility with everyday conversation and other means of communication (e.g. reading the newspaper).

Several appendices are included: common English abbreviations, a list of numerals, ordinal numbers, fractional numbers, as well as American measurements and their international (Metric System) equivalents. The appendices should serve many practical uses, helping the user with matters such as clarifying confusing abbreviations, writing checks, citing addresses, or understanding bank statements or financial reports.

Approximately 8,500 entries have been included. Words that are internationally recognized as well as words that are obscure have been omitted. For entries with more than one definition, a comma has been inserted between definitions that are synonyms and a semi-colon between definitions with completely different meanings.

The most unique feature of this dictionary consists of its "common-sense," easy-to-use system of pronunciation in the English-Bosnian section. It is designed to simplify the pronunciation of English words for Bosnian speakers as much as possible. Instead of using international phonetic symbols, Bosnian-specific symbols are used. For the long "neutral" sound, especially at the beginning of a word (abroad/e,bro:d/; earth/e,:rth/) the letter "e" followed by a comma is used. For the indication of a long sound, the colon sign (":") is used. To represent the "a" sound (open "a") as in "sand," the sign "ae" is used.

For English speakers, a guide to pronunciation is provided at the beginning of the Bosnian-English portion.

I hope that this dictionary will be your useful companion.

Nikolina Uzicanin

List of Abbreviations in Dictionary
Popis skraćenica u Rječniku

abbr.	abbreviation	skraćenica
adj.	adjective	pridjev
adv.	adverb	prilog
Am.	Americanism	amerikanizam
art.	article	član
con.	conjunction	sveza
coll.	colloquial	familijaran
fig.	figurative	figurativno
f.	feminine	ženski rod
int.	interjection	uzvik, usklik
irr.	irregular	nepravilan
m.	masculine	muški rod
n.	neuter	srednji rod (in Bosnian-English)
noun	imenica	(in English-Bosnian)
num.	numeral	broj
pl.	plural	množina
prep.	preposition	prijedlog
pron.	pronoun	zamjenica
v.	verb	glagol

BOSNIAN-ENGLISH DICTIONARY
BOSANSKO-ENGLESKI RJEČNIK

Guide to Bosnian Pronunciation

Sound in Bosnian word	Pronounced like	Same Sound in English
a	a	father
b	b	
c	tz	pretzel
ćč	ch	child
d	d	
đ(dj),dž	g	gentle
e	e	end
f	f	
g	g	go
h	h	hat
i	i	machine
j	y	you
k	k	
l	l	
lj	li	million
m	m	
n	n	new
nj	ni	opinion
o	o	note
p	p	
r	r	root
s	ss	glass
š	sh	English
t	t	
u	oo	moon
v	v	
z	z	
ž	s	treasure

A

abeceda *f.* alphabet
adaptacija *f.* adaptation
administracija *f.* administration
adresa *f.* address
adut *m.* trump (card)
advokat *m.* attorney, lawyer
afirmacija *f.* recognition
agencija *f.* agency
agonija *f.* agony
agresija *f.* aggression
akademija *f.* academy
akademski *adj.* academic
akcija *f.* action
ako *conj.* if
akrobacija *f.* acrobatics
aktivan *adj.* active
aktuelan *adj.* topical, current
akumulator *m.* battery
akustika *f.* acoustics
akutan *adj.* acute
akvarel *m.* water-color
akvarij *m.* aquarium
akviziter *m.* solicitor
alat *m.* tool
album *m.* album
alergija *f.* allergy
ali *conj.* but
alibi *m.* alibi
alimentacija *f.* alimony
alkohol *m.* alcohol
alkoholičar *m.* alcoholic
aludirati *v.* allude to

aluminij *m.* aluminium
aluzija *f.* allusion
amater *m.* amateur
ambalaža *f.* packing
ambulanta *f.* out-patient department
amnestija *f.* amnesty
amo *adv.* here, this way
amputirati *v.* amputate
analfabet *m.* illiterate
analitički *adj.* analytical
analogija *f.* analogy, parallel
ananas *m.* pineapple
anarhija *f.* anarchy
anatomija *f.* anatomy
andjeo *f.* angel
anemija *f.* anemia
angažirati *v.* engage
angina *f.* tonsillitis
anketa *f.* poll
ansambl *m.* troupe, ensemble
antena *f.* aerial
antibiotik *m.* antibiotic
antikvarnica *n.* second-hand bookshop
antilop *m.* suede
antipatičan *adj.* unlikable
apartman *m.* suite
apoteka *f.* chemist's, drug store
april *m.* April
apsolutan *adj.* absolute
arak *m.* sheet
arija *f.* tune
arogantan *adj.* arrogant
asfalt *m.* asphalt
asistent *m.* assistant
astma *f.* asthma
atentat *m.* assassination

ateriati *v.* land
august *m.* August
autor *m.* author
autostop *m.* hitchhiking
avet *f.* ghost
avion *m.* airplane

B

baba   *f.* grandmother
baciti   *v.* throw, cast
badem   *m.* almond
bajka   *f.* fairy-tale, fable
bakar   *m.* copper
baklja   *f.* torch
balkon   *m.* balcony
balon   *m.* balloon
balvan   *m.* log
balzam   *m.* balm
bankrotstvo   *n.* bankruptcy
bara   *f.* pond, pool
baterija   *f.* battery
batina   *f.* stick, club
baviti   *se v.* occupy oneself with
bazen   *m.* swimming pool
baš   *adv.* just, exactly
beba   *f.* baby
bedro   *n.* thigh
berba   *f.* vintage
berza   *f.* stock exchange
besanica   *f.* insomnia
beskonačan   *adj.* endless, infinite
beskućnik   *m.* homeless
besmislen   *adj.* absurd, senseless
besplatan   *adj.* gratis, free of charge
besposlen   *adj.* unemployed; idle
besposličariti   *v.* loiter
bespravan   *adj.* rightless, illegal
beton   *m.* concrete, cement
bez   *prep.* without
bezbrižan   *adj.* care-free, lightminded

bezkoristan *adj.* useless
beznačajan *adj.* insignificant
beznadan *adj.* hopeless
bezobrazan *adj.* impudent
bezobziran *adj.* careless, reckless
bezopasan *adj.* harmless
bezvoljan *adj.* apathetic, indifferent
bič *m.* whip
biber *m.* pepper
biblioteka *f.* library
bibliotekar *m.* librarian
bicikl *m.* bicycle
bicikl *f.* (Am.) bike
bijel *adj.* white
bijeli *luk* m. garlic
bijeliti *v.* bleach
bijes *m.* fury, rage, wrath
bijesan *adj.* furious, mad
bik *m.* bull
bolje *adv.* & adj. better
bilježiti *v.* record, note
bilješka *f.* note, memo
biljka *f.* plant; herb
bilo *m.* pulse
bilo *kada* adv. whenever
bilo *kako* adv. anyway, anyhow
bilo *ko* pron. whoever
bilo *što* adv. anything
birati *v.* choose, select; elect
biser *m.* pearl
bistar *adj.* lucid, clever
bitan *adj.* essential
biti *v.* be, exist
bitka *f.* battle
bivši *adv.* former
bizon *m.* buffalo

biće *n.* being, creature
bježati *v.* escape, flee
bjesniti *v.* rage, storm
blag *adj.* mild
blago *n.* treasure ; cattle
blagosiljati *v.* bless
blatnjav *adj.* muddy
blato *n.* mud
blijed *adj.* pale
blijedilo *n.* paleness
blistati *v.* glitter
blistav *adj.* glittering; brilliant
blitva *f.* Swiss chard
blizak *adj.* near, close (to)
blizanac *m.* twin
bluza *f.* blouse
božanski *adj.* divine
bočni *adj.* lateral
boca *f.* bottle
bodež *m.* dagger
bog *m.* god
bogalj *m.* cripple
bogat *adj.* rich, wealthy
bogatstvo *n.* wealth
boja *f.* paint, color
bojažljiv *adj.* timid
bojiti *v.* paint, color
bok *m.* hip
bol *m.* pain, ache
bolan *adj.* painful
bolest *f.* illness, disease, sickness
bolestan *adj.* sick, ill
bolje *adj.* better
boljeti *v.* hurt, ache, pain
bolnica *f.* hospital
bolnicka kola *f.* ambulance

bombon *m.* sweet
bor *m.* pine
bora *f.* wrinkle, line
boraviti *v.* stay
borba *f.* fight, struggle, combat
boriti *se* v. struggle, fight
borovnica *f.* blueberry
bosonog *adj.* barefoot
brada *f.* beard; chin
bradavica *f.* nipple
brak *m.* marriage
brana *f.* dam
braniti *v.* defend
brat *m.* brother
brava *f.* lock
brašno *n.* flour
brbljati *v.* chatter, chat
brdo *n.* hill
breme *n.* burden, load
breskva *f.* peach
breza *f.* birch
brid *m.* edge
briga *f.* worry, trouble
brijač *m.* barber
brijati *(se)* v. shave
brinuti *(se)* v. care, worry
brinuti *se* za v. look after
britva *f.* razor
brk *m.* moustache
brod *m.* ship, vessel
broj *m.* number, numeral
brojčanik *m.* dial, face
brojati *v.* count
bronza *f.* brass
brz *adj.* quick, fast, rapid, prompt
brz pogled *m.* glance

brzina *f.* speed, velocity
bršljan *m.* ivy
bučan *adj.* noisy
buba [vabo *m.* cockroach
bubanj *m.* drum
bubreg *m.* kidney
bubuljica *f.* pimple
budala *f.* fool
budan *adj.* awake
budilnik *m.* alarm clock
budučnost *f.* future
buha / buva *f.* flea
buka *f.* noise
buljiti *v.* stare
buntovnik *m.* rebel
bure *n.* barrel
burence *n.* keg

C

car *m.* emperor
carevina *f.* empire
carina *f.* customs
carski *adj.* imperial
cedulja *f.* note, slip
cement *m.* cement
centar grada *m.* city
centrifuga (za veš) *f.* dryer, drier
ceriti *se* v. grimace
cesta *f.* road, highway
cestarina *f.* toll
Ciganin *m.* Gipsy
cigareta *f.* cigarette
cigla *f.* brick
cijediti *v.* strain, filter
cijeli *adj.* whole
cijena *f.* price
cijeniti *v.* esteem; appreciate, value
cijepati *v.* split
cijepiti *v.* vaccinate
cijev *f.* pipe, tube
cilj *m.* goal, aim
cink *m.* zink
cio *adj.* whole, entire
cipela *f.* shoe
cisterna *f.* tank
citat *m.* quotation
citirati *v.* quote
cjelina *f.* whole, totality; gross
cjelokupan *adj.* total
cjelovit *adj.* integral, entire
cjenkati se *v.* bargain, haggle
cjenovnik *m.* price list

cjevanica *f.* shin bone
crijep *m.* tile
crijevni *adj.* intestinal
crknuti *v.* die
crkva *f.* church
crn *adj.* black
crta *f.* line
crtati *v.* draw; design
crtež *m.* drawing
crtica *f.* hyphen
crv *m.* worm
crven *adj.* red
crvenilo *n.* blush
curica *f.* little girl
curiti *v.* run, flow
cvasti *v.* bloom, flower
cvijet *m.* flower
cvjećara *f.* florist
cvrčak *m.* cricket

č

čaj *m.* tea
čajnik *m.* teapot
čak *ad.* even
čamac *m.* boat
čar *m.* charm
čarapa *f.* sock, hose, stocking
čarobnjak *m.* wizard
čaršav *m.* sheet
čas *m.* moment, minute
častan *adj.* honorable
časopis *m.* periodical, journal, magazine
čast *f.* honor
čavka *f.* jackdaw
čaša *f.* glass
čežnja *f.* longing
ček *m.* check
čekaonica *f.* waiting room
čekati *v.* wait
čekić *m.* hammer
čelik *m.* steel
čeljust *f.* jaw
čelo *n.* forehead; front
čemu *pron.* why
čep *m.* cork
česma *f.* fountain; well
čestica *f.* particle, fragment
čestit *adj.* honest
čestitati *v.* congratulate
često *adv.* frequently, often
češalj *m.* comb
češati se *v.* scratch
češnjak *m.* garlic
češče *adv.* pretty often

četiri *num.* four
četka za kosu *f.* hairbrush
četka za zube *f.* toothbrush
četka *f.* brush
četrdeset *num.* forty
četrnaest *num.* fourteen
četvrti *num.* fourth
četvrt *f.* district; quarter
četvrtak *m.* Thursday
čeznuti *v.* yearn, seek
čiji, čija, čije *pron.* whose
čin *m.* act
činjenica *f.* fact
čipka *f.* lace
čir *m.* ulcer
čist *adj.* clean; pure; kosher
čistionica *f.* cleaner's
čistka *f.* purge
čitak *adj.* readable, legible
čitati *v.* read
čitav *adj.* whole, complete, intire
čizma *f.* boot
član *m.* member
čanak *m.* article; ankle
članstvo *n.* membership
čopor *m.* herd
čorba *f.* broth, soup
čovječan *adj.* humane
čovječanstvo *n.* humankind
čovjek *m.* man
čudan *adj.* strange, odd, peculiar
čuditi se *v.* wonder
čudjenje *n.* suprise
čudo *n.* miracle
čudovište *n.* monster
čulo *n.* sense

čupati *v.* pluck
čuvati *v.* keep, protect; preserve
čuven *adj.* famous, well known
čvor *m.* knot
čvorište *n.* junction
čvoruga *f.* bump
čvrst *adj.* firm, solid

ć

ćaskati *v.* chatter
ćelav *adj.* bald
ćelija *f.* cell
ćilim *m.* carpet, rug
ćirilica *f.* Cyrillic script
ćorav *adj.* one-eyed
ćorsokak *m.* dead-end, blind alley
ćud *f.* temper
ćup *m.* jar
ćurka *f.* turkey
ćuška *f.* slap
ćuti *v.* hear

D

da *conj.* yes, that
dabar *m.* beaver
dadilja *f.* nanny, nurse
dah *m.* breath
dakle *adv.* well; therefore
daktilograf *m.* typist
dalek *adj.* remote, distant
daleko *adv.* faraway
dalekovod *m.* overhead line
dalje *adj.* farther, further
dama *f.* lady
dan (24 sata) *m.* day
danas *adv.* today, nowdays
dapače *adv.* on the contrary
dar *m.* present, gift, grant
darovati *v.* make a present; donate
darovit *adj.* gifted, talented
daska *f.* board; plank
dati *v.* give, provide, supply
datirati *v.* date
datum *m.* date
daviti (se) *v.* choke, suffocate
davno *adv.* long ago
debljati *se v.* fatten, put on weight
debljina *f.* fatness, obesity
deblo *n.* trunk
decembar *m.* December
decimalni razlomak *m.* fraction
dečko *m.* boy; boy-friend
definicija *f.* definition
deformisati *v.* deform
deka *f.* blanket
dekada *f.* decade

dekan *m.* dean
dekorisati *v.* decorate
demokratija *f.* democracy
demonstrirati *v.* demonstrate
demontirati *v.* dismantle
depilator *m.* hair- remover
derati *v.* tear, rip, pull apart
derati se *v.* scream
derište *n.* brat
desert *m.* dessert
deset *num.* ten
desni (oko zuba) *pl.* gum
destinacija *f.* destination
deterdžent *m.* detergent
deva *f.* camel
devet *num.* nine
devize *pl.* foreign currency
dezen *m.* pattern, design
dijabetis *m.* diabetes
dijagnosticirati *v.* diagnose
dijagram *m.* diagram, chart
dijamant *m.* diamond
dijapozitiv *m.* slide
dijeliti *v.* divide, separate; share
dijeljenje *n.* division
dijeta *f.* diet
dijete (djeca) *n.* child (pl. children)
diktirati *v.* dictate
dim *m.* smoke
dimiti *se* v. smoke
dimnjak *m.* chimney
dinja *f.* melon
dinstati *v.* stew
dio *m.* part, share; spare part
dionica *f.* share, stock
diplomirati *v.* graduate

dirati *v.* touch
director *m.* manager; principal
direkcija *f.* headquarters, main office
dirigent *m.* conductor
dirigovati *v.* conduct
disati *v.* breathe, respire
diskutovati *v.* debate, discuss
dispanzer *m.* health center
dišni *adj.* respiratory
div *m.* giant
divan *adj.* wonderful, marvelous
diverzant *m.* commando
diviti se *v.* admire
divljak *m.* savage
divlji *adj.* wild, fierce
divljina *f.* wilderness
dizalica *f.* crane
dizalo *n.* elevator
djavo *m.* devil
dječak *m.* boy
djed *m.* grandfather
djelatnost *f.* activity
djeljiv *adj.* divisible
djelo *n.* work, deed, act
djelokrug *m.* scope, domain; range
djelomičan *adj.* partial
djelotvoran *adj.* efficient, effective
djelovanje *n.* action, activity
djelovati *v.* work, perform; operate
djetelina *f.* clove
djetinjast *adj.* childish
djetinjstvo *n.* childhood
djevica *f.* virgin
djevojka *f.* girl
dlaka *f.* hair
dlakav *adj.* hairy

dlan *m.* palm
dnevna soba *f.* sitting-room
dnevni *adj.* daily
dnevnik *m.* diary
dno *n.* bottom
do sada *adv.* hereto, hitherto
dok *conj.* while
doživotan *adj.* lifelong
dob *f.* age
dobar *adj.* good, well
dobitak *m.* gain, profit
dobiti *v.* get, obtain, receive, gain
dobitnik *m.* winner
dobrobit *f.* welfare, benefit
dobrodošlica *f.* welcome
dobrodošao *adj.* welcome
dobrota *f.* goodness
dobrotvoran *adj.* benevolent
dobrovoljac *m.* volunteer
dobrovoljan *adj.* voluntary
dobrovoljno *adv.* voluntarily
docent *m.* assistant professor
dočekati *v.* meet
doći *v.* come
dodatak *m.* addition, appendix
dodatan *adj.* additional
dodati *v.* add
dodatni *adj.* extra
dodavanje *n.* addition
dodijati *v.* be fed up with
dodijeliti *v.* assign
dodirnuti *v.* touch
dogadjaj *m.* event, experience
dogoditi se *v.* happen, occur, take place
dogovor *m.* arrangement, agreement
dohvat rukom *m.* grip

dohvatiti *v.* reach
dojam *m.* impression
dok *m.* dock
dokaz *m.* proof, evidence
dokle *conj.* until
dokle *adv.* how long
dokle god *conj.* while
dokolica *f.* leisure
dolazak *m.* arrival
dole *adv.* down, below, downstairs
dolina *f.* valley
doliti *v.* add, fill up
dom *m.* home; club; dormitory
domaći *adj.* home, domestic
domaćica *f.* housewife, hostess
domaćin *m.* host
domišljat *adj.* ingenious
domorodac *m.* native
domovina *f.* homeland
donijeti *v.* bring
donje rublje *pl.* underwear
donji *adj.* lower
dopis *m.* official letter
dopisivati se *v.* correspond
dopisnica *f.* postal card, post card
dopisnik *m.* correspondent, reporter
dopratiti *v.* escort
dopremiti *v.* supply; transport
dopust *m.* vacation
dopustenje *n.* permission
dopustiti *v.* allow, permit
doručak *m.* breakfast
dosadan *adj.* boring, dull; tedious
dosadjivati *v.* annoy, bother, bore
dosije *m.* file
dosjetiti se *v.* have an idea, understand

doskora *adv.* shortly, soon
dosljedan *adj.* consistent
doslovan *adj.* literal
dosta *adv.* enough
dostaviti *v.* deliver
dostojanstven *adj.* dignified
dostojanstvo *n.* dignity
dotle *adv.* till then, as far as
dovdje *adv.* this far
dovesti *v.* bring over
dovidjenja (part of speech) good-bye
dovoljan *adj.* sufficient
dovršiti *v.* finish, complete
doza *f.* dose
doznačiti (novac) *v.* remit
doznaka *f.* voucher, mail order
doznati *v.* learn, find out, hear
dozreti *v.* mature; ripen
dozvati *v.* call back, send for
dozvola(vozačka) *f.* driving licence
dozvola *f.* permission
dozvoliti *v.* permit
doći *v.* come; arrive
drag *adj.* dear, sweet
dragulj *m.* jewel; gem
dragocjen *adj.* precious; costly
draguljar *m.* jeweller
drastičan *adj.* drastic
dražba *f.* auction
dražestan *adj.* charming, lovely
dražiti *v.* irritate; provoke
držanje *n.* carriage; bearing;attitud
držati *v.* hold; support; keep
država *f.* state, country
državljanin *m.* citizen

državni *adj.* government
drevan *adj.* ancient
drmati *v.* shake, agitate, jolt
drobiti *v.* crash
drogerija *f.* drugstore, chemist's
drug *m.* fellow, mate, comrade
drugi *adj.* other, another, second
društven *adj.* sociable
društvo *n.* society, community
drven *adj.* wooden
drvo *n.* tree, wood, lumber
drzak *adj.* arrogant
dućan *m.* shop, store
dubina *f.* depth
dubok *adj.* deep
dug *m.* debt
dug *adj.* long
duga *f.* rainbow
dugme *n.* button
dugotrajan *adj.* long-lasting, durable
dugovati *v.* owe
duguljast *adj.* elongated; oblong
duh *m.* spirit; ghost
duhovit *adj.* witty
duhovitost *f.* wit
duhovni *adj.* spiritual
dukat *m.* gold coin
duplikat *m.* duplicate
dur (muz.) *m.* major
duša *f.* soul
dušek *m.* mattress
dušmanin *m.* enemy, foe
duvan *m.* tobacco
duvati *v.* blow
dužina *f.* length

dužnost *f.* duty
dva *num.* two
dvadeset *num.* twenty
dvanaest *num.* twelve
dvorana *f.* auditorium, hall
dvoriti *v.* attend
dvosmislen *adj.* ambiguous
dvostruk *adj.* double

Dž

džamija *f.* mosque
džemper *m.* sweater, pullover
džep *m.* pocket
dževrek *m.* bagel
džez *m.* jazz
džezva *f.* coffe pot
džigerica *f.* liver
džokej *m.* jockey
džumbir *m.* ginger
džungla *f.* jungle

Đ

đak *m.* pupil

đavo *m.* devil

đon *m.* sole

đubre *n.* garbage

đurđevak *m.* lily of the valley

đuture *adv.* in-bulk; wholesale

đuvegija *m.* bridegroom

E

efikasan   *adj.* effective
egzaltiran   *adj.* hyper sensitive
egzistirati   *v.* exist
eho   *m.* echo
ekipa   *f.* team
ekonomija   *f.* economy, economics
ekran   *m.* screen
ekspeditivan   *adj.* prompt
eksplozija   *f.* bang
eksponat   *m.* exhibit
elaborat   *m.* survey, presentation
elan   *m.* enthusiasm
elastičan   *adj.* elastic, flexible
električar   *m.* electrician
električni   *adj.* electrical
elektricitet   *m.* electricity
električna centrala   *f.* power plant
elektrotehnika   *f.* electrical engineering
emajl   *m.* enamel
emisija   *f.* broadcast; transmission
energičan   *adj.* energetic
energija   *f.* energy
Engleska   *f.* Great Britain, United Kingdom
eno   *adv.* there
epruveta   *f.* test tube
eskurzija   *f.* excursion
etapa   *f.* stage
etički   *adj.* ethical
etiketa   *f.* label, tab
evandjelje   *n.* Gospel
eventualan   *adj.* possible
Evropa   *f.* Europe

F

faktura *f.* invoice
fakultet *m.* college, faculty, school
faliti *v.* lack, missing
falsifikovanje *n.* forgery
fantazija *f.* imagination, fantasy
farba *f.* dye
farmaceut *m.* pharmacist
farovi *pl.* headlights
fasada *f.* front, facade
fascikl *m.* folder
fašistički *adj.* fascist
faza *f.* stage, step, phase
fazan *m.* pheasant
februar *m.* February
fen *m.* hair-dryer
fenjer *m.* lantern
ferije *n.* vacation, holidays
filijala *f.* branch
fin *adj.* fine, good-mannered
firma *f.* firm, company
fitilj *m.* wick, fuse
fizičar *m.* physicist
fizički *adv.* physical
fizika *f.* physics
flaster *m.* plaster
folija *f.* foil
fond *m.* fund
forma *f.* shape, form
formular *m.* form
fotelja *f.* arm-chair, easy chair
fotografski aparat *m.* camera
fotografski snimak *m.* snapshot
Francuska *f.* France

fratar   *m.* monk, friar
fraza   *f.* idiom, phrase
freska   *f.* mural
frizer   *m.* hairdresser
fričider   *m.* refrigerator
funta   *f.* pound
furnir   *m.* veneer
futrola   *f.* case

G

gaće *pl.* pants, briefs
gadan *adj.* disgusting
gaditi se *v.* make sick
gadjati *v.* aim
gadjenje *n.* disgust
gajiti *v.* cherish, nurse, breed
galama *f.* noise, fuss
galamiti *v.* make noise, scream, roar
galerija *f.* gallery
galon *m.* gallon
gangster *m.* gangster
ganuti *v.* touch
garancija *f.* guarantee
garderoba *f.* wardrobe
gas *m.* gas
gasiti *v.* extinguish
gavran *m.* raven
gazda *m.* landlord; boss
gazdarica *f.* landlady
gdje *adv.* where
gegati se *v.* toddle
generacija *f.* generation
genije *m.* genius
gibak *adj.* flexibile
gimnazija *f.* high school
ginuti *v.* be killed, perish
gips *m.* gypsum
glačalo *n.* iron
glad *f.* hunger; famine
gladak *adj.* smooth
gladan *adj.* hungry
gladovanje *n.* starvation
gladovati *v.* starve

glagol *m.* verb
glas *m.* voice; tone
glasan *adj.* loud, noisy
glasanje *n.* vote; ballot
glasati *v.* vote
glasnik *m.* messenger
glasno *adv.* aloud
glava *f.* head; chapter
glavni *adj.* main; principal; cardinal
glavni put *m.* highway
glavnica *f.* capital, principal
glavobolja *f.* headache
glazba *f.* music
gledalac *m.* spectator
gledati *v.* watch, look at
gležanj *m.* ankle
glina *f.* clay
gljiva *f.* mushroom
globus *m.* globe
glodati *v.* gnaw; nibble
gluh/gluv *adj.* deaf
glumac *m.* actor
glumica *f.* actress
glup *adj.* stupid, dumb; fullish, silly
glupost *f.* nonsense, stupidity
gmizavac *m.* reptile
gnijezdo *n.* nest
gnjaviti *v.* bother, make a fuss
gnjev *m.* anger, wrath
gnjuranje *n.* dive
gnoj *m.* dung, manure
go/gol *adj.* naked, nude; bare
godina *f.* year
godisnji *adj.* annual
godišnje doba *n.* season
golem *adj.* huge, immense

golub(ica) *f.* dove; pigeon
gomila *f.* crowd, mob
goniti *v.* chase, pursue
gora *f.* mountain
gorak *adj.* bitter
gore *adv.* up; above; upstairs
gori *adj.* worse
gorivo *n.* fuel
gorjeti *v.* burn
gorljiv *adj.* eager
gornji *adj.* upper
gospodar *m.* lord, master, boss
gospodin *m.* gentleman; Mister; sir
gospodja *f.* lady, Mrs.; madam
gospodjica *f.* Miss
gost *m.* guest
gostionica *f.* inn
gostitii *v.* treat
gostoprimstvo *n.* hospitality
gotovina(novac) *f.* cash
govedina *f.* beef
govor *m.* speech
govoriti *v.* speak
govornik *m.* speaker
gozba *f.* feast, banquet
grablje *pl.* rake
grad *m.* town; city
graditi *v.* build, construct
gradivo *n.* material
gradjanin *m.* citizen
gradjanski *adj.* civil, civic
gradonačelnik *m.* mayor
grah *m.* bean
gramofon *m.* record player
grana *f.* branch
granata *f.* shell

granica *f.* border, boundary, frontier
grašak *m.* pea
grba *f.* hump, hunch
grč *m.* cramp, spasm, convulsion
Grčka *f.* Greece
greška *f.* mistake, fault, error
greda *f.* timber
grepsti *v.* scratch
grickati *v.* nibble
grijalica *f.* heater
gripa *f.* flu
griva *f.* mane
grliti *v.* embrace
grlo *n.* throat
grm *m.* bush, shrub
grmiti *v.* thunder
grob *m.* grave, tomb
groblje *n.* cemetery
groza *f.* horror
grozd *m.* bunch, cluster
groznica *f.* fever, shiver
grozota *f.* atrocity
gročdčice *f.* raisin
gročdje *n.* grapes
grub *adj.* rude; harsh
grudi *pl.* breasts
grudnjak *m.* bra
grupa *f.* group
gubitak *m.* loss
gubiti *v.* lose
guma *f.* rubber; tire
gundjati *v.* mutter
gungula *f.* riot
gurati *v.* push
gusar *m.* pirate
gusjenica *f.* caterpillar

guska   *f.* goose
gust   *adj.* thick, dense
gustoća   *f.* thickness, density
gutljaj   *m.* sip, drink, swallow
gušiti   *v.* choke, suffocate
gušter   *m.* lizard

H

hađija *m.* pilgrim
hajde come on!
hajduk *m.* outlaw
hajka *f.* chase
haljina *f.* dress, robe, gown
hambar *m.* barn, grainary
hanuma *f.* lady, Mrs.
hapsiti *v.* arrest
hapšenik *m.* prisoner
harati *v.* devastate; rage
harmonika *f.* accordion
hauba *f.* bonnet, hood
heftati *v.* baste
heksnšus *m.* stiff back (neck)
hemijski *adj.* chemical
higijena *f.* hygiene
higijenski *adj.* sanitary
hiljada *f.* thousand
himber *m.* raspberry juice
himna *f.* anthem, hymn
hipoteka *f.* mortgage
hir *m.* caprice, whim
hirurgija *f.* surgery
hitac *m.* gunshot, shot
hitan *n.* adj. urgent
hlače *pl.* trousers
hladiti *v.* cool
hladnjača *f.* cold storage
hladnjak *m.* refrigerator
hladno *adv.* cold, chilly
hladnoća *f.* cold
hladovina *f.* shade
hlapiti *v.* evaporate

hljeb *m.* bread
hodža *m.* Moslem priest
hodati *v.* walk
hodnik *m.* corridor, hall
hodozčasnik *m.* pilgrim
horizont *m.* horizon
hozntregeri *pl.* suspenders
hrabar *adj.* brave, valiant
hram *m.* temple
hrana *f.* food
hraniti *v.* feed, nourish
hranjiv *adj.* nutritious
hrapav *adj.* rough
hrast *m.* oak
hrkati *v.* snore
hropac *m.* death rattle
hrpa *f.* pile
hrskati *v.* crunch
hrt *m.* grayhound
Hrvat *m.* Croat
hrvati se *v.* wrestle
Hrvatska *f.* Croatia
htjeti *v.* want
hučati *v.* roar, boom
hujati *v.* whistle
hulja *f.* villain, scoundrel
hvala *f.* thank you, thanks
hvalisati *se v.* boast, brag
hvatati *v.* catch; snatch at

ITEM CHARGED

LIB#: *1000192730*
GRP: STUDENT

Due: 5/11/2011 08:00 PM

Title: Bosnian-English, English-Bosnian
dictionary / Nikolina S. Uzicanin.
Auth: Uzicanin, Nikolina S.
Call #: 491.82321 UZICANI 1995
Enum
Chron
Copy:
Item *0025067K*

I

i *conj.* and
iako *conj.* although, though
ići *v.* go, walk
idealan *adj.* ideal
ideja *f.* idea
igla *f.* pin, needle
igra *f.* play; game
igračka *f.* toy
igralište *n.* playground
ikada *adv.* ever
iko *adv.* any, anybody, anyone
ili *conj.* or
imanje *n.* property, estate
imati *v.* have, possess, own
ime *n.* name
imenica *f.* noun, substantive
imenik *m.* directory, register
imenjak *m.* namesake
imenovati *v.* appoint; nominate
imitirati *v.* imitate
imovina *f.* fortune, assets
impozantan *adj.* impressive
impregniran *adj.* waterproof
inače *adv.* otherwise, anyway
invalid *m.* invalid, disabled person
inženjer *m.* engineer
ipak *conj.* nevertheless, however
ironija *f.* irony
iscrpan *adj.* exhaustive, thorough
iscrpiti *v.* exhaust
iseliti *v.* emigrate; evacuate
ishlapiti *v.* evaporate
isijavati *v.* radiate

iskaz *m.* statement
isklesati *v.* sculpture
isključiti *v.* exclude; expel; disconnect
iskopati *v.* dig out, excavate
iskra *f.* spark
iskren *adj.* sincere, frank, open
iskreno *adv.* sincerely
iskrvariti *v.* lose much blood
iskustvo *n.* experience
iskušati *v.* try out, test
iskušenje *n.* temptation
iskvariti *v.* corrupt
ispaliti *v.* fire, discharge
ispariti *v.* evaporate
ispirati *v.* rinse
ispit *m.* exam
ispitivati *v.* examine
isplahnuti *v.* rinse
isplata *f.* payment
ispljunuti *v.* spit out
ispod *adv.* under, below, underneath
isporučiti *v.* deliver
ispraćaj *m.* farewell, seeing off
isprava *f.* document, papers
ispraviti *v.* rectify
ispred *adv.* before, in front of
ispričati *se v.* apologize
isprika *f.* excuse; apology
ispružiti(se) *v.* stretch
isprva *adv.* at first
ispucati *v.* crack
ispuhati *v.* deflate
ispuniti *v.* fill (up, out); fulfill
ispustiti *v.* drop, let out
istaći *v.* emphasize, stress, point
istaknut *adj.* prominent, outstanding

isteći *v.* run out; expire
isti *adj.* same, likewise, identical
istina *f.* truth
istinit *adj.* true
istjerati *v.* drive out, expel
istok *m.* east
istorija *f.* history
istovariti *v.* unload
istraga *f.* inquiry, investigation
istrajati *v.* persist, endure
istraživati *v.* investigate, explore
istrljati *v.* rub
iščašiti *v.* dislocate, sprain
iščetkati *v.* brush (out)
iščeznuti *v.* disappear
itd. *abbr.* etc. (et cetera)
ivica *f.* edge, rim
iz *prep.* out, from, of
iza *prep.* behind, after
izabrati *v.* choose, select; elect
izaslanik *m.* delegate, deputy
izazov *m.* provocation; challenge
izazvati *v.* provoke, challenge
izbezumiti *v.* drive crazy
izbjegavati *v.* avoid
izbjeglica *f.* refugee
izblijediti *v.* fade, lose color
izbor *m.* choice, selection
izbori *pl.* election
izbrisati *v.* wipe, erase
izdahnuti *v.* exhale
izdaja *f.* treason, treachery
izdajica *m.* traitor
izdajnički *adj.* treacherous
izdanje *n.* edition, issue
izdašan *adj.* abundant; economical

izdatak *m.* expense
izdati knjigu *v.* publish
izdavač *m.* publisher
izdržavanje *n.* livelihood
izdvojiti *v.* separate
izgled *m.* appearance; outlook
izgnanstvo *n.* exile
izgovarati *v.* pronounce
izgovor *m.* excuse; pronunciation
izgubljen *adj.* lost, missing
izići *v.* come out, go out
izjava *f.* statement
izjaviti *v.* state, declare
izlaz *m.* exit, way out; outlet
izlazak sunca *m.* sunrise
izlet *m.* trip, excursion
izliti *v.* pour out, spill, flood
izlizan *adj.* worn out
izlog *m.* shop window
izložba *f.* exhibition
izložiti *v.* exhibit, display; expose
izlučivati *v.* secrete
izmedju *prep.* between, among
izmisliti *v.* invent
izmjenican *adj.* alternate
izmjenicna struja *f.* alternating current
izmlatiti *v.* beat up; thrash
iznad *adv.* above; over
iznajmiti *v.* hire, rent, lease
iznenada *adv.* suddenly
iznenadan *adj.* sudden
iznenaditi *v.* suprise
iznos *m.* amount, sum
iznova *adv.* anew, afresh
izopćiti *v.* excommunicate
izradjivati *v.* make, manufacture, fabric

izraz *m.* expression, idiom
izraziti *v.* express
izreći *v.* say, utter
izručiti *v.* deliver, hand over
izum *m.* invention
izumro *adj.* extinct
izuzetak *m.* exception
izuzeti *v.* except, exempt
izvaditi *v.* take out, extract
izvan *adv.* out, outside
izvanredan *adj.* extraordinary, terrific
izvedivost *f.* feasibility
izvesti *v.* perform
izvidjač *m.* scout
izvjestan *adj.* certain, positive
izvještač *m.* reporter
izvještavati *v.* report
izvječbanost *f.* routine
izvor *m.* source; resource; well
izvorno *adv.* originally
izvoz *m.* export
izvršiti *v.* carry out, perform

J

ja *pron.* I
jabuka *f.* apple
jačina *f.* strength, vigor, power
jad *m.* grief, distress, woe
jadan *adj.* poor, miserable
jadikovati *v.* complain, lament
jagoda *f.* strawberry
jahati *v.* ride
jahta *f.* yacht
jaje *n.* egg
jajnik *m.* ovary
jak *adj.* strong, powerful
jakna *f.* jacket
jalov *adj.* sterile; barren
jama *f.* pit, hole
janja *f.* daisy
janje *m.* lamb
januar *m.* January
jarak *m.* ditch, tranch
jard (0.914 metara) *m.* yard
jare *n.* young goat, kid
jasan *adj.* clear, obvious; bright
jastog *m.* lobster
jastreb *m.* hawk
jastučnica *f.* pillowcase
jastuk *m.* pillow
jato *n.* flock
jauk *m.* cry of pain, yell
javan *adj.* public
javiti *v.* notify; inform
javor *m.* maple
jaz *m.* gap, gulf
jecati *v.* sob

ječam *m.* barley
jedan *num.* one; an; a
jedanaest *num.* eleven
jedanput *adv.* once
jedar *adj.* fresh, vigorous
jedinica *f.* unit
jedino *adv.* only, solely
jedinstven *adj.* unique
jednadžba *f.* equation
jednak *adj.* equal; equivalent; alike
jednakost *f.* equality
jednina *gram.* singular
jednjak *m.* gullet
jednoglasno *adj.* unanimously
jednoličan *adj.* monotonous, uniform
jednostavan *adj.* simple; plain
jedro *m.* sail
jedva *adv.* hardly, scarcely, barely
jeftin *adj.* cheap, inexpensive
jegulja *f.* eel
jeka *f.* echo
jelen *m.* deer
jelovnik *m.* menu
jenjati *v.* abate, go down
jer *conj.* because, as, for
jesen *f.* autumn, fall
jesti *v.* eat
jestivo *adj.* edible
jetra *f.* liver
Jevrej *m.* Jew
jevrejski *adj.* Jewish
jezero *n.* lake
jezgra *f.* nucleus, core, heart
jezik *m.* language; tongue
jorgan *m.* comforter, quilt
jorgovan *m.* lilac

još *adv.* still, yet
jubilej *m.* anniversary, jubilee
jučer *adv.* yesterday
jug *m.* South
juha *f.* soup
juli *m.* July
junak *m.* hero
juni *m.* June
juriti *v.* rush, run; speed
jutro *n.* morning

K

ka   *prep.* to, towards
kabanica   *f.* raincoat
kabel   *m.* cable
kabina   *f.* cabin, cockpit, fitting
kaciga   *f.* helmet
kada   *adv.* when
kada   *f.* bathtub
kadar   *m.* able
kadulja   *f.* sage
kafa/kahva/kava   *f.* coffee
kafana   *f.* cafe
kaiš   *m.* belt
kajanje   *n.* regret, remorse
kajgana   *f.* scrambled eggs
kajsija   *f.* apricot
kakav   *adj.* what kind of ?
kako   *adv.* how
kaldrma   *f.* cobbles
kalem   *m.* spool, reel
kalendar   *m.* calendar
kalij   *m.* potassium
kaludjer   *m.* monk
kaludjerica   *f.* nun
kalup   *m.* mold
kamata   *f.* interest
kamen   *m.* stone; rock
kamila   *f.* camel
kamilica   *f.* camomile
kamin   *m.* fireplace
kamion   *m.* truck, lorry
kamp   *m.* camp
kampanja   *f.* campaign
kanal   *m.* channel; canal

kancelarija *f.* office
kandidat *m.* candidate; applicant
kandža *f.* claw
kao *conj.* like, as
kap(lja) *f.* drop; stroke
kapa *f.* cap, beret, bonnet
kapara *f.* deposit
kapati *v.* drop, drip
kapetan *m.* captain; master
kapija *f.* gate
kapuljača *f.* hood
kaput *m.* coat, overcoat
karakter *m.* character
karakteristika *f.* characteristic, feature
karanfil *m.* carnation
karfiol *m.* cauliflower
karijera *f.* career
karika *f.* link
kariran *adj.* plaid
karlica *f.* pelvis
karniša *f.* curtain rod
karoserija *f.* auto body
karta *f.* card; ticket
karter *m.* oil-pan
karton *m.* cardboard
kasa *f.* cashier, cash-box
kasarna *f.* barracks
kaskati *v.* jog
kasni *adj.* late
kasnije *adv.* later, afterwards
kaša *f.* porridge, gruel; pulp
kašalj *m.* cough
kašika *f.* spoon
kašljati *v.* cough
kat *m.* floor, story
katastrofa *f.* disaster

katedrala   *f.* cathedral
katkad   *adv.* sometimes
katran   *m.* tar
kaucija   *f.* deposit
kavez   *m.* cage
kavga   *f.* fight
kazalište   *n.* theater
kazaljka   *f.* hand
kazalo   *n.* index
kazati   *v.* say
kazna   *f.* punishment, penalty
kazniti   *v.* punish; fine
kažiprst   *m.* index-finger, forefinger
kefa   *f.* brush
kelj   *m.* kale, savoy cabbage
kelner   *m.* waiter
kengur   *m.* kangaroo
kepec   *m.* dwarf
kesa   *f.* bag, purse
kesten   *m.* chestnut
kičma   *f.* backbone, spine
kifla   *f.* croissant
kihati   *v.* sneeze
kiki-riki   *m.* peanuts
kikotati   *se v.* giggle
kila   *f.* hernia (med.)
kiml   *m.* caraway (seeds)
kino   *n.* movies, cinema, theater
kip   *m.* statue, sculpture
kipiti   *v.* boil, seethe; simmer
kiselina   *f.* acid
kiseo   *adj.* sour
kisik   *m.* oxygen
kist   *m.* bush
kiša   *f.* rain
kišobran   *m.* umbrella

kit   *m.* whale; putty (window)
kita   *f.* bunch
kititi   *v.* decorate
klada   *f.* log
klanje   *n.* slaughter
klasa   *f.* class
klasičan   *adj.* classic
klavijatura   *f.* keyboard
klavir   *m.* piano
klečati   *v.* kneel
kleti   *v.* curse, swear
kleveta   *f.* slander, libel
klica   *f.* germ; shoot, sprout
klicati   *v.* cheer
klijent   *m.* client
klima   *f.* climate
klimav   *adj.* loose, shaky
klimnuti   *v.* nod
klin   *m.* wedge; nail, peg
klip   *m.* cob; piston
klistir   *m.* enema
klizalište   *n.* skating rink
klizati se   *v.* skate
klizav   *adj.* slippery
kliziti   *v.* glide, slide, skim
klješta   *f.* tweezers
ključ   *m.* key
kljucati   *v.* peck
klopka   *f.* trap
klovn   *m.* clown
klub   *m.* club
klupa   *f.* bench; desk
klupko   *n.* clue
knjiga   *f.* book
knjigovodstvo   *n.* bookee
književni   *adj.* literary

ITEM CHARGED

LIB#: *1000168540*
GRP: STUDENT

Due: 6/3/2010 08:00 PM

Title: Bosnian-English, English-Bosnian
dictionary / Nikolina S. Uzicanin.
Auth: Uzicanin, Nikolina S.
Call #: 491.82321 UZICANI 1995
Enum
Chron
Copy:
Item *0025067K*

književnost *f.* literature
ko *pron.* who
koban *adj.* fateful, disastrous
kobasica *f.* sausage
kocka *f.* cube
kockar *m.* gambler
kockati se *v.* gamble
kočnica *f.* brake
kod *m.* code
kod *prep.* at
kofer *m.* suitcase
koga *prep.* whom
koještarija *f.* nonsense
koji *pron.* which; who; that
koketirati *v.* flirt
kokoš *f.* hen
kola *f.* automobile, car; cart
kolač *m.* cake; pastry
kolega *m.* colleague
koliba *f.* hut; cottage, cabin, lodge
kolica *f.* hand-truck; wheel-chair
količina *f.* quantity, amount
koliko *adv.* how much; how many
koljeno *n.* knee
koljevka *f.* cradle, cot
kolona *f.* column
kolovoz *m.* August
komad *m.* piece
komandovati *v.* command
komarac *m.* mosquito
komoda *f.* dresser
komora *f.* chamber
komotan *adj.* comfortable; loose
kompanjon *m.* partner
kompot *m.* stewed fruit
komunalni *adj.* municipal, public

konac *m.* thread; end
konačan *adj.* final, ultimate
koncept *m.* draft
konfekcija *f.* ready-made clothes
konj *m.* horse
konkurencija *f.* competition
konobar *m.* waiter
konopac *m.* rope, line, cord, string
kontura *f.* outline
konvenirati *v.* suit
konzerva *f.* can
kopar *m.* dill
kopati *v.* dig
kopča *f.* buckle
kopija *f.* duplicate
kopile *n.* bastard
kopito *n.* hoof
kopkati *v.* bother
kopno *n.* land
kora *f.* bark, rind, crust, peel
koračati *v.* step, march
korak *m.* step, pace
korijen *m.* root
korist *f.* advantage, benefit
koristan *adj.* useful, beneficial
korištenje *n.* use, utilization
korjenit *adj.* radical
kormilariti *v.* steer
kornjača *f.* turtle
korov *m.* weed
korpa *f.* basket; hamper, dust-bin
kos *adj.* inclined
kos *m.* blackbird
kosa *f.* hair
kositi *v.* mow
kosmat *adj.* hairy

kost *f.* bone
kostim *m.* suit
kostur *m.* skeleton
košnica *f.* bee-hive
koštati *v.* cost
košulja *f.* shirt
kotao *m.* kettle; boiler
kotlet *m.* chop, cutlet
kotlina *f.* hollow, depression
kotrljati *v.* roll
koturaljke *pl.* roller-skates
kovač *m.* blacksmith
kovati *v.* forge, hammer
koverta *f.* envelope
kovina *f.* metal
kovrčav *adj.* curly
koza *f.* goat
kozmetičar *m.* beautician
koža *f.* leather; skin
kradja *f.* theft; shop-lifting
kragna *f.* collar
kraj *m.* end, close; area
krajnik *m.* tonsil
krajnji *adj.* extreme
krajolik *m.* landscape
kralj *m.* king
kraljevski *adj.* royal
kraljevstvo *n.* kingdom
krasan *adj.* wonderful; beautiful
krasta *f.* crust, scab
krastavac *m.* cucumber
krasti *v.* steal
kratak *adj.* short, brief
kratica *f.* abbreviation
kratkovidan *adj.* short-sighted
krava *f.* cow

kravata *f.* tie; bow-tie
krčma *f.* pub, bar, saloon
kreacija *f.* design
kreč *m.* lime
kreda *f.* chalk
kredenac *m.* cupboard, kitchen cabinet
krema *f.* filling; cream
krepak *adj.* sturdy; hearty
krepost *f.* virtue
kretanje *n.* motion
kreten *m.* cretin
krevet *m.* bed
krezub *adj.* toothless; gap-toothed
krhotina *f.* fragment, splinter
krijumčar *m.* smuggler
krijumčariti *v.* smuggle
krilo *n.* wing; lap
kriška *f.* slice
kriti *v.* hide
kriv *adj.* guilty
krivac *m.* culprit
krivica *f.* guilt
kriviti *v.* blame
krivokletstvo *n.* perjury
krivotvorina *f.* forgery
krivulja *f.* curve
krofna *f.* doughnut
krojač *m.* tailor
krojačica *f.* seamstress
krompir/krumpir *m.* potato
krošnja *f.* tree (top)
krotak *adj.* meek
krov *m.* roof
kroz *adv.* through
krpa *f.* rag
krpelj *m.* tick

krsni list *m.* birth certificate
krstiti *v.* baptize, christen
krtica *f.* mole (animal)
krug *m.* circuit, circle, ring
kruh *m.* bread
kruna *f.* crown
krupan *adj.* big, large
kruška *f.* pear
krut *adj.* stiff; solid; rigid
krv *f.* blood
krvariti *v.* bleed
krzno *n.* fur
kucati *v.* knock
kučka *f.* bitch (animal)
kuća *f.* house
kućevlasnik *m.* landlord
kuda *adv.* where
kuga *f.* plague
kugla *f.* sphere, bowl, ball
kuhar *m.* cook, chef
kuhinja *f.* kitchen
kuka *f.* hook
kunić *m.* rabbit
kupac *m.* buyer, purchaser
kupati se *v.* have a bath
kupatilo *n.* bathroom
kupaći kostim *m.* swimming/bathing suit
kupina *f.* blackberry
kupiti *v.* buy, purchase
kupola *f.* dome
kupovina *f.* shopping, purchase
kupus *m.* cabbage; cole
kurir *m.* messenger
kurje oko *n.* corn
kut *m.* corner; angle
kutija *f.* box

kutljača *f.* ladle, scoop
kutnjak *m.* molar
kvačilo *n.* clutch
kvadrat *m.* square
kvaka *f.* handle, doorknob
kvalitet *m.* quality
kvantitet *m.* quantity
kvar *m.* breakdown, fault
kvariti *v.* spoil, corrupt
kvasac *m.* leaven, yeast
kvrga *f.* bump

L

labav   *adj.* loose; slack
labilan   *adj.* unstable
labilan   *adj.* unstable
labud   *m.* swan
ladica   *f.* drawer
ladja   *f.* boat; ship, vessel
lagati   *v.* lie, tell lies
lahor   *m.* breeze
lajati   *v.* bark
lak   *m.* varnish
lak   *adj.* easy; light
lakat   *m.* elbow
lako   *adv.* easily
lakomislen   *adj.* light-minded, though
lampa   *f.* lamp
lan   *m.* flax
lanac   *m.* chain
larma   *f.* noise, fuss
laskati   *v.* flatter
lastavica   *f.* swallow
latica   *f.* petal
latinica   *f.* Latin characters
lav   *m.* lion
lavina   *f.* avalanche
lavor   *m.* bowl
lažan   *adj.* false, fake
lažov/lažljivac   *m.* liar
lebdjeti   *v.* float
led   *m.* ice
ledenica   *f.* icicle
ledja   *f.* back
leglo   *m.* hatch
legura   *f.* alloy

lekcija *f.* lesson
leptir *m.* butterfly
let *m.* flight
letjeti *v.* fly
ležati *v.* lie
lice *n.* face; person; party
licemjer *m.* hypocrite
lična karta/legitimacija *f.* identification card
lično *adv.* personally
lift *m.* lift; elevator
liječiti *v.* heal, treat, cure
lijek *m.* medicine, drug, remedy
lijen *adj.* lazy
lijep *adj.* beautiful, handsome
lijevati *v.* pour
lim *m.* sheet; tin
limun *m.* lemon
linija *f.* line
lisica *f.* fox
list *m.* leaf; sheet; calf
livada *f.* meadow
lizati *v.* lick
lobanja *f.* skull
lokva *f.* puddle, pool
loman *adj.* fragile, frail
lonac *m.* pot
lopata *f.* shovel, spade
lopov *m.* thief
lopta *f.* ball
losos *m.* salmon
loš *adj.* bed
lov *m.* hunt
lubenica *f.* watermelon
lud *adj.* mad, insane
ludilo *n.* lunacy, madness
ludjak *m.* lunatic, madman

luk *m.* arc; bow
luk *m.* onion
luka *f.* port; harbour
lukav *adj.* sly, shrewd
luksuz *m.* luxury
lutati *v.* wander, stroll
lutka *f.* doll
lutrija *f.* lottery

LJ

ljaga *f.* blemish, spot, blot
ljekar *m.* physician, doctor
ljekarski *adj.* medical
ljekovit *adj.* healing
ljenčariti *v.* loaf, idle
ljepilo *m.* glue
ljepljiv *adj.* sticky, adhesive
ljepota *f.* beauty; grace
ljestve *n.* ladder
ljetina *f.* crops, harvest
ljeto *n.* summer
ljetovalište *n.* summer resort
lješnik *m.* hazelnut
ljiljan *m.* lily
ljubav *f.* love
ljubavnik *m.* lover
ljubaznost *f.* kindness
ljubičica *f.* violet
ljubljen *adj.* darling
ljubomora *f.* jealousy
ljubomoran *adj.* jealous
ljudi *pl.* people
ljudožder *m.* cannibal
ljudski *adj.* human
ljuljačka *f.* swing
ljuštiti *v.* peal, shell
ljut *adj.* mad, angry
ljutnja *f.* anger, fury

M

mač *m.* sword
mače *n.* kitten
mačka *f.* cat
maćeha *f.* step-mother
madež *m.* mole (body pigmentation)
madjijski *adj.* magic
madjioničar *m.* magician
madrac *m.* mattress
Madžar *m.* Hungarian
magacin *m.* store, shop, magazine
magarac *m.* donkey; ass
magla *f.* fog; mist; smog
maglovit *adj.* foggy; hazy; nebulous
magnetofon *m.* tape-recorder
mahati *v.* swing
mahovina *f.* moss
mahuna *f.* pod; green beans
maj *m.* May
majčinstvo *n.* motherhood, maternity
majica *f.* t-shirt; undershirt
majka *f.* mother
majmun *m.* monkey; ape
majstor *m.* master
mak *m.* poppy
makar *conj.* even if
makaze *pl.* scissors
maknuti se *v.* move
malaksao *adj.* exhausted
malen *adj.* small, little
malina *f.* raspberry
malo *adv.* a little; few
maloljetan *adj.* underage
maloumnik *m.* imbecile

malte ne   *conj*. almost
malter   *m*. mortar
mamiti   *v*. lure
mamuran   *adj*. drowsy
mana   *f*. fault; disadvantage
manastir   *m*. monastery
mandarina   *f*. tangerine
manjak   *m*. shortage; deficit
manje   *adv*. less; fewer
manji   *adj*. smaller; minor
manjina   *f*. minority
mapa   *f*. map; portfolio
marama   *f*. scarf
marelica   *f*. apricot
mariti   *v*. care
marka   *f*. stamp; brand, mark
marljiv   *adj*. hard-working, diligent
marmelada   *f*. jam
mart   *m*. March
marširati   *v*. march
masa   *f*. mass
masirati   *v*. massage
maskirati   *v*. mask
maslac   *m*. butter
maslina   *f*. olive
masnica   *f*. bruise, wale
mastan   *adj*. greasy
mašina   *f*. engine, machine
mašina za sudje   *f*. dishwasher
mašna   *f*. bow
mašta   *f*. imagination, fantasy
materijal   *m*. material; cloth
maternica   *f*. womb
maziti   *v*. cherish
mazivo   *n*. lubricant
med   *m*. honey

medeni mjesec *m.* honeymoon
medja *f.* boundary, border, frontier
medju *pr.* between; among
medjunarodni *adj.* international
medjutim *adv.* meanwhile
medjuvrijeme *n.* meantime, interim
medvjed *m.* bear
mehanički *adj.* mechanical
mekan *adj.* soft; tender
mekinje *pl.* bran
melodija *f.* melody, tune
mene; meni *pron.* me
mesar *m.* butcher
meso *n.* meat; flesh
mesti *v.* sweep
meta *f.* target
metilj *m.* liver-fluke
metla *f.* broom
metnuti *v.* place
mešava *f.* snowstorm
mi *pron.* we
mijenjanje *n.* change, modification
mijenjati, promijeniti *v.* change, modify
mijesiti *v.* knead
miješati *v.* mix
miješati(se), pačati(se) *v.* interfere, mingle
milijarda *f.* billion
milja (1,609 km) *f.* mile
miljenik *m.* favorite, pet
milosrdan *adj.* charitable
milost *f.* mercy, grace
milostiv *adj.* merciful
mina *f.* mine
minijaturan *adj.* midget
mir *m.* peace
miran *adj.* peaceful; quiet; calm

miris *m.* scent; odor
miris *m.* fragrance; smell
mirisati *v.* smell
mirodjija *f.* spice
misao *f.* thought; idea
misliti *v.* think
miš *m.* mouse
mišić *m.* muscle
mišljenje *n.* opinion, view
miteser *m.* blackhead
miting *m.* rally
mitraljez *m.* heavy machine-gun
mizeran *adj.* lousy
mjehur *m.* bubble; bladder (urine)
mjenjačnica *f.* exchange office
mjera *f.* measure
mjerenje *n.* measurement
mjesečni *adj.* monthly
mjesec (nebesko tijelo) *m.* moon
mjesec (kalendarski) *m.* month
mjesečina *f.* moonlight
mjesto *n.* place, spot, location; sit
mješati *v.* stir
mlad *adj.* young
mlada *f.* bride
mladelački *adj.* youthful, juvenile
mladi luk *m.* chives
mladost *f.* youth
mlak *adj.* lukewarm
mlaz *m.* jet
mlijeko *n.* milk
mlin *m.* mill
mljekara *f.* dairy
mljeti *v.* grind
mljeveno meso *n.* minced-meat
mlohav *adj.* flabby

mnogi *adj.* many
mnogo *adv.* a lot
mnogobrojan *adj.* numerous
mnogostran *adj.* versatile
močvara *f.* swamp
moć *f.* power, might
moćan *adj.* powerful, mighty
moći *v.* be able to
moda *f.* fashion, vogue
mogućnost *f.* possibility
moguć *adj.* possible, eventual
molitva *f.* prayer
moj *pron.* my
mokar *adj.* wet; damp
mokraća *f.* urine
mokraćni mjehur *m.* bladder
molba *f.* request; application
molitelj *m.* applicant
moliti *v.* ask, beg, request
moliti se *v.* pray
moljac *m.* moth
molo *n.* pier
montaža *f.* fitting, installation
mora *f.* nightmare
morati *v.* have to, must
more *n.* sea
mornar *m.* sailor
morski *adj.* sea, maritime
morski rak/jastog *m.* lobster
most *m.* bridge
motati *v.* wind
motka *f.* pole
motor *m.* engine
mozak *m.* brain
možda *conj.* maybe, perhaps
mračan *adj.* dark; gloomy

mramor *m.* marble
mrav *m.* ant
mraz *m.* frost
mrena *f.* cataract
mreža *f.* net
mrkva *f.* carrot
mrlja *f.* spot, stain
mrmljanje *n.* murmur
mršav *adj.* thin, skinny; meager; lean
mrštiti se *v.* frown
mrtav *adj.* dead
mrvica *f.* crumb
mrziti *v.* hate
mrznuti *se* v. freeze
mržnja *f.* hatred
mucati *v.* stutter
mučan *adj.* painful
mučenje *n.* torture
mučiti *v.* torture, torment
mučiti *se* v. suffer
mućkati *v.* shake
mućnina *f.* nausea
mudar *adj.* smart, wise
mudrost *f.* wisdom
muha *f.* fly
muka *f.* torment
mumlati *v.* grumble
municija *f.* ammunition
munja *f.* lightning
mutan *adj.* vague
muškarac *m.* man, male
muški *adj.* male, masculine
mušterija *f.* customer
muzičar *m.* musician
muzika *f.* music
muč *m.* husband

N

na *prep.* on, at
na gore *prep.* upon
nabavljač *m.* supplier
nabavljati *v.* supply; purchase, acquire
nabor *m.* fold; wrinkle; pleat
nacija *f.* nation
nacrt *m.* outline; draft; design
načelo *n.* principle
način *m.* way, manner
nad *prep.* above, over
nada *f.* hope
nadahnuti *v.* motivate
nadimak *m.* nickname
nadlaktica *f.* upper arm
nadležan *adj.* competent
nadmašiti *v.* surpass; excel
nadmoćan *adj.* superior
nadnica *f.* wage
nadobudan *adj.* promising; ambitious
nadoknada *f.* compensation
nadoknaditi *v.* make-up for; reimburse
nadomjestiti *v.* substitute
nadoći *v.* rise
nadražaj *m.* stimulus; irritation
nadvožnjak *m.* overpass
nadzirati *v.* inspect, control, supervise
nadživjeti *v.* outlive
nafta *f.* oil, petroleum
nagadjati *v.* guess
nagao *adj.* sudden; hasty
naginjati *v.* incline
naglasak *m.* accent
naglasiti *v.* emphasize, accent

naglo *adv.* suddenly, quickly
nagluh *adj.* deaf
nagnuti (se) *v.* incline, tilt, lean over
nagomilati *v.* accumulate
nagon *m.* instinct
nagovjestiti *v.* announce; hint(at); herald
nagovoriti *v.* persuade; urge
nagrada *f.* reward, prize, award
nahraniti *v.* feed
naime *adv.* namely
najam *m.* rent; hire
najaviti *v.* announce
najbolji *adj.* the best
naježiti se *v.* get goose pimples
najgori *adj.* worst
najmanje *adv.* at least
najmiti *v.* hire, rent, lease
najviše *adj.* most
najzad *adv.* lastly
nakit *m.* jewelery
naklon *m.* bow
naknadno *adv.* later on, subsequently
nalaz *m.* finding
naličje *n.* reverse (side)
nalijepiti *v.* stick on
naljepnica *f.* label, sticker
namakati *v.* soak
nametljiv *adj.* intrusive
nametnuti se *v.* intrude
namignuti *v.* wink
namirisati *se* v. perfume oneself
namiriti *v.* settle
namjera *f.* intention
namjeran *adj.* deliberate
namjeravati *v.* intend
namjerno *adv.* on purpose, intentionally

namjestiti *v.* fix, mount; set
namještaj *pl.* furniture
namotavati *v.* wind
nana *f.* grandmother; mint
naniže *adv.* down
nanjušiti *v.* smell
nanos *m.* deposit, drift
nanula *f.* wooden-soled sandal
naočare *pl.* glasses, spectacles
naoko *adv.* seemingly
naokolo *adv.* around
naopako *adv.* upside-down; wrong
naoruzati *v.* arm
napad *m.* aggression; attack
napakostiti *v.* spite
napamet *adv.* by heart
napasti *v.* attack, assault; invade
napet *adj.* tense; tight
napetost *f.* tension
naplatiti *v.* charge; collect
napokon *adv.* finally
napomena *f.* mark, note
napon *m.* tension
napor *m.* effort, endeavor
napor *m.* effort
napredak *m.* progress; growth, development
napredan *adj.* progressive; advanced
napredovati *v.* make progress; grow
naprezati *v.* strain
naprijed *adv.* forward, ahead
naprotiv *adv.* on the contrary
napuhati *v.* inflate
napuniti *v.* fill (up); stuff
napustiti *v.* abandon, give up; withdraw
naranča/narandža *f.* orange
narasti *v.* grow

narav *f.* nature; temper
naredba *f.* order
narječje *n.* dialect
narkoman *m.* drug addict
naročito *adv.* especially
narod *m.* people, folks
narukvica *f.* bracelet
nasamo *adv.* in private
nasilje *n.* violence
nasip *m.* embankment, bank
naslaga *f.* layer
naslijediti *v.* inherit; succeed
nasljedan *adj.* hereditary
nasljednik *m.* heir, inheritor
nasljedstvo *n.* inheritance, heritage
naslonjač *m.* armchair
naslov *m.* title, headline
nasrtljiv *adj.* aggressive
nastati *v.* begin, originate
nastava *f.* instruction, teaching
nastaviti *v.* go on, continue, resume
nastavnik *m.* teacher, instructor, tutor
nastran *adj.* eccentric, peculiar, odd
nastup *m.* appearance
nasumce *adj.* at random
naš *pron.* our
naći *v.* find
natalitet *m.* birth rate
natašte *adv.* on an empty stomach
nateći *v.* swell
natenane *adv.* leisurely
natrij *m.* sodium
naučnik *m.* scholar
nauka *f.* science
navesti *v.* specify, list; quote
navijač *m.* supporter, fan

navika *f.* habit; custom
navodnjavanje *n.* irrigation
navratiti *v.* drop in, look in
nazad *adv.* back, backwards
nazdraviti *v.* toast
naziv *m.* name; term
naznačiti *v.* indicate, mark, denote
nazor *m.* idea, view, opinion
nažalost *adv.* unfortunately
ne *adv.* no, not
nečitljiv *adj.* illegible
nebesa *pl.* heavens
nebo *n.* sky
neboder *m.* skyscraper
nećak *m.* nephew
nećakinja *f.* niece
nedaleko *adv.* nearby
nedavno *adv.* recently
nedelja *f.* Sunday
nedirnut *adj.* intact
nedorastao *adj.* immature
nedosljedan *adj.* inconsistent
nedostajati *v.* lack
nedostatak *m.* lack; shortcoming
nedruštven *adj.* unsociable
negdje *adv.* somewhere
nego *adv.* than, but
neishranjenost *f.* malnutrition
neiskren *adj.* insincere, false
neispravan *adj.* faulty, out of order
neistinit *adj.* unfaithful
neizlječiv *adj.* incurable
neizvjestan *adj.* dubious, uncertain
nejasan *adj.* not clear, vague, obscure
nejednak *adj.* unequal; uneven
nekada *adv.* formerly, long ago

nekako *adv.* somehow
neki *pron.* a, some, a certain, any
neko *pron.* someone, somebody
nekoliko *pron.* several, a few, some
nekoristan *adj.* useless; worthless
nekretnina *f.* real estate
nekuda *adv.* somewhere, anywhere
nemar *m.* indolence
nemaran *adj.* indolent; careless
neminovan *adj.* inevitable
nemir *m.* unrest; anxiety
nemoguć *adj.* impossible
nemoj (part of speech) do not
nemoćan *adj.* helpless; unable
neobičan *adj.* unusual, uncommon
neobuzdan *adj.* rampant
neočekivan *adj.* unexpected
neodgojen *adj.* ill-mannered
neodločan *adj.* urgent
neodlučan *adj.* indecisive
neodredjen *adj.* indefinite; vague
neograničen *adj.* unlimited, absolute
neopravdan *adj.* unjustified
neosnovan *adj.* groundless
neosporan *adj.* indisputable
neoženjen *adj.* single
neparan *adj.* odd
nepažljiv *adj.* inattenive; absent-minded
nepce *n.* palate
nepismen *adj.* illiterate
neplodan *adj.* fruitless
nepodnošljiv *adj.* unbearable, intorelable
nepokretan *adj.* motionless, still; fixed
nepomićan *adj.* stationary
nepomirljiv *adj.* implacable
nepopustljiv *adj.* relentless, resolute

nepošten *adj.* dishonest; unfair
nepotreban *adj.* unnecessary
nepouzdan *adj.* unreliable
nepovjerenje *n.* distrust
nepoznat *adj.* unknown
nepravda *f.* injustice
nepravedan *adj.* unjust
nepredvidjen *adj.* unforeseen
neprekidan *adj.* continual; unbroken
neprihvaljiv *adj.* unacceptable
neprijatelj *m.* enemy
neprijateljski *adj.* hostile
neprijateljstvo *n.* hostility, animosity
neprijazan *adj.* unkind, unfriendly
neprikladan *adj.* unsuitable, inappropriate
neprilika *f.* trouble
nepristojan *adj.* impolite; indecent
nepristrasan *adj.* impartial, objective
neprocjenjiv *adj.* priceless
nepropustan *adj.* air-tight, water-tight
neproziran *adj.* opaque, non-transparent
nerazuman *adj.* unreasonable, irrational
nerazvijen *adj.* underdeveloped
nerc *m.* mink
nerdjajući *adj.* rust proof; stainless steel
nered *m.* disorder
nesanica *f.* insomnia
neskroman *adj.* immodest
neslaganje *n.* disagreement
neslan *adj.* unsalted, salt-free
neslužben *adj.* informal, casual
nespokojan *adj.* uneasy
nesporazum *m.* misunderstanding
nesposoban *adj.* incapable
nesposobnost *f.* inability
nespretan *adj.* clumsy; awkward

nesreća *f.* disaster; misfortune
nesreća *f.* bad luck, unhappiness
nestašica *f.* shortage
nestati *v.* disappear, vanish; wane
nestrpljiv *adj.* impatient
nestvaran *adj.* unreal
nesuglasica *f.* disagreement
nesumnjiv *adj.* doubtless, undoubted
nesvjestan *adj.* unaware
nesvjestica *f.* faint
neškodljiv *adj.* harmless
nešto *adv.* something
neudata *adj.* single
neugodan *adj.* embarassing; troublesome
neukusan *adj.* tasteless
neumoran *adj.* tireless
neuporediv *adj.* incomparable; incompatible
neuredan *adj.* untidy
neustrašiv *adj.* fearless, intrepid
nevidljiv *adj.* invisible
nevin *adj.* innocent; virgin
nevjerovatan *adj.* unbelievable, incredible
nevjesta *f.* bride
nevolja *f.* trouble
nevrijeme *n.* bad weather, storm
nezaboravan *adj.* unforgettable
nezadovoljstvo *n.* discontent
nezahvalan *adj.* ungrateful
nezakonit *adj.* illegal
nezaposlen *adj.* unemployed
nezaposlenost *f.* unemployment
nezavisan *adj.* independent
nezdrav *adj.* unhealthy
nezdrava hrana *f.* junk-food
nezgoda *f.* accident
neznatan *adj.* insignificant; negligible

nezreo *adj.* immature; unripe

neženja *m.* bachelor

nigdje *adv.* nowhere

nijem *adj.* mute, dumb

Nijemac *m.* German

nikada *adv.* never

nikako *adv.* not at all

niko *pron.* nobody

nit *f.* thread

niti *conj.* neither, nor

nivo *m.* level

niz *m.* row, series

nizak *adj.* low

Nizozemska *f.* The Netherlands, Holland

nizvodno *adv.* downstream

ništa *adv.* nothing

noć *f.* night

noćna mora *f.* nightmare

noga *f.* leg

nogomet *m.* soccer

nokat *m.* nail

nos *m.* nose

nosač *m.* porter

nositi *v.* carry; wear

nošnja *f.* costume; folk costume

notes *m.* memo-pad

nov *adj.* new

novčanik/šlajpek/buđelar *m.* wallet; purse

novčić *m.* penny pl. pence

novac *m.* money

novela *f.* short story

novembar *m.* November

novinar *m.* journalist

novorodjenče *n.* newborn child

novost *f.* news

nozdrva *f.* nostril

nož *m.* knife
nuditi *v.* offer, bid
nula/ništica *f.* zero, nil

NJ

njedra *pl.* breast
njega *f.* care; nursing
njegov *pron.* his; its
Njemačka *f.* Germany
njemu *pron.* him
njezin *pron.* her, hers
nježan *adj.* gentle; tender
njihati *v.* swing
njihov *pron.* their, theirs
njiva *f.* field
njuh *m.* sense of smell
njuška *f.* snout
njuškati *v.* smell, sniff

O

o *prep.* about
oba *adv.* either, both
obala *f.* coast, shore; bank
obasjati *v.* to illuminate, lihgt up
obasuti *v.* shower, flood; overwhelm
obaveza *f.* obligation, engagement
obavezati se *v.* commit oneself; engage
obavijestiti *v.* inform
obaviti *v.* do, perform, carry out
obdanište *n.* kindergarten
obeshrabriti *v.* discourage
obećati *v.* promise
običaj *m.* custom; habit
obično *adv.* usually
obilan *adj.* plentiful, abundant
obilazak *m.* tour, round
obilaznica *f.* detour
obilje *n.* abundance
obilovati *v.* abound
obim *m.* circumference
običan *adj.* ordinary, common; usual
objašnjenje *n.* explanation, comment
objasniti *v.* explain
objesiti *v.* hang (up)
oblak *m.* cloud
oblik *m.* shape
oblizati *v.* lick
oblog *m.* compress
obmanuti *v.* delude
obnoviti *v.* restore
obogatiti *v.* make rich; enrich
obostran *adj.* mutual
obozavati *v.* adore

obračun *m.* settlement; showdown
obrada *f.* processing; treatment
obradovati *v.* delight, make happy
obrati *v.* pick; skim
obratiti *se* v. apply to
obraz *m.* cheek
obrazac *m.* form
obrazovanje *n.* education
obrazovati *v.* educate; form
obred *m.* ritual
obrisati *v.* wipe
obrnuto *adv.* upside-down
obrok *m.* meal
obruč *m.* ring
obrva *f.* eyebrow
obuka *f.* training
obuti se *v.* put on shoes
obuzdati(se) *v.* restrain, control
obuća *pl.* footwear
obući(se) *v.* dress
obveznica *f.* bond
obzir *m.* regard, consideration
ocat *m.* vinegar
ocijeniti *v.* evaluate, assess; grade
očaj *m.* despair
očajan *adj.* desperate
očekivati *v.* expect
očetkati *v.* brush (off)
očit *adj.* obvious, evident
očarati *v.* fascinate, enchant, thrill
očekivati *v.* expect
očigledno *adv.* obviously
očuh *m.* stepfather
od *prep.* of; from; off
odabrati *v.* select
odakle *adv.* from where

odan *adj.* devoted
odašiljač *m.* transmitter
odazvati se *v.* respond to; call back
odbaciti *v.* throw off; discard, reject
odbojka *f.* volley ball
odbor *m.* committee
odbrana *f.* defense
odgadjati *v.* postpone, delay, put off
odgoj *m.* upbringing
odgovarajući *adj.* suitable; compatible
odgovarati *v.* suit; fit
odgovor *m.* answer, reply
odgovoran *adj.* responsible; liable
odgovoriti *v.* answer, reply; respond
odgristi *v.* bite off
odgurnuti *v.* push away
odigrati se *v.* take place
odijelo *n.* suit
odjaviti *v.* check out
odjednom *adv.* suddenly; all at once
odjek *m.* echo
odjeća *f.* clothes, garment, apparel
odlazak *m.* departure
odlediti *v.* defrost
odličan *adj.* excellent
odlijepiti *v.* unstick; pull off
odlikovanje *n.* decoration
odliti *v.* pour off
odložiti *v.* put aside
odlučan *adj.* determined, resolute
odlučiti(se) *v.* decide
odluka *f.* decision
odmah *adv.* at once, immediately
odmor *m.* rest; vacation
odnos *m.* relation
odobravanje *n.* approval; acclamation

odobrenje *n.* permission
odoljeti *v.* resist
odrastao čovjek *m.* adult, grown-up
odraz *m.* reflection
odražavati *v.* reflect
odredište *n.* destination
odrediti *v.* determine, define, fix
odredjen *adj.* definite, certain
odrezak *m.* steak
održavati *v.* maintain
odsjek *m.* department
odskočiti *v.* jump back; rebound
odstraniti *v.* remove
odsutan *adj.* absent, missing
oduljiti se *v.* drag on, linger
odustati *v.* give up
oduvijek *adj.* always
oduzeti *v.* take away; subtract; deduct
oduševljen *adj.* enthusiastic
odvesti *v.* take to; take away
odvezati *v.* untie, undo
odvojiti *v.* separate; detach
odvratan *adj.* disgusting
odvrnuti *v.* turn off; unscrew
ogladniti *v.* become hungry
oglas *m.* advertisment, announcement
oglasiti *v.* announce; advertise
ogledalo *n.* mirror
ognjište *n.* fireplace
ogovarati *v.* gossip
ograda *f.* fence
ogranak *m.* branch
ograničen *adj.* narrow-minded
ograničiti *v.* bound; terminate; restrict
ogrebotina *f.* scratch
ogrjev *m.* fuel; firewood

ogrlica *f.* necklace
ogroman *adj.* huge, immense, enormous
ogrtač *m.* overcoat
oguliti *v.* peel
ohladiti (se) *v.* cool (off)
ohol *adj.* haughty
ohrabriti *v.* encourage
okaniti se *v.* give up
okean *m.* ocean
okinuti *v.* trigger
okliznuti *se v.* slip
okljevati *v.* hesitate
oko *n.* eye
oko *adv.* around
okolina *f.* environment, surroundings
okolnost *f.* circumstance
okomit *adj.* perpendicular, vertical
okovati *v.* chain
okrečiti *v.* whitewash
okret *m.* turn, rotation
okretati *v.* turn, revolve, spin
okretati (se) *v.* rotate
okriviti *v.* blame; accuse
okrugao *adj.* round
oktobar *m.* October
okupiti (se) *v.* gather
olabaviti *v.* slacken, loosen
olakšanje *n.* relief
olovka *f.* pencil
olovo *n.* lead
oluja *f.* storm, thunderstorm
oluk *m.* gutter
olupina *f.* wreck
omča *f.* loop
ometati *v.* hamper; thwart
omiljen *adj.* popular, favorite

omjer *m.* proportion; ratio
omogučiti *v.* make possible, enable
on *pron.* he
on lično *adv.* himself
ona *pron.* she
onaj *pron.* that
onesposobiti *v.* disable; knock out
onesvjestiti *se* v. faint
oni *pron.* they
ono *pron.* it
ono samo *pron.* itself
opadati *v.* decline, decrease
opak *adj.* wicked; vicious
opasan *adj.* dangerous
opasač *m.* belt
opasnost *f.* danger; emergency
opažanje *n.* perception
opeći (se) *v.* burn (oneself)
operacija *f.* surgery, operation
opet *adv.* again
opip *m.* (sense of) touch
opipljiv (fig.) *adj.* tangible; palpable
opis *m.* description
opisati *v.* describe
opklada *f.* bet
opkoliti *v.* surround
oplakivati *v.* mourn, lament
opna *f.* membrane
opomena *f.* warning
oporaviti se *v.* recover, get better
oporezovati *v.* tax
opravdan *adj.* justified, legitimate
opravdati *v.* justify
oprema *f.* equipment
oprez *m.* precaution
opruga *f.* spring

opsada *f.* siege
opseg *m.* degree; extent
opsezan *adj.* extensive
optičar *m.* optician
optužiti *v.* accuse(of), charge(with)
opustiti se *v.* relax
opšiti *v.* edge; ham
orah *m.* walnut
orao *m.* eagle
ordinacija *f.* (doctor's) office
orkan *m.* hurricane
ormar *m.* wardrobe; closet; cupboard
ortak *m.* partner
oružje *pl.* arms, weapons
osa *f.* wasp
osakatiti *v.* cripple
osam *num.* eight
osamdeset *num.* eighty
osamnaest *num.* eighteen
osiguranje *n.* insurance
osigurati *v.* ensure
osigurač *m.* fuse
osijediti *v.* turn grey (hair)
osim *prep.* besides, except
osim da *prep.* morover
osip *m.* rash
osjeka *f.* low tide
osjetljiv *adj.* sensitive; sensible
osjećanje *n.* feeling, sentiment
osjećati *v.* feel
oslabiti *v.* weaken
osladiti *v.* to sweeten, make sweet
osloboditi (se) *v.* get rid of, release
osloniti se *v.* rely on; lean (on)
osmjeh *m.* smile
osnivač *m.* founder

osnova *f.* basis; foundation
osnovni *adj.* basic, prime
osoba *f.* person
osobina *f.* characteristic
osoblje *n.* personnel, staff
osovina *f.* axle; axis
ospice *pl.* measles
osposobiti *v.* fit; train, qualify
ostariti *v.* grow old
ostatak *m.* left over; residue
ostaviti *v.* abandon; give up; leave
ostavka *f.* resignation
ostriga *f.* oyster
ostrvo *n.* island
ostvariti *v.* realize
osuda *f.* sentence
osvajač *m.* conqueror
osvetiti se *v.* revenge
osvježenje *n.* refreshment
osvježiti *v.* refresh
ošamariti *v.* slap
ošamutiti *v.* daze
ošišati *v.* cut hair
oštar *adj.* sharp; keen; severe;
oštećenje *n.* damage
oštrica *f.* blade, cutting edge
otac *m.* father
oteklina *f.* swelling
otiži *v.* go away; leave, apart
otirač *m.* doormat; mop
otkako *adv.* as long as, since
otključati *v.* unlock
otkopčati (se) *v.* unbutton
otkriće *n.* discovery
otkriti *v.* discover; detect; reveal
otmica *f.* abduction; kidnapping

otpaci *pl.* garbage
otpor *m.* resistance
otprilike *adv.* about, approximately
otpustiti *v.* dismiss; discharge, fire
otrov *m.* poison
otuda *adv.* from there, hence
otvaranje *n.* opening
otvoriti *v.* open; turn on
ovaj *pron.* this
ovakav *adj.* such
ovca *f.* sheep; ewe
ovdje *adv.* here
ovlažiti *v.* moisten
ozbiljan *adj.* serious
ozdraviti *v.* get well, recover
ožedniti *v.* become thirsty
oženiti se *v.* marry
oženjen *adj.* married
ožiljak *m.* scar
oživiti *v.* revive; enliven

P

pa *conj.* well; and
pacijent *m.* patient
pacov *m.* rat
pad *m.* fall; decline; drop
padati *n.* fall
padina *f.* slope
padobran *m.* parachute
pahuljica *f.* flake, fluff
pakao *m.* hell
paket *m.* parcel
pakostan *adj.* malicious, spiteful
pakovati *v.* pack
palac *m.* thumb
palačinka *f.* pancake
palata *f.* palace
palma *f.* palm
paluba *f.* deck
pamćenje *n.* memory
pamet *f.* mind
pametan *adj.* smart; clever; wise
pamtiti *v.* remember
pamuk *m.* cotton
panj *m.* stump; block
pantalone *pl.* pants, trousers
papa *m.* pope
papagaj *m.* parrot
papir *m.* paper
paprika *f.* pepper
papuča *f.* slipper
par *m.* pair; couple
para *f.* steam; vapour
paradajz *m.* tomato
parcela *f.* lot

parfem *m.* perfume
parnica *f.* law-suit
pas *m.* dog
pasoš *m.* passport
pastrmka *f.* trout
pasulj *m.* kidney-bean
patiti *v.* suffer
patka *f.* duck
patuljak *m.* gnome
paučina *f.* web
pauk *m.* spider
paun *m.* peacock
pauza *f.* recess, intermission
pazar *m.* bargain
paziti *v.* keep watch; take care
pazuh *m.* armpit
pažljiv *adj.* careful
pažnja *f.* attention; care; interest
pčela *f.* bee
pečat *m.* seal
pecati *v.* fish
pečurka *f.* mushroom
peć *f.* stove, oven, furnace
peći *v.* bake, roast, toast, grill
pećina *f.* cave
pedeset *num.* fifty
pegla *f.* iron
pejsaž *m.* landscape
pekara *f.* bakery
pekmez *m.* jam; marmelade
pelena *f.* diaper
penjati se *v.* climb
penkalo *n.* pen
penzija *f.* retirement; pension
pepeljara *f.* ashtray
pepeo *m.* ash

perad *pl.* poultry
perika *f.* wig
period *m.* period, interval
pero *n.* feather
pertla *f.* shoelace
perut *f.* dandruff
peršin *m.* parsley
pesnica *f.* fist
peškir *m.* towel
peta *f.* heel
petak *m.* Friday
peteljka *f.* stalk; stem
petlja *f.* loop
petnaest *num.* fifteen
piće *n.* drink
pidjama *f.* pajamas
pihtija *f.* jelly
pijaca *f.* market
pijan *adj.* drunk
pijanica *m.* drunkard; bum
pijesak *m.* sand
pijetao *m.* rooster, cock
pila *f.* saw
pile *n.* chicken
pipa *f.* faucet, tap
pipati *v.* touch; feel
pire krompir *m.* mashed potato
pisac *m.* writer
pisaća mašina *f.* typewriter
pisaći sto *m.* desk
pisati *v.* write
pismenost *f.* literacy
pismo *n.* letter
pita *f.* pie
pitati *v.* ask, question
piti *v.* drink

pitom *adj.* tame
pivo *n.* beer
pjega *f.* spot; freckle
pjena *f.* foam
pjesma *f.* song; poem
pješak *m.* pedestrian
pješke/pješice *adv.* on foot
pjevač *m.* singer
pjevati *v.* sing
plafon *m.* ceiling
plakati *v.* cry; weep
plamen *m.* flame
plan *m.* design, plan
planina *f.* mountain
planuti *v.* catch fire
plata *f.* payment, wages, salary
platiti *v.* pay
platno *n.* linen; canvas
plav *adj.* blue
plavuša *f.* blonde
plaža *f.* beach
pleča *pl.* shoulder
pleme *n.* tribe
plemenit *adj.* noble
plemić *m.* nobleman, aristocrat
ples *m.* dance
plesti *v.* knit; braid; weave
pletenica *f.* braid
plijen *m.* prey; booty
plijesan *f.* mildew
plin *m.* gas
plitak *adj.* shallow
pliš *m.* plush
plivati *v.* swim
pljeskati *v.* clap
pljusak *m.* shower

pljuvati *v.* spit
ploča *f.* plate; board
pločnik *m.* pavement
plod *m.* produce; fruit
plomba *f.* plumb; filling
plosnat *adj.* flat; level
plot *m.* fence
ploviti *v.* float; navigate
plug *m.* plough
pluvačka *f.* saliva
pluća *f.* lungs
pobačaj *m.* miscarriage
pobijediti *v.* win; defeat
pobjeda *f.* victory; triumph
pobjednik *m.* winner
pobjeći *v.* escape
poblijediti *v.* turn pale
poboljšati *v.* improve; amend
pobožan *adj.* religious
pobuna *f.* mutiny
počast *f.* honors
početak *m.* beginning
početi *v.* begin; start
početnica *f.* primer
počiniti *v.* commit
pod *m.* floor
pod *prep.* under, below; beneath
podaci *pl.* data
podcijeniti *v.* underestimate
poderati *v.* tear
podesan *adj.* appropriate; opportune
podgrijati *v.* warm-up
podići *v.* raise
podijeliti *v.* divide; share; split
podkošulja *f.* undershirt, vest
podloga *f.* base; support; foundation

podmazati *v.* lubricate
podmititi *v.* bribe
podmladiti(se) *v.* rejuvenate
podmornica *f.* submarine
podmukao *adj.* sneak; mean person
podne *n.* noon, midday
podnijeti *v.* withstand, bear, stand
podrezati *v.* trim
podrignuti *v.* belch
podrum *m.* basement
podsjetiti *v.* remind
podstanar *m.* tenant
podsvijest *f.* subconsciouness
podučavati *v.* teach; tutor
podupirati *v.* support
podvrgnuti *v.* submit
podvući *v.* underline
podzemni *adj.* underground
poezija *f.* poetry
pogadjati *v.* guess
poginuti *v.* perish; die
pogled *m.* look; view; glimpse; sight
pogodan *adj.* favorable
pogoršati *v.* make worse; aggravate
pogostiti *v.* entertain
pogreb *m.* funeral
pogrešan *adj.* wrong
pogubiti *v.* execute
pohlepan *adj.* greed, avidity, eagerness
pohvala *f.* praise
pojačati *v.* strengthen; amplify
pojam *m.* notion, idea, concept
pojas *m.* belt
pojaviti se *v.* appear; emerge
pojedinost *f.* detail
pojednostaviti *v.* simplify

pojesti *v.* eat up
pokazati *v.* show, demonstrate, display
pokisnuti *v.* get wet
poklon *m.* present, gift; donation
pokloniti *v.* gift; donate
poklopac *m.* lid
pokojni *adj.* the late; dead; deceased
pokolj *m.* slaughter, massacre
pokopati *v.* bury
pokret *m.* movement; motion; gesture
pokrivač *m.* blanket; comforter
pokupiti *v.* collect; gather; pick up
pokus *m.* experiment
pokušati *v.* try; attempt
pokvaren *adj.* bad; corrupt; vicious
pokvariti *v.* spoil; ruin; corrupt
pokvasiti *v.* wet; moisten
polica *f.* shelf
polje *n.* field
poljoprivreda *f.* agriculture
poljubac *m.* kiss
položaj *m.* position; situation; stand
položiti *v.* lay
polovina *f.* half
poluga *f.* lever, bar
poluostrvo *n.* peninsula
Poljska *f.* Poland
pomagati *v.* help, assist, aid
pomaknuti *v.* shift; move
pomesti *v.* sweep up
pomiriti *v.* reconcile; make it up
pomnožiti *v.* multiply
pomoć *f.* help, aid
pomoćnik *m.* assistant
ponašanje *n.* behaviour
ponašati se *v.* behave

ponedeljak   *m.* Monday
ponekada   *adv.* sometimes
poništiti   *v.* cancel
ponizan   *adj.* humble
poniziti   *v.* humilate; humble; abase
ponoć   *f.* midnight
ponos   *m.* pride
ponosan   *adj.* proud
ponoviti   *v.* repeat
ponuda   *f.* offer; bid
ponuditi   *v.* offer
pop   *m.* priest
popis   *m.* list; inventory
poplava   *f.* flood
popločati   *v.* pave
popraviti   *v.* fix, repair; correct
poprečan   *adj.* oblique; transversal
popuniti   *v.* fill, fill out
popust   *m.* discount
poraz   *m.* defeat
porcelan   *m.* china
pored   *adv.* beside; besides; as well
poredak   *m.* order; sequence
poredati   *v.* arrange
poredjenje   *n.* comparison
porez   *m.* tax
poricati   *v.* deny; dispute
porijeklo   *n.* origin
porodica   *f.* family
porodjaj   *m.* childbirth
porok   *m.* vice
porota   *f.* jury
porub   *m.* hem; border
poručnik   *m.* lieutenant
poruka   *f.* message
porušiti   *v.* demolish

posada *f.* crew
posaditi *v.* plant; set
posao *m.* job; business; deal
posijati *v.* saw
posipati *v.* sprinkle; strew
posjeći *v.* fell; cut down
posjedovati *v.* possess; own
posjetilac *m.* visitor
posjetiti *v.* visit
poslati *v.* send; dispatch
poslije *prep.* after; afterwards
poslije podne *n.* afternoon
posljedica *f.* outcome; consequence
posljednji *adj.* the last, final
poslodavac *m.* employer
poslovica *f.* proverb, saying
poslovodja *m.* manager; chief
poslušan *adj.* obedient
posmatrač *m.* observer
posmatrati *v.* watch; observe
posoliti *v.* salt
pospan *adj.* sleepy; drowsy
pospremiti *v.* put in order, tidy up
posrednik *m.* mediator; agent
postati *v.* become
postava *f.* lining
postaviti *v.* set; place
posteljina *f.* bedding
postepen *adj.* gradual
postići *v.* achieve
postidjen *adj.* ashamed
postotak *m.* percent
postojati *v.* exist
postolje *n.* stand
postupati *v.* treat; deal with
posuda *f.* dish; vessel

posuditi   *v.* lend; borrow
posvetiti   *v.* devote; dedicate
pošiljalac   *m.* sender
pošiljka   *f.* shipment; parcel
pošta   *f.* post, mail
poštar   *m.* mailman, postman
poštarina   *f.* postage
pošten   *adj.* honest; fair; just
pošto   *adv.* after, when, as
pošto?   how much?
poštovan   *adj.* respected; honored
poštovanje   *n.* respect
potapšati   *v.* tap
poticaj   *m.* encouragement; impulse
poticati   *v.* stimulate
potiljak   *m.* nape
potjera   *f.* chase
potkopati   *v.* undermine
potkovica   *f.* horseshoe
potok   *m.* brook
potomak   *m.* descendant; off-spring
potopiti   *v.* immerse; sink
potpaliti   *v.* set fire to; light
potpetica   *f.* heel
potpis   *m.* signature
potplatiti   *v.* bribe
potpun   *adj.* complete; full; thorough
potražnja   *f.* demand; requirement; claim
potreba   *f.* need; necessity
potreban   *adj.* necessary
potres   *m.* earthquake
potrošač   *m.* consumer
potrošiti   *v.* expend
potvrda   *f.* certificate; confirmation
potvrditi   *v.* confirm; verify
pouzdan   *adj.* reliable; trustworthy

povećati *v.* increase
povijest *f.* history
povik *m.* shout
povjerenje *n.* trust; confidence
povjerljiv *adj.* confidental
povjetarac *m.* breeze
povod *m.* occasion
povraćati *v.* vomit
povreda *f.* injury
povremen *adj.* occasional
površina *f.* surface; area
povrće *n.* vegetable
povući se *v .* withdraw; retire
pozadina *f.* background; rear
pozdrav *m.* greeting; salute
pozdraviti *v.* salute; greet
poziv *m.* call; summons; invitation
poznanstvo *n.* acquaintance
pozorište *n.* theater
pozornica *f.* stage
pozvati *v.* invite; summon
požar *m.* fire
poželjan *adj.* desirable
pradjed *m.* great-grandfather; ancestor
prag *m.* threshold
pramen *m.* tuft; lock
praonica *f.* laundry
prasa *f.* leek
prasak *m.* burst
prasetina *f.* pork
prašina *f.* dust
prašnjav *adj.* dusty
prašuma *f.* rain forest
prati *v.* wash
pratiti *v.* escort; follow; accompany
pravda *f.* justice

pravi *adj.* genuine, original
pravično *adv.* right; justice, fair
pravilo *n.* rule
praviti *v.* make; produce; manufacture
pravo *n.* law; justice; right
pravopis *m.* spelling
pravougaonik *m.* rectangle
prazan *adj.* empty; blank; vacant
praznik *m.* holiday
praznina *f.* vacancy
praznovjerje *n.* superstition
prebivalište *n.* residence
preboljeti *v.* get over, get well
prečica *f.* short cut
prečka *f.* bar; rung
pričvrstiti *v.* fasten; attach
pred *prep.* before; in front of
predak *m.* ancestor
predati se *v.* surrender
predavanje *n.* lecture
predgovor *m.* introduction; foreword
predgradje *n.* suburb; outskirts
predhodan *adj.* preliminary; previous
predhoditi *v.* precede
predja *f.* yarn
predjašnji *adj.* prior
predložiti *v.* propose; suggest
predmet *m.* object; subject
prednji *adj.* forward
prednost *f.* advantage; privilege
predomisliti *se v.* change one's mind
predrasuda *f.* prejudice
predsjednik *m.* president
predsoblje *n.* hall
predstava *f.* performance; show
predstaviti *v.* introduce

predstavljati *v.* represent
preduzeće *n.* enterprise
preduzeti *v.* undertake
predvorje *n.* lobby
pregovarati *v.* negotiate
prehlada *f.* cold
prekidač *m.* switch
prekinuti *v.* break; interrupt
preko *prep.* across; over
prekoriti *v.* blame
prekrasan *adj.* wonderful; magnificent
prekriti *v.* cover (with)
prekršaj *m.* offense; breach
prekršiti *v.* violate
prelaz *m.* crossing; transit
preljub *m.* adultery
prelom *m.* fracture; break
prema *prep.* accordingly; against
premda *conj.* although
preminuti *v.* die; pass away
prenos *m.* transfer
prepasti *v.* frighten; scare
prepasti *v.* scare
prepisati *v.* prescribe
preporučiti *v.* recommend
preporuka *f.* recommendation; reference
prepoznati *v.* recognize
prepravka *f.* modification
prepreka *f.* barrier; obstacle
preskočiti *v.* skip
presoliti *v.* oversalt
prespavati *v.* oversleep
prestati *v.* cease; stop; finish
presuda *f.* verdict; judgment; decree
presušiti *v.* dry up
pretinac *m.* locker; drawer

pretjerati *v.* overdo; exaggerate
pretplatiti(se) *v.* subscribe
pretpostaviti *v.* suppose, assume
pretpostavka *f.* assumption; presumption
pretrpjeti *v.* undergo; endure; suffer
pretvarati se *v.* pretend, simulate
prevara *f.* fraud; cheat
prevariti *v.* cheat; deceive
previše *adv.* too much
prevod *m.* translation
prevoditi *v.* translate
prevoz *m.* transportation
prevrnuti (se) *v.* tumble
prezime *n.* family name, surname
prezir *m.* contempt
prezirati *v.* contempt, scorn
preživjeti *v.* survive
pribaviti *v.* provide
približiti se *v.* approach
približan *adj.* approximate
pribor *m.* accessories; kit
pričekati *v.* wait for
pričuvati *v.* reserve
pridikovati *v.* preach
pridjev *m.* adjective
pridodati *v.* append
prići *v.* come up to; approach
prigovor *m.* objection
prihod *m.* income; revenue; profit
prihvatiti *v.* accept (take)
prihvatljiv *adj.* acceptable
prijatan *adj.* pleasant
prijatelj(ica) *f.* friend
prijateljski *adj.* friendly
prijateljstvo *n.* friendship
prijava *f.* report; denunciation

prijašnji *adj.* former; previous
prije *prep.* before; ago; formerly
prijedlog *m.* proposal; suggestion
prijesto *m.* throne
prijestonica/prijestolnica *f.* metropolis, capital
prijetiti *v.* threaten
prijetnja *f.* threat; menace
prikaz *m.* review
prikladan *adj.* suitable, convenient
priključak *m.* connection
prilagoditi *v.* adjust , adapt
prilagodljiv *adj.* adaptable
prilaz *m.* access; entrance; approach
prilično *adv.* rather; fairly
prilika *f.* chance, opportunity
primalac *m.* receiver
primanje *n.* reception
primijeniti *v.* apply
primirje *n.* truce
primiti *v.* receive
primjedba *f.* remark; comment; note
primjena *f.* application
primjer *m.* example
primjerak *m.* specimen
primorje *n.* seaside
pripadati *v.* belong
pripaziti *v.* look after
pripovjetka *f.* short story; tale
pripremiti *v.* prepare
pripovjedač *m.* narrator
priroda *f.* nature
prirodan *adj.* natural
priručnik *m.* textbook
prisan *adj.* intimate
prisiliti *v.* force, compel
pristojan *adj.* decent; proper; polite

pristup *m.* admission; access
pristupaćan *adj.* accessible
pristupiti *v.* approach; join, enter
prisutan *adj.* present
prišiti *v.* sew on; stich on
pritisak *m.* pressure
priuštiti *v.* afford
prividan *adj.* apparent
priviknuti *v.* accustom
privjesak *m.* pendant; tag
privlačan *adj.* attractive
privlačiti *v.* attract, draw
privreda *f.* economy; business
privremen *adj.* temporary
priznanje *n.* acknowledgment
priznati *v.* admit; confess
prizor *m.* scene; spectacle; sight
prkos *m.* defiance, spite
prkositi *v.* defy
prljav *adj.* dirty
proba *f.* trial; test; rehearsal
probava *f.* digestion
problijediti *v.* turn pale
probosti *v.* pierce; stitch
probuditi se *v.* awake
probušiti *v.* pierce; perforate; stitch
procijeniti *v.* estimate; evaluate
procjena *f.* appraisal; assessment
pročelje *n.* front; facade
pročistiti *v.* clean; purify; purge
pročitati *v.* read
proći *v.* pass by, go by
prodati *v.* sell
prodavac *m.* salesperson
prodrijeti *v.* penetrate
produžiti *v.* extend, prolong

proglasiti *v.* proclaim
prognati *v.* banish
prognoza *f.* forecast
progoniti *v.* prosecute
progutati *v.* swallow
proizvod *m.* product
proklet *adj.* damned
proliti *v.* spill
proljev *m.* diarrhea
proljeće *n.* spring
promet *m.* traffic
promijeniti *v.* change
promjenjiv *adj.* variable
promjer *m.* diameter
promocija *f.* graduation
promukao *adj.* hoarse; husky
pronalazak *m.* invention
pronaći *v.* find out; invent; discover
propis *m.* rule, regulation
proplanak *m.* clearing; lawn
propovjedaonica *f.* pulpit
propust *m.* omission; negligence; fail
propustiti *v.* miss; omit
prorez *m.* slot, slit
proreći *v.* predict
prosipati *v.* waste; scatter; spill
prosječan *adj.* average, ordinary
proslava *f.* jubilee
prost *adj.* rude, vulgar
prostor *m.* room; space
proširiti *v.* expand
protiv *prep.* against
protivnik *m.* antagonist; opponent
provesti *v.* spend; carry out
providan *adj.* transparent
provjeriti *v.* examine, check

provjetriti *v.* ventilate; air
prozor *m.* window
proždrljiv *adj.* greedy
prsa *f.* chest; breast
prskati *v.* sprinkle; splash
prst *m.* finger; toe
prsten *m.* ring
pršut *m.* smoked ham
prtljag *m.* luggage, baggage
prvak *m.* champion
prvenstvo *n.* priority
prvi *adj.* first
pržiti *v.* fry
psihijatar *m.* psychiatrist
pšenica *f.* wheat
ptica *f.* bird
puž *m.* snail
pubertet *m.* puberty
pucati *v.* shoot, fire
pučina *f.* high sea
puder *m.* powder
puhati *v.* blow
pukotina *f.* crack; gap; leak
pumphozne *pl.* knickerbockers
pun *adj.* full
punac *m.* father-in-law
punica *f.* mother-in-law
puno *adv.* much
punomoć *f.* warrant
pupak *m.* navel
pupoljak *m.* bud
pust *adj.* waste
pustinja *f.* desert
pustiti *v.* leave
pustolovina *f.* adventure
pustoš *f.* havoc

pustošiti   *v.* devastate
pušač   *m.* smoker
puška   *f.* rifle, gun
put   *m.* way, road; route
putanja   *f.* orbit
puter   *m.* butter
putnik   *m.* passenger, traveler
putokaz   *m.* sign post
putovanje   *n.* travel, journey, voyage
putovati   *v.* travel
puzati   *v.* crawl, creep

R

račun *m.* account; bill; invoice
računar *m.* computer
računati *v.* calculate; reckon
računovodja *m.* accountant
račvati se *v.* fork, bifurcate
rad *m.* work; labor; job
radi *conj.* because of
radije *adv.* rather; sooner
radionica *f.* workshop
raditi *v.* do; work
radnik *m.* worker
rado *adv.* gladly, willingly
radost *f.* joy, delight
radostan *adj.* glad, joyful
radoznao *adj.* curious
raj *m.* paradise
rajsferšlus *m.* zipper
rak *m.* crab; shrimp; cancer
raka *f.* grave, tomb
raketa *f.* rocket
rakija *f.* brandy
rakun *m.* raccoon
ram *m.* frame
rame *n.* shoulder
rana *f.* wound, sore; injury
raniji *adj.* former
ranjav *adj.* vulnerable; sore
rano *adv.* early
rashladiti se *v.* cool off
rashod *m.* expenses, expenditure
rasipan *adj.* wasteful
raskinuti *v.* disrupt
raskliman *adj.* shaky

raskoš *f.* luxury; splendor
raskršće *n.* crossing; intersection
raspad *m.* crumbling, decay
raspeće *n.* crucifix
raspitati se *v.* make inquiries
rasplakati se *v.* burst into tears
rasplinuti se *v.* fade away, dissolve
raspodjela *f.* distribution
raspolagati *v.* dispose of
raspoloženje *n.* temper, mood
raspoloživ *adv.* available
raspon *m.* span; range
raspored *m.* scheme, program; schedule
rasporediti *v.* arrange, sort out
rasporiti *v.* rip (off), unstitch
raspoznati *v.* identify; recognize
raspravljati *v.* debate; discuss; argue
raspremiti *v.* clear away; dismantle
rasprodaja *f.* sale, clearance
rasprsnuti se *v.* burst, blow up, explode
raspući *v.* split
raspust *m.* vacation
raspustiti *v.* dismiss
rastegnuti *v.* stretch; draw
rasteretiti *v.* unburden
rastezati *v.* stretch, extend
rasti *v.* grow
rastojanje *n.* distance
rastopiti *v.* dissolve; melt; thaw
rastresen *adj.* absent-minded
rastrgati *v.* tear to pieces
rasuti *v.* scatter; spill; waste
rasvijetliti *v.* light up, illuminate
raširiti *v.* spread; extand, expand
rat *m.* war
rata *f.* installment

ratarstvo   *n.* agriculture
ratnik   *m.* warrior; fighter
ratoboran   *adj.* militant; aggressive
ravan   *f.* plain, plateau
ravan   *adj.* level, flat; straight
ravnalo   *n.* ruler
ravnica   *f.* plain
ravnodusan   *adj.* indifferent, apathetic
razbiti   *v.* break in pieces, smash
razbjesniti   *v.* infuriate
razblažiti   *v.* dilute
razbojnik   *m.* robber, bandit
razboljeti se   *v.* become ill
razborit   *adj.* sensible; reasonable
razboritost   *f.* common sense; prudence
razdražiti   *v.* provoke; irritate; enrage
razdražljiv   *adj.* irritable
razgledati   *v.* view; look at
razgovor   *m.* talk, conversation
razgovorljiv   *adj.* talkative
razjasniti   *v.* explain; clarify
različit   *adj.* different, various
razlika   *f.* difference
razlikovati se   *v.* distinguish, differ
razlog   *m.* reason; ground; cause
razlomak   *m.* fraction
razmak   *m.* distance; interval
razmažen   *adj.* spoiled
razmisliti   *v.* consider, think over
razmjena   *f.* exchange
razmnožiti   *se v.* multiply
razmotati   *v.* unfold, unpack
raznolikost   *f.* diversity; variety
raznositi   *v.* deliver
raznovrstan   *adj.* miscellaneous
razočarati   *v.* disappoint

razoriti *v.* destroy; demolish
razred *m.* grade; classroom
razriješiti *v.* solve
razrok *adj.* cross-eyed
razum *m.* intellect, reason, sense
razuman *adj.* rational; intelligent
razumijevanje *n.* understanding, comprehens
razumjeti *v.* understand, comprehend
razvedriti se *v.* clear up; brighten up
razviti *v.* develop; evolve
razvod *m.* divorce
razvoj *m.* development, progress
raž *f.* rye
ražalostiti *v.* make sad, sadden, afflict
rdja *f.* rust
režiser *m.* director
rešetka *f.* grate, grid
reagovati *v.* react
rebro *n.* rib
recept *m.* recipe; prescription
rečenica *f.* sentence, clause
reći *v.* say, tell
red *m.* order
reklama *f.* publicity; advertisement
religija *f.* religion
remen *m.* strap; belt
rentgen *m.* x-rays
rep *m.* tail
rerna *f.* oven
rever *m.* lapel
revnosan *adj.* eager
rezanac *m.* noodle
rezati *v.* cut, slice; carve
rezime *m.* summary
rezultat *m.* result; effect
riba *f.* fish

ribati *v.* scrub
ribnjak *m.* fish-pond
ricinus *m.* castor oil
rigati *v.* vomit; belch
riječ *f.* word; term; expression
rječit *adj.* eloquent
rječnik *m.* dictionary; vocabulary
rijedak *adj.* rare, scarce; thin
rijeka *f.* river
riješiti *v.* solve; settle
rijetko *adv.* rarely, seldom
rikati *v.* roar
rizik *m.* risk; hazard; venture
riža *f.* rice
rješenje *n.* solution; decision
rob *m.* slave
roba *f.* goods; merchandise; ware
rodan *adj.* fruitful; fertile
rodbina *f.* relatives, kin
roditelj *m.* parent
roditi *v.* bear, give birth to
rodjak *m.* relative
rodjen *adj.* born
rodjendan *m.* birthday
rodjenje *n.* birth, delivery
rodni *adj.* native
rodoljub *m.* patriot
rok *m.* deadline; term
roman *m.* novel
roniti *v.* dive, plunge
rosa *f.* dew
rotkvica *f.* radish
rasadnik *m.* nursery
rub *m.* edge; rim; margin; border
rubac *m.* napkin, handkerchief
rublje *n.* underwear; linen

ručak *m.* dinner, lunch
ručati *v.* dine, have dinner(lunch)
ručka *f.* handle
ručni *adj.* manual, by hand
ručni zglob *m.* wrist
ruda *f.* ore, mineral
rudar *m.* miner
rudnik *m.* mine, pit
rugati se *v.* mock
rujan *m.* September
ruka *f.* arm; hand; wrist
rukav *m.* sleeve
rukavica *f.* glove
rukopis *m.* handwriting; manuscript
rukovati *v.* manipulate, handle, operate
rukovodilac *m.* manager
rukovodstvo *n.* management
rupa *f.* hole; gap; puncture
ruševina *f.* ruin
ruž za usne *m.* lipstick
ruža *f.* rose
ružan *adj.* ugly; nasty
ružiti *v.* blemish
ružnoća *f.* ugliness

S

sa   *s* prep. with
sablja *f.* sabre
sabor *m.* parliament, congress
sačuvati *v.* preserve; keep from; save
sada *adv.* now, at present
saditi *v.* plant
sadržaj *m.* contents, summary
sadržavati *v.* contain; hold; include
sadržina *f.* contents; volume
saft *m.* sauce
sagraditi *v.* build, erect
sahrana *f.* burial
sahraniti *v.* bury
sajam *m.* fair, market
sakat *adj.* crippled
sako *m.* jacket
sakriti *v.* hide, conceal
sakupljati *v.* collect, gather
salata *f.* lettuce; salad
sam *adj.* alone; sole; only
samljeti *v.* grind
samo *adv.* only; just; merely
samoglasnik *m.* vowel, vocal
samoodbrana *f.* self-defense
samoubistvo *n.* suicide
samovoljan *adj.* arbitrary; obstinate
samoća *f.* loneliness, solitude
samt *m.* velvet
san *m.* sleep; dream
sanduk *m.* trunk, chest; coffin
sanjati *v.* dream
sanke *pl.* sleigh, sledge
santa *f.* iceberg

saobraćaj *m.* traffic, transportation
saopštiti *v.* announce; make known
sapun *m.* soap
saradjivati *v.* cooperate; collaborate
sastanak *m.* appointment; meeting
sastaviti *v.* put together; join
sastojak *m.* ingredient; component
sastojati *se* v. consist (of)
sasvim *adv.* entirely; quite; fully
sat *m.* clock; watch; hour
sašiti *v.* sew up (together)
satnica *f.* time table
saučešče *n.* condolence; sympathy
sav *adj.* all, whole, entire
savez *m.* union; association
saviti *v.* fold, bend
savjest *f.* conscience, consciousness
savjet *m.* advice; council
savjetovati *v.* advise; counsel; consult
savladati *v.* overcome
savremen *adj.* contemporary, current
savršen *adj.* perfect; faultless
sazreti *v.* ripen, mature
sažaljenje *n.* compassion, pity
sažetak *m.* resume
sažeti *v.* contract; compress
sebičan *adj.* selfish
sedam *num.* seven
sedamdeset *num.* seventy
sedamnaest *num.* seventeen
sedlo *n.* saddle
sedmica *f.* week
seliti se *v.* move; migrate
seljak *m.* peasant, farmer
selo *n.* village; country
semafor *m.* traffic lights

senf *m.* mustard
sestra *f.* sister
sestričina *f.* niece
sestrić *m.* nephew
sgnuti se *v.* bend
shvatiti *v.* understand, comprehend
sići *v.* get down
sidro *n.* anchor
siguran *adj.* sure, safe; positive
sigurnost *f.* safety; security
sijati *v.* sow; seed; sift
siječanj *m.* January
sijed *adj.* gray-haired
sijelo *n.* meeting
sijevati *v.* lighten, flash
sila *f.* power; force; strength
silovanje *n.* rape
silovit *adj.* violent, brutal
simpatičan *adj.* nice, attractive, likable
simulirati *v.* simulate, pretend
sin *m.* son
sinoć *adv.* previous night
sir *m.* cheese
siroče *n.* orphan
siromašan *adj.* poor, needy
siromaštvo *n.* poverty, neediness
sirov *adj.* raw, uncooked
sisa *f.* breast, bust
sisar *m.* mammal
sisati *v.* suck
sit *adj.* full; sick of, tired of
sitan *adj.* tiny; petty
siv *adj.* gray
sjaj *m.* brightness, shine
sjajan *adj.* shining, radiant
sjati *v.* shine; glare; glow

sjeckati *v.* mince; chop
sjedititi *v.* sit, be seated
sjednica *f.* meeting; session
sjekira *f.* axe, hatchet
sjeme *n.* seed
sjena *f.* shadow; shade
sjeno *n.* hay
sjesti *v.* sit down, take a seat
sjeta *f.* melancholy; sadness
sjetan *adj.* blue, melancholic
sjetiti se *v.* remember
sjetva *f.* sowing
sjever *m.* north
sjećanje *n.* memory; remembrance
skakati *v.* jump, spring, leap, hop
skapavati *v.* starve; perish
skela *f.* ferry
skica *f.* draft, sketch
skijati se *v.* ski
skitnica *f.* tramp, vagabond
skladan *adj.* harmonious
skladište *n.* warehouse; depot
sklonište *n.* shelter
sklonost *f.* favour; affection
sklopiti *v.* fold; close; clasp
skoro *adv.* almost, nearly; soon
skratiti *v.* shorten
skrenuti *v.* turn
skrojiti *v.* cut out
skroman *adj.* modest
skroz *adv.* through
skuhati *v.* boil; prepare; make
skup *adj.* expensive, costly
skupa *adv.* together; jointly
skupiti (se) *v.* shrink
skupljati *v.* gather, collect; raise

skupština *f.* meeting; assembly
skuša *f.* mackerel
slab *adj.* weak, faint, feeble
slabiti *v.* weaken
sladak *adj.* sweet
sladoled *m.* ice-cream
slagati se *v.* agree
slama *f.* straw
slan *adj.* salted
slanina *f.* bacon
slap *m.* waterfall
slast *f.* delight; zest; sweet
slastan *adj.* delicious
slava *f.* fame, glory
slavan *adj.* famous, glorious
slavina *f.* tap, faucet
slaviti *v.* celebrate; glorify
sličan *adj.* similar, like, alike
sličiti *v.* resemble, be like
sličnost *f.* resemblance
slijedeći *adj.* next; the following
slijediti *v.* follow; succeed
slijep *adj.* blind
slijepi miš *m.* bat
slika *f.* picture; image; painting
slina *f.* saliva
sljepilo *n.* blindness
sljepoočnica *f.* temple
sloboda *f.* liberty; freedom
slobodan *adj.* free
slog *m.* syllable
sloga *f.* harmony
sloj *m.* layer
slomiti *v.* break; fracture; crash
slon *m.* elephant
slovo *n.* letter

slučaj *m.* case; incident
slučajno *adv.* accidentally
sluga *m.* servant
sluh *m.* hearing; ear
slušaoci *pl.* audience, public
slušati *v.* listen to; obey
sluškinja *f.* maid
služba *f.* employment; service
službeni *adj.* official
službenik *m.* officer; employee
služiti *v.* serve; attend; wait
smanjiti *v.* diminish, lessen; reduce
smatrati *v.* consider, think
smedj *adj.* brown
smetati *v.* disturb; annoy; interrupt
smetljište *n.* dump
smeće *pl.* rubbish, garbage, litter
smijati se *v.* smile; laugh
smijeh *m.* laugh
smiješan *adj.* funny, ridiculous
smisao *m.* sense; meaning
smjena *f.* shift
smjer *m.* direction, course; trend
smjerati *v.* tend towards
smjesa *f.* mixture; blend
smjestiti *v.* place; accommodate
smjeti *v.* may; dare; be allowed
smještaj *m.* position; accommodation
smokva *f.* fig
smola *f.* resin; pitch
smrditi *v.* stink, smell badly
smrskati *v.* crash, smash
smrt *f.* death
smrtonosan *adj.* lethal, deadly, fatal
smršati *v.* lose weight, slim
snažan *adj.* strong, powerful, vigorous

snabdjevati *v.* supply, provide
snaha *f.* daughter-in-law
snaći se *v.* find one's way
snijeg *m.* snow
snop *m.* bundle
so *f.* salt
soba *f.* room, chamber
sočan *adj.* juicy
sok *m.* juice
sokna *f.* sock
soko *m.* falcon, hawk
soliti *v.* salt
sonda *f.* probe
sova *f.* owl
spaliti *v.* burn down
spas *m.* salvation; liberation
spasiti *v.* rescue
spavati *v.* sleep
spavaća soba *f.* bedroom
spavaćica *f.* nightgown
spljoštiti *v.* flatten
spoj *m.* joint, connection
spoljašnji *adj.* outside
spoljašnjost *f.* outside, exterior
spoljnji *adj.* outer
spomenik *m.* memorial
spomenuti *v.* mention
spor *m.* slow
sporazum *m.* agreement
sposoban *adj.* capable; fit for
sposobnost *f.* ability, capability; skill
sprava *f.* apparatus; appliance
spreman *adj.* ready; prepared
spriječiti *v.* prevent, obstruct
sprijeda *adv.* in front of, before, ahead
spužva *f.* sponge

sramota *f.* disgrace
srce *n.* heart
srdačan *adj.* kind; cordial, hearty
srebro *n.* silver
sreća *f.* happiness; luck
srećom *adv.* luckily, fortunately
srednji *adj.* medium; middle
srednjovjekovni *adj.* medieval
sresti *v.* meet
sretan *adj.* happy; lucky
srijeda *f.* Wednesday
srkati *v.* sip
srna *f.* doe
srodan *adj.* related
srodstvo *n.* relationship
srpanj *m.* July
srž *f.* core, pit
stabilan *adj.* stable, firm
stabljika *f.* stalk, stem
stablo *n.* tree
stado *n.* herd
staja *f.* stable
stajati *v.* stand
staklo *n.* glass
stalan *adj.* steady, permanent
stan *m.* apartment
stanica *f.* station
stanovati *v.* live, reside
stanovništvo *n.* population
star *adj.* old, aged
stariji *adj.* elder; senior
starina *f.* antique
stariti *v.* age, get old
staromodan *adj.* old-fashioned
starost *f.* old age
stav *m.* attitude

staviti *v.* put, place
stavka *f.* item
staza *f.* path; trail; track
stepen *m.* grade; degree
stepenica *f.* stair
stići *v.* arrive, come, get to
stid *m.* shame
stidljiv *adj.* shy; bashful
stih *m.* verse, line; rhyme
stijena *f.* rock; cliff
stipendija *f.* scholarship
stisnuti *v.* squeeze; shrink
stjenica *f.* bug
sto *m.* table
stoka *f.* cattle
stolica *f.* chair
stoljnjak *m.* tablecloth
stomak *m.* stomach
stopalo *n.* foot
stopiti (se) *v.* merge; unit
stotina *f.* hundred
straža *f.* guard
strah *m.* fear, fright
strana *f.* side
stranac *m.* stranger; foreigner
stranica *f.* page
stranka *f.* party; faction
strast *f.* passion
strašan *adj.* terrible; awful
strašilo *n.* scarecrow
strašiti *v.* terrify
strijela *f.* arrow
strina *f.* aunt
strm *adj.* steep
strog *adj.* strict, severe, harsh
strpljenje *n.* patience

struganje *n.* scrape
struja *f.* stream; current
struk *m.* waist
stubište *n.* staircase
stručnjak *m.* expert
stvar *f.* thing; matter; stuff
stvaran *adj.* real, actual
subota *f.* Saturday
sud *m.* court of justice
sudar *m.* collision, crash; impact
sudbina *f.* fate, destiny
sudija *m.* judge
sudje *n.* dishes; vessels
sudjenje *n.* trial
sudnica *f.* court, courtroom
sudoper *m.* sink
suglasnik *m.* consonant
sujeta *f.* vanity
sujetan *adj.* vain
suknja *f.* skirt
sukob *m.* conflict, clash
sumnja *f.* doubt, suspicion
sumnjati *v.* suspect, doubt
sumnjičav *adj.* doubting, suspicious
sumoran *adj.* sombre, dull, gloomy
sunčan *adj.* sunny
sunčev sjaj *m.* sunshine
sunce *n.* sun
supa *f.* soup
suparnik *m.* rival, competitor
suprotan *adj.* opposite, contrary
supružnik *m.* spouse
suprug *m.* husband
supruga *f.* wife
surov *adj.* rude, brutal; severe
susjed *m.* neighbor

susjedan *adj.* adjacent; next door

susjedstvo *n.* neighborhood

suša *f.* drought

sušiti *v.* dry

suština *f.* essence, substance

sutra *adv.* tomorrow

suza *f.* tear

svađa *f.* quarrel; dispute

svakako *adv.* by all means; of course

svaki *adv.* every; each

svako *adv.* everybody

svakodnevni *adj.* everyday, daily, regular

svanuće *n.* dawn; daybreak

svastika *f.* sister-in-law

sve *adj.* all, everything

svečan *adj.* festive

svejedno *adv.* nevertheless

svemir *m.* universe; space

sveštenik *m.* priest; clergyman

svet *adj.* saint, holy, sacred

svezati *v.* tighten; bind

svi *adj.* all; everbody

svijet *m.* world; the universe

svijetao *adj.* bright, light

svijeća *f.* candle

svila *f.* silk

svinja *f.* pig, hog, swine

svinjetina *f.* pork

svitati *v.* dawn

svjedočenje *n.* testimony

svjedočiti *v.* testify

svjedodžba *f.* report; certificate

svjedok *m.* witness

svjestan *adj.* conscious; aware

svjetina *f.* mob, rabble

svjetionik *m.* lighthouse

svjetovni *adj.* secular
svjež *adj.* fresh; cool, chilly
svojina *f.* property; belonging
svota *f.* sum, total; amount
svrbiti *v.* itch
svrha *f.* purpose, aim, object
svrstavati *v.* classify
svuda *adv.* everywhere, throughout

Š

šablon   *m.* stereotype; model
šadrvan / vodoskok   *m.* fountain
šah   *m.* chess
šah-mat   *m.* checkmate
šaht   *m.* manhole
šaka   *f.* fist
šal   *m.* shawl
šala   *f.* fun, joke
šaliti se   *v.* joke
šalter   *m.* window (bank, post office); switch (electric)
šaljiv   *adj.* funny, humorous
šamar   *m.* slap; blow
šamarati / ošamariti šamlica   *f.* stool
šampinjon   *m.* mushrooms
šampion   *m.* champion
šampita   *f.* whipped cream pie
šamrolna   *f.* whipped cream roll
šansa   *f.* chance
šapa   *f.* paw
šaptati   *v.* whisper
šapat   *m.* whisper
šara   *f.* hue, tinge
šaraf   *m.* screw
šarafziger   *m.* screwdriver
šaran   *m.* carp
šarati   *v.* scratch, scribble
šaren   *adj.* colorful
šargarepa / mrkva   *f.* carrot
šarka / šarnir   *f.* hinge
šarlah   *m.* scarlet fever
šaržer   *m.* clip, magazine (on a weapon)
šasija   *f.* chasis, frame

šašav *adj.* crazy
šator *m.* tent
šatra / šatrovački jezik *f.* slang
ščepati *v.* seize, grab, grip
šećer *m.* sugar
šećerlema *f.* sugar candy
šega *f.* jeer, taunt, jest, gibe
šegrt *m.* apprentice
sejtan / đavo *m.* devil
šema *f.* scheme, plan, outline
šepati *v.* limp
šepav *adj.* lame
šeprtlja *f.* bungler, fumbler
šeret *m.* jokester
šerpa / ranljika *f.* pot
šesnaest *num.* sixteen
šest *num.* six
šešir *m.* hat
šetati *v.* walk, stroll
ševrdati *v.* stagger, zigzag; vacillate
šezdeset *num.* sixty
šiba *f.* rod; birch; wicker
šibica *f.* match
šifon *m.* chiffon
šifra *f.* code
šija *f.* nape
šikanirati *v.* harass
šiljak *m.* peak, point; tip
šiljat *adj.* pointed, pointy; jagged
šiljiti *v.* sharpen
šimšir *m.* box; barberry(divlji)
šina *f.* rail
šintor / šinter *m.* fleecer
šipka *f.* bar, stick, rod
širina *f.* width
širiti(se) *v.* spread, propagate

širm   *m.* shade; lampshade (na lampi)

širok   *adj.* broad, wide

šišati   *v.* cut, trim, crop

šiti   *v.* sew, stitch

šišmiš   *m.* bat

škakljati   *v.* tickle

škembe   *n.* tripe

škembići   *m.pl.* tripes

škiljav   *adj.* cross-eyed

škoditi   *v.* harm

škola   *f.* school

školjka   *f.* shell

škrt   *adj.* mean, stingy; miserly

škrtac   *m.* miser

šlafrok   *m.* dressing gown

šlager   *m.* hit

šlajer / veo / vala   *m.* veil

šljem   *m.* helmet

šljiva   *f.* plum; prune

šljivovica   *f.* plum-brandy

šljunak   *m.* gravel, pebbles

šminka   *f.* make-up

šnajder   *m.* tailor

šnajderica   *f.* dressmaker

šnala   *f.* buckle; hairpin (za kosu)

šnešue / galoše / kaloše   *pl.* galoshes

šnicla   *f.* steak

šofer   *m.* driver

šoferšajbna   *f.* windshield

šojka   *f.* jay

šok   *m.* shock

šolja   *f.* cup

šorc   *m.* shorts

šovinist(a)   *m.* chauvinist

špaga   *f.* string

špajz(a)   *m.* pantry

španija španija

španija *f.* Spain
špediter *m.* shipper
špenadla *f.* straight pin
šperploča *f.* plywood
špic *m.* sharp point, end
špijun *m.* spy
špil *m.* deck
špinat *m.* spinach
šporet *m.* range
šrapnel *m.* shrapnel
šta *prep.* what
štab *m.* staff; headquarters
štampa *f.* press
štamparska greška *f.* misprint
štand *m.* stand, exhibit, display; boot
štap *m.* cane, stick
štedjeti *v.* save, spare
štedljiv *adj.* saving, thrifty
štene *n.* puppy
šteta *f.* damage, harm; loss
štetan *adj.* harmful; damaging
štipati *v.* pinch, nip
štititi *v.* protect; shield
štof *m.* fabric, material, cloth; textile
štokrla *f.* stool
štopati *v.* darn, mend
štucati *v.* hiccup
šubara *f.* fur-cap
šuljati se *v.* sneak; slink
šum *m.* noise, murmur
šuma *f.* wood; forest
šunka *f.* ham
šupa *f.* shed
šupalj *adj.* hollow
šura *m.* brother-in-law
šuškati *v.* rustle; lisp

šut (sport)   *m.* shot; kick; v. shoot
šutjeti   *v.* be silent
švaler   *m.* lover, paramour
švedska   *f.* Sweden
švercer   *m.* smuggler, black marketer; v. smuggle
švicarska / švajcarska   *f.* Switzerland
švrljati   *v.* liter; roam

T

taban *m.* sole
tabela *f.* list
tableta *f.* pill, tablet
tacna *f.* tray
tačan *adj.* exact, accurate; precise
tačka *f.* point, full stop; dot
tačno *adv.* properly
tačnost *f.* accuracy; precision
tada *adv.* than, in that case
taj *prep.* this
tajanstven *adj.* mysterious
tajna *f.* secret, mystery
takav *adj.* such; like that, sort of
takmičiti se *v.* compete, contest
tako *adv.* so, thus, in this way
takodje *adv.* too; also
taksa *f.* tax; due; rate
taksi *m.* cab, taxi
talas *m.* wave
talog *m.* sediment
tama *f.* darkness, dusk
taman *adj.* dark, dusky, dim
tamnica *f.* prison, jail
tamo *adv.* there
tanak *adj.* thin; slim; slender
tanjirić *m.* saucer
tanjur *m.* plate
tantijema *f.* royalty
taoc *m.* hostage
tapeta *f.* wallpaper
tapšati *v.* pat
tast *m.* father-in-law
tata *m.* dad, daddy

tava *f.* frying-pan
tavan *m.* attic; loft
tašta *f.* mother-in-law
tečan *adj.* liquid; fluent
tečnost *f.* liquid, fluid
teći *v.* flow, run, stream
tegla *f.* jar
tegliti *v.* tow, haul, tug, drag
tegoba *f.* difficulty, hardship
tehnika *f.* technique
tehnologija *f.* technology
tele *n.* calf
telefon *m.* phone
telegram *m.* cable
teletina *f.* veal
temelj *m.* foundation, basis, base
tempo *m.* rate
teniske *pl.* sneakers
tepih *m.* carpet, rug
teško *adv.* heavily; hard; badly
tetiva *f.* ligament
tetka *f.* aunt
tezga *f.* booth
težak *adj.* heavy; tough, hard
težina *f.* weight; load
ti, vi *pron.* you
tih *adj.* still, quiet, silent
tijelo *n.* body; constitution
tijesan *adj.* tight; narrow; close
tijesto *n.* dough, pastry
tikva *f.* pumpkin
tinta *f.* ink
tip *m.* type, character
tipka *f.* key
tišina *f.* silence, quiet, stillness
titrati *v.* oscillate, vibrate

tjeme *n.* top of head
tjerati *v.* chase; pursue; drive
tjeskoba *f.* anxiety
tješiti *v.* console, comfort
tkanina *f.* fabric, textile; cloth
tkivo *n.* tissue
tlo *n.* ground, earth, soil
toalet *m.* restroom, toilet
točak *m.* wheel
točiti *v.* pour out
tok *m.* course; flow; stream
tona *f.* ton
tonuti *v.* sink
top *m.* gun, cannon
topao *adj.* warm
topiti (se) *v.* thaw; melt; dissolve
toplina *f.* warmth
toranj *m.* tower
torba *f.* bag
torta *f.* layer cake
tovar *m.* load, cargo, freight
tovariti *v.* load, freight
traženje *n.* searching, seeking
tražiti *v.* look for, seek; claim
tračati *v.* gossip
tragati *v.* trace
trajan *adj.* durable, lasting
trajna *f.* permanent (hair treatment)
traka *f.* band, strip, ribbon; tape
tramvaj *m.* tram
trava *f.* grass
travanj *m.* April
trbuh *m.* belly, abdomen
trener *m.* coach
trenerka *f.* sweatshirt
trenje *n.* friction

trenutak *m.* moment, instant
trepavice *pl.* eyelash
treperiti *v.* twinkle, flicker, flutter
tresak *m.* bang, slam, crash
tresti *v.* shake; agitate
trešnja *f.* cherry
trčati *v.* run, race
trg *m.* market; square
trgovac *m.* merchant, dealer
trgovačka roba *pl.* merchandise
trgovački *adj.* trade, commercial
trgovati *v.* trade
trgovina *f.* trade, commerce
tri *num.* three
trica *f.* trifle
tričav *adj.* petty, trivial
trijem *m.* porch
trijezan *adj.* sober
triko *m.* tights
trka *f.* race
trljati *v.* rub, massage
trn *m.* thorn
trokut *m.* triangle
trostruk *adj.* triple
trošak *m.* expense, cost
trošiti *v.* spend; consume
trotoar *m.* sidewalk
trpati *v.* stuff
trpezarija *f.* dining room
trska *f.* reed, cane
truba *f.* trumpet
trud *m.* effort; pains; trouble
trudna *adj.* pregnant
trunuti *v.* decay, rot
truo / truho *adj.* rotten
trzaj *m.* jerk, twitch

tržište   *n.* market
tu   *adv.* here
tucati   *v.* pound, crush
tučnjava   *f.* fight
tuči   *v.* beat; whisk
tudj   *adj.* strange, foreign
tuga   *f.* sorrow, sadness, grief
tumačiti   *v.* explain, interpret
tup   *adj.* blunt, dull, stupid
turpija   *f.* file, rasp
Turska   *f.* Turkey
turšija   *f.* pickles
tuš   *m.* shower
tužan   *adj.* sad, sorrowful
tužba   *f.* accusation; complaint
tužilac   *m.* prosecutor, plaintiff
tvoj, vaš   *pron.* your; yours
tvor   *m.* skunk
tvrd   *adj.* hard; solid; rigid
tvrditi   *v.* affirm, assert
tvrdjava   *f.* fortress, stronghold
tvrdoglav   *adj.* stubborn, obstinate

U

u   *prep.* in, at; by; into
ubaciti   *v.* inject
ubica   *m.* murderer, killer
ubistvo   *n.* homicide, murder
ubiti   *v.* kill, murder, slay
ublažiti   *v.* soothe, alleviate
ubod   *m.* sting, stab; bite
ubrati   *v.* pick, gather
ubrzati   *v.* accelerate, speed up
ubuduće   *adv.* in future
ucijeniti   *v.* blackmail
ucjenjivač   *m.* racketeer
učestvovati   *v.* participate, take part in
učionica   *f.* classroom
učitelj   *m.* teacher
učiti   *v.* teach; learn, study
učtiv   *adj.* polite; respectful
učvrstiti   *v.* fix, fasten, make firm
ući   *v.* enter, come in, get in
udaja   *f.* marriage
udaljen   *adj.* far, distant, remote
udarac   *m.* blow, stroke; kick; shock
udariti   *v.* strike, hit, kick
udebljati   *se v.* grow fat
udisati   *v.* inhale, breathe in
udo   *n.* limb
udoban   *adj.* comfortable, cozy
udovac   *m.* widower
udovica   *f.* widow
udruženje   *n.* association; society
udubina   *f.* hollow; niche
udžbenik   *m.* textbook
uganuti   *v.* sprain, dislocate

ugao   *m.* corner; angle
ugasiti   *v.* extinguish; turn off
uginuti   *v.* perish
uglavnom   *adv.* mainly, chiefly
ugled   *m.* prestige, reputation
ugledan   *adj.* distinguished, eminent
ugodan   *adj.* pleasant, agreeable
ugovor   *m.* contract; treaty
ugrijati   *v.* heat, warm
ugušiti   *v.* suffocate, choke
uhapsiti   *v.* arrest
uho, uvo   *n.* ear
uhvatiti   *v.* catch, seize, capture
ujak   *m.* uncle
ujediniti   *se* v. unite
ujna   *f.* aunt
ukinuti   *v.* cancel, abolish
ukiseliti (se)   *v.* pickle; turn sour, acidify
uključiti (se)   *v.* include, comprise
uključujući   *adv.* including
ukloniti   *v.* remove
ukočen   *adj.* stiff, rigid
ukras   *m.* ornament, decoration
ukrasti   *v.* steal
ukrcati se   *v.* embark, go aboard
ukupno   *adv.* entirely, totally
ukus   *m.* flavor; taste
ukusan   *adj.* tasty
ulaz   *m.* entry; entrance
ulaznica   *f.* ticket
ulegnuti se   *v.* sag, curve
ulica   *f.* street
ulje   *n.* oil
uljepšati   *v.* beautify
ulog   *m.* stake; deposit
uloga   *f.* role, part

uložak *m.* refill
um *m.* mind; intellect
umalo *adv.* almost, nearly
umanjiti *v.* lessen, diminish, reduce
umetnuti *v.* insert
umiješati se *v.* intervene
umirujući *adj.* soothing
umivaonik *m.* sink, lavatory
umjeren *adj.* moderate; medium
umjesto *adv.* instead
umjetan *adj.* artificial
umjetnik *m.* artist
umjetnost *f.* art
umor *m.* fatigue, exhaustion
umoran *adj.* tired, exhausted
umrijeti *v.* pass away, die
unapredjenje *n.* advancement, promotion
unaprijed *adv.* in advance
uništenje *n.* destruction, demolition
unuk/unuka *m./f.* grandchild
unutar *adv.* within; inside; indoors
unutrašnji *adj.* internal, interior
uobičajen *adj.* usual, habitual
uokviriti *v.* frame
uopće/uopšte *adv.* generally, altogether
uostalom *adv.* after all
upala *f.* inflammation
upaliti *v.* set fire to; turn on
upaljač *m.* lighter
upečatljiv *adj.* impressive
upisati se *v.* register, enroll
upiti *v.* soak; absorb
uplašen *adj.* frightened, scared
uplata *f.* payment
uplesti *v.* involve
uporan *adj.* persistent; stubborn

uporediti *v.* compare
uporediv *adj.* comparable
upotreba *f.* use, usage
upotrebljavan *adj.* secondhand
upotrebljavati *v.* use
upoznati *v.* meet, get acquainted with
upozorenje *n.* warning; alert
upozoriti *v.* warn
uprava *f.* administration
upravo *adv.* exactly, just
uprkos *adv.* despite, in spite of
uprljati *v.* dirty; contaminate
upropastiti *v.* ruin, wreck
upućen *adj.* informed
uputa *f.* instruction, direction
uputiti na *v.* refer
uraditi *v.* do, commit
uragan *m.* hurricane
uredan *adj.* neat, tidy
uredjaj *m.* equipment
urednik *m.* editor
urezati *v.* make a cut, engrave
urodjen *adj.* inborn, innate; native
usamljen *adj.* lonely, solitary
useknuti se *v.* blow one's nose
usidjelica *f.* old maid, spinster
uskoro *adv.* soon, shortly
Uskrs *m.* Easter
uskrsnuće *n.* resurrection
uslov *m.* condition
usluga *f.* favor, service
usmen *adj.* oral, verbal
usmjeriti *v.* aim, head; direct
usna *f.* lip
uspinjača *f.* railway
uspjeh *m.* success

uspješan *adj.* successful; efficient
usplahiren *adj.* agitated; fussy
uspomena *f.* memory
uspon *m.* climb; rise; ascent
usporiti *v.* slow down
uspravan *adj.* vertical, upright
usput *v.* by the way
usred *adv.* in the middle of, among
usresrediti *v.* focus, concentrate
usta *f.* mouth
ustanak *m.* rebellion, uprising
ustanoviti *v.* settle; establish
ustati *v.* get up, rise; stand up
ustav *m.* constitution
ustručavati (se) *v.* hesitate
ustupiti *v.* concede
usuditi se *v.* dare, have the courage
ususret *adv.* towards
usvojiti *v.* adopt
utirkati *v.* starch
uticaj *m.* impact, influence
utisnuti *v.* impress, imprint
utjecati *v.* affect
utočište *n.* shelter, resort
utopiti se *v.* get drowned
utorak *m.* Tuesday
uvala *f.* bay, gulf
uvažavan *adj.* respectable
uvažavati *v.* appreciate; respect
uvećati *v.* increase; magnify
uvenuti *v.* fade
uvid *m.* insight, inspection
uvijek *adv.* always
uvjeravati *v.* assure
uvod *m.* introduction,
uvoz *m.* import

uvreda *f.* offend, insult, outrage
uvredljiv *adj.* resentful
uvrijediti *v.* offend, insult, hurt
uzajamno *adv.* mutually
uzak *adj.* narrow; tight
uzaludan *adj.* useless
uzastopan *adj.* consecutive
uzbudjenje *n.* excitement
uzbudljiv *adj.* exciting, thrilling
uzbuna *f.* alarm
uzburkan *adj.* stormy, rough
uzdisati *v.* sigh
uzduž *adv.* along
uzeti *v.* take
uzgajati *v.* bring up, grow
uznemiravati *v.* disturb
uznemiren *adj.* agitated, restless
uzorak *m.* sample; pattern
uzrečica *f.* saying, proverb
uzrok *m.* cause, reason
užas *m.* horror
užasan *adj.* horrible, terrible, dreadful
užina *f.* light meal
uživati *v.* enjoy

V

vaditi   *v.* take out, pull out
vaga   *f.* scale, balance
vagati   *v.* weigh; balance
vagon   *m.* wagon, carriage, coach
val   *m.* wave
valjati se   *v.* roll over
valjda   *adv.* perhaps, maybe
valovit   *adj.* wavy
valuta   *f.* currency
van   *adv.* out
vanbračni   *adj.* illegitimate
vani   *adv.* out
vanjski   *adj.* outside, outdoor, exterior
varati   *v.* cheat, swindle
variti   *v.* boil; digest
varivo   *n.* boiled vegetables
varka   *f.* trick
varnica   *f.* spark
vaspitanje   *n.* up bringing
vašar   *m.* fair, market
vaška   *f.* louse
vatra   *f.* fire
vatrogasac   *m.* fireman
vazduh   *m.* air
vazna   *f.* vase
važan   *adj.* important
veče   *n.* evening
večera   *f.* dinner; supper
večeras   *adv.* tonight
već   *m.* already
većina   *f.* majority
većinom   *adv.* mostly; mainly
vedar   *adj.* serene; clear; cheerful

vedro   *n.* bucket, pail
velegrad   *m.* large town, big city
velesila   *f.* great power
veličanstven   *adj.* gorgeous, magnificent
veličina   *f.* size; dimension
velik   *adj.* big, large; great
veliko slovo   *n.* capital letter
velikodušan   *adj.* generous
veljača   *f.* February
vena   *f.* vein
ventil   *m.* valve
venuti   *v.* wilt, wither
veo   *m.* veil
verati se   *v.* climb
veresija   *f.* credit, loan
veseliti se   *v.* be glad
veseo   *adj.* jolly, cheerful, merry
veslati   *v.* row
veslo   *n.* oar; paddle
vez   *m.* embroidery
veza   *f.* connection; link; relation
vezati   *v.* bind, fasten, tie
veznik   *m.* conjunction
vid   *m.* eye sight
vidik   *m.* view; vista
vidjenje   *n.* vision; seeing
vidjeti   *v.* see
vidljivost   *f.* visibility
vidokrug   *m.* horizon
vijavica   *f.* blizzard, snowstorm
vijek   *m.* century
vijest(i)   *adj.* news
vikati   *v.* shout, cry; yell
vilica   *f.* jaw
viljuška   *f.* fork
vino   *n.* wine

vinova loza *f.* grapevine
violina *f.* violin
viriti *v.* peek; peep, peer
viseći *adj.* hang
visibaba *f.* snowdrop
visina *f.* hight, altitude
visok *adj.* high, tall
višak *m.* surplus, excess
više *adv.* more; higher
više voljeti *v.* prefer
višegodišnji *adj.* perennial
višnja *f.* cherry
vitak *adj.* slim, slender
viteški *adj.* knightly
vitez *m.* knight
vječan *adj.* eternal, everlasting
vječno *adv.* forever
vječnost *f.* eternity
vjenčanje *n.* wedding
vjera *f.* religion, belief, faith
vjeran *adj.* faithful, loyal, true
vjerodostojan *adj.* reliable; authentic
vjerovati *v.* believe
vjerovatno *adv.* probably, likely
vjerski *adj.* religious
vješala *pl.* gallows
vještica *f.* witch
vještina *f.* skill; proficiency
vjetar *m.* wind
vjetrovito *adj.* windy
vjeverica *f.* squirrel
vježba *f.* exercise, practice, drill
vježbati *v.* train, exercise, practice
vlada *f.* government
vladar *m.* ruler
vladati *v.* rule, govern

vlak *m.* train
vlakno *n.* fibre
vlasnik *m.* owner, proprietor
vlasništvo *n.* ownership, possession
vlast *f.* power; authority
vlažan *adj.* moist, damp, wet
vlažnost *f.* humidity
voćnjak *m.* orchard
voda *f.* water
vodič *m.* guide
voditi *v.* lead; guide
vodja *m.* leader
vodoinstalater *m.* plumber
vodonik *m.* hydrogen
vojni *adj.* military
vojnik *m.* soldier
vojska *pl.* army
vol *m.* ox
volan *m.* steering wheel
volja *f.* will
voljan *adj.* willing; ready
voljeti *v.* love, like, be fond of
vosak *m.* wax
voz *m.* train
vozačka dozvola *f.* driver's license
vozač *m.* driver
vozilo *n.* vehicle
voziti *v.* drive, ride
vrabac *m.* sparrow
vrag *m.* devil, satan
vrana *f.* crow
vrat *m.* neck
vrata *f.* door; gate
vratiti(se) *v.* return
vrba *f.* willow
vrebati *v.* lurk, spy upon

vreća *f.* sack, bag
vrećast *adj.* baggy
vrelo *n.* spring, well, source
vremenski *adv.* time
vrh *m.* top, peak, summit
vrhnje *n.* sour cream
vrhunac *m.* culmination, climax
vrijedan *adj.* valuable; worth; diligent
vrijedjati *v.* offend, insult
vrijednost *f.* value; worth
vrijeme *n.* time
vrijeme (atm.) *n.* weather
vrijeme (gram.) *n.* tense
vrijeme (hron.) *n.* time
vriskati *v.* scream, shriek
vriti *v.* boil; simmer
vrlina *f.* virtue
vrlo *adv.* very, very much; extremely
vrpca *f.* ribbon, tape, band
vrsta *f.* type, kind, species
vrt *m.* garden
vrtiti *v.* rotate, revolve; whirl
vrtlar *m.* gardener
vrtlog *m.* whirlpool
vrtoglav *adj.* dizzy
vrtoglavica *f.* dizziness
vrućina *f.* heat
vući *v.* draw; drag, pull
vuk *m.* wolf
vuna *f.* wool

Z

za *prep.* for
zabava *f.* party; entertainment
zabavan *adj.* amusing, funny
zabavljati *v.* amuse, entertain
zabilježiti *v.* notate
zabluda *f.* delusion, misconception
zaborav *m.* oblivion
zaboravan *adj.* forgetful, oblivious
zaboraviti *v.* forget
zabrana *f.* ban, prohibition
zabraniti *v.* forbid, prohibit
zabranjen prolaz *m.* trespass
zabrinut *adj.* concerned, worried
zabrinutost *f.* anxiety, worry, concern
zabuna *f.* mistake, misunderstanding
zabušavati *v.* shirk
zacijeliti *v.* heal
zacrveniti se *v.* blush
začarati *v.* bewitch
začepiti *v.* stop(up), plug
začin *m.* spice, seasoning; dressing
začinjen *adj.* spicy
začuditi *v.* surprise, astonish, amaze
zadatak *m.* task
zadirkivati *v.* tease
zadnji *adv.* last, latest, final
zadovoljan *adj.* satisfied, content
zadovoljavajući *adj.* satisfactory
zadovoljiti *v.* satisfy
zadovoljstvo *n.* pleasure
zadruga *f.* community; cooperative
zadržati *v.* retain, detain

zagadjenje *n.* pollution
zagadjivati *v.* pollute
zagonetka *f.* puzzle, riddle, enigma
zagrada *f.* bracket, parenthesis
zagrijati *v.* warm up
zagrijavanje *n.* heating
zagrliti *v.* hug, embrace
zagušljiv *adj.* stale
zahod *m.* restrooms, toilet
zahrdjati *v.* rust
zahvala *f.* acknowledgement
zahvalan *adj.* grateful
zahvaliti *v.* thank
zahvalnost *f.* gratitude
zainteresovan *adj.* interested in
zaista *adv.* really, indeed, truly
zajam *m.* loan; advance
zajedljiv *adj.* sarcastic, bitter
zajednica *f.* community
zajedno *adv.* together; in common
zakasniti *v.* be late
zakleti se *v.* swear, take an oath
zakletva *f.* promise
zaključak *m.* conclusion
zaključati *v.* lock up
zaključiti *v.* conclude
zakon *m.* law
zakonit *adj.* lawful, legal
zakonodavstvo *n.* legislature
zakopčati *v.* button up
zakrčiti *v.* obstruct; bar, jam
zakrpa *f.* patch
zakup *m.* lease; rent
zakuska *f.* snack
zalazak sunca *m.* sunset

zalediti *v.* freeze up
zaliha *f.* reserve, supply, stock
zalijevati *v.* water, irrigate
zaliv *m.* bay
zaljubiti se *v.* fall in love with
zalogaj *m.* bite, snack
založiti *v.* pawn; pledge; mortgage
zalupiti *v.* slam
zalutati *v.* stray
zamak *m.* castle
zamazan *adj.* dirty, filthy
zametak *m.* embryo
zamijeniti *v.* replace; exchange
zamisao *f.* idea; conception
zamisliti *v.* imagine
zamišljen *adj.* thoughtful
zamjeriti *v.* resent
zamka *f.* trap
zamoliti *v.* ask, beg
zamotati *v.* wrapup
zamrsiti *v.* entangle; ruffle
zamršen *adj.* intricate
zanat *m.* craft, handicraft
zanemariti *v.* neglect; omit
zanijeti *v.* become pregnant
zanimanje *n.* interest; profession
zanimljiv *adj.* interesting
zanovijetati *v.* nag
zao *adj.* bad, wicked, evil
zaokružiti *v.* surround; encircle
zaova *f.* sister-in-law
zapad *m.* west
zapaliti *v.* light, ignite; turn on
zapamtiti *v.* memorize, remember
zapanjiti *v.* astonish

zapanjujuci *adj.* amazing

zapeta/zarez *f./m.* comma

zapis *m.* note; entry; record

zapljeniti *v.* confiscate; capture

zaposleni *pl.* employee

zaposlenost *f.* employment

zaposliti *v.* employ

zarada *f.* earnings, income

zaraditi *v.* earn

zaraza *f.* infection, epidemic

zarobiti *v.* capture

zaručiti se *v.* get engaged

zaručnica *f.* fiancee

zaručnik *m.* fiance

zasjeda *f.* ambush

zasluga *f.* merit, credit

zaslužiti *v.* deserve; earn

zaspati *v.* fall asleep, go to sleep

zastario *adj.* obsolete; conservative

zastava *f.* flag, banner

zastoj *m.* standstill; jam

zastor/zavjesa *m./f.* curtain; blind

zastrašiti *v.* frighten, scare

zaštita *f.* protection

zaštititi *v.* protect

zaštitnik *m.* patron

zašto *adv.* why

zatim *adv.* than, after that

zato *adv.* therefore; consequently

zatvor *m.* prison, jail

zatvoriti *v.* shut, close; turn off

zauvijek *adv.* forever

zaušnjaci *pl.* mumps

zavesti *v.* seduce

zavidan *adj.* envious, jealous

zavisiti *v.* depend
zavist *f.* envy
zavjera *f.* conspiracy
zbir *m.* sum, total
zbirka *f.* collection
zbog *prep.* because of
zbog toga *prep.* therefore
zbogom! good-bye!
zbor *m.* assembly, meeting; rally
zbrka *f.* mess, confusion, chaos
zbuniti *v.* embarress; confuse
zdrav *adj.* healthy
zdravica *f.* toast
zdravlje *n.* health
zdravo! hi!
zec *m.* hare; rabbit
zelen *adj.* green
zelje *n.* spinach
zemlja *f.* country; land, ground
zemljak *m.* country person
zemljoradnik *m.* farmer
zemljotres *m.* earthquake
zet *m.* son-in-law
zglob *m.* joint
zgnječiti *v.* smash; squash
zgodan *adj.* handsome, nice, pretty
zgoditak *m.* lucky hit, prize
zgrabiti *v.* grab, seize
zgrada *f.* building
zgužvati *(se)* v. crease, wrinkle
zid *m.* wall
zidar *m.* mason
ziherica *f.* safety pin
zijevati *v.* yawn
zima *f.* winter; cold, chill

zimzelen *adj.* evergreen
zjapiti *v.* gape
zjenica *f.* pupil
zlatan *adj.* golden
zlato *n.* gold
zlo *n.* evil, mischief
zloban *adj.* malice, wicked
zločin *m.* crime
zločudan *adj.* malignant, malevolent
zloslutan *adj.* ominous
zloupotreba *f.* abuse
zmaj *m.* dragon; kite
zmija *f.* snake
značajan *adj.* notable, significant
značenje *n.* meaning
značka *f.* badge
znak *m.* sign, symbol, mark
znamenitost *f.* landmark; importance
znanje *n.* knowledge
znati *v.* know
znatiželjan *adj.* curious, inquisitive
znoj *m.* sweat
znojiti se *v.* perspire
zob *f.* oat
zora *f.* dawn
zračiti *v.* air; radiate
zrak *m.* air; beam; ray
zreo *adj.* ripe; mature
zrno *n.* grain; kernel; bullet
zub *m.* tooth
zubar *m.* dentist
zubobolja *f.* toothache
zujati *v.* buzz, hum
zupčanik *m.* gear
zvaničan *adj.* formal

zvanje   *n.* profession
zvati   *v.* call
zvijezda   *f.* star
zviždati   *v.* whistle
zvoniti   *v.* ring; tingle
zvono   *n.* bell
zvuk   *m.* sound

Ž

žaba *f.* frog; toad
žaljenje *n.* regret; pity
žalost *f.* sorrow, sadness
žalostan *adj.* sad, pathetic
žamor *m.* murmur, din
žaoka *f.* sting
žar *m.* glow; live coal
žarulja *f.* electric bulb
žbun *m.* bush, shrub
ždrijebe *n.* foal
ždrijelo *n.* throat; gullet
žedan *adj.* thirsty
žedj *f.* thirst
želja *f.* wish, desire
željeti *v.* want
željeznica *f.* railroad, railway
željezo *n.* iron
želudac *m.* stomach
žemička *f.* roll
žena *f.* woman; wife
ženidba *f.* marriage
ženski *adj.* female, feminine
žensko rublje *pl.* lingerie
žeton *m.* token
žetva *f.* harvest
žgaravica *f.* heartburn
žiža *f.* focus
žica *f.* wire; string
židak *adj.* liquid, running
židov/Jevrej *m.* Jew
žig *m.* stamp; brand
žila *f.* vein; artery

žilav *adj.* tough, muscular
žilet *m.* razor blade
žiri *m.* jury
žitarica *f.* cereal
žitnica *f.* grianary; barn
žito *n.* corn, grain, cereals
živ *adj.* live (alive)
živac *m.* nerve
živčan *adj.* nervous
živahan *adj.* vivid
živahan *adj.* lively, brisk, vivid
živio! long live! cheers!
živjeti *v.* live
život *m.* life, existence
životinja *f.* animal, beast
životni *adj.* vital
žlijezda *f.* gland
žmirkati *v.* blink
žohar *m.* cockroach
žrtva *f.* victim
žrtvovati *v.* sacrifice
žuč *f.* gall
žulj *m.* blister, callus
žumance *n.* yolk
žurba *f.* hustle, hurry, urgency
žuriti se *v.* hurry
žut *adj.* yellow
žvakati *v.* chew

ENGLISH-BOSNIAN DICTIONARY
ENGLESKO-BOSANSKI RJEČNIK

English Alphabet

A,a	(ei:)
B,b	(bi:)
C,c	(si:)
D,d	(di:)
E,e	(i:)
F,f	(ef)
G,G	(dži:)
H,h	(eič)
I,i	(ai)
J,j	(džei)
K,k	(k)
L,l	(el)
M,m	(em)
N,n	(en)
O,o	(ou)
P,p	(pi:)
Q,q	(kju:)
R,r	(a:)
S,s	(es)
T,t	(ti:)
U,u	(ju:)
V,v	(vi:)
W,w	(dabl-ju)
X,x	(eks)
Y,y	(vaj)
Z,z	(zi:)

A

aback /e'baek/ *adv.* natrag, straga
abandon /e'baendn/ *v.* ostaviti, prepustiti
abase /e'bejz/ *v.* poniziti
abate /'ebejt/ *v.* smanjiti, utažiti
abbreviation /e'bri:viejšn/ *n.* skraćenica, kratica
abbey /'aebi/ *n.* opatija
abdomen /'aebdomen/ *n.* trbuh
abduct /aeb'dakt/ *v.* ugrabiti
abide /e'bajd/ *v.* ostati, ustrajati, održati riječ
ability /e'biliti/ *n.* sposobnost
able /'ejbl/ *adj.* kadar, sposoban; *v.* be-/bi-/moći, biti u stanju
abnormal /aeb'no:ml/ *adj.* neobičan, nepravilan, nakazan
aboard /e'bo:d/ *adv.* na brodu, all-! /ol-/ svi u vlak!
abolish /e'boliš/ *v.* ukinuti
abortion /e'bo'šn/ *n.* izjalovljenje, neuspjeh, abortus
abound /e'baund/ *v.* obilovati, -with/-vid/ vrvjeti od
about /e'baut/ *adv.* naokolo, u blizini, približno
about /e'baut/ *prep.* o, okolo, po
above /e'bav/ *adv.* iznad, gore, više
abrade /e'breid/ *v.* ogrepsti, oderati
abreast /e'brest/ *adv.* uporedo, rame uz rame
abridge /e'bridj/ *v.* pokratiti, stegnuti
abroad /e'bro:d/ *adv.* napolju, u inostranstvu, u inozemstvu, vani
abrupt /e'brapt/ *adj.* prekinut, strm, nesuvisao, nenadan
absent /'aebsnt/ *adj.* odsutan
absent-minded /'aebsnt'majndid/ *adj.* rastresen, duhom odsutan
absolute /'aebsolju:t/ *adj.* bezuvjetan, potpun; (alkohol) čist
absorb /eb'zorb/ *v.* upiti,zaokupiti, svega obuzeti
abstain /ebs'tejn/ *v.* sustegnuti se, kloniti se (pića)
abstract /'aebstrekt/ *v.* oduzeti, načiniti izvadak, umanjiti
absurd /aeb'surd/ *adj.* besmislen, budalast, smiješan

abundance /e'bandns/ *n.* obilje, preobilje
abuse /e'bju:z/ *n.* zloupotreba, grdnja
abuse /e'bjuz/ *v.* zloupotrijebiti, grditi, psovati, prevariti
academic /ae'kedemik/ *adj.* akademski
accede /eksid/ *v.* pristupiti
accelerate /aek'selerejt/ *v.* ubrzati, pospješiti
accent /'aeksent/ *n.* naglasak, prizvuk tudjeg izgovora
accent /'aeksent/ *v.* naglasiti, istaći
accept (take) /aek'sept/ *v.* prihvatiti, odobriti
acceptable /aek'septbl/ *adj.* prihvatljiv
acceptance /aek'septns/ *n.* prihvat, odobrenje
access (entrance) /'aekses/ *n.* prilaz, pristup, napadaj
accessible /aek'sesibl/ *adj.* pristupačan
accessory /aek'sesori/ *n.* dodatak
accident /'aeksident/ *n.* nezgoda, slučaj, nesreća
accidentally /'aeksidentli/ *adj.* slučajno
acclaim /e'kleim/ *v.* klicanjem pozdravljati
accommodate /e'komedejt/ *v.* smjestiti, prilagoditi
accommodation /ekome'dejšn/ *n.* smještaj, prilagođjenje
accompany /e'kampeni/ *v.* pratiti, uslijediti istodobno
accomplish /e'kampliš/ *v.* izvršiti, ispuniti, postići
accomplishment /e'kamplišment/ *n.* izvršenje, postignuće
according /e'ko:rding/ *prep.* prema, u skladu sa
accordingly /e'ko:rdingli/ *adv.* dakle, prema tome
account /e,kaunt/ *n.* račun, računanje, izvještaj
accountant /e'kauntent/ *n.* računovodja, knjigovodja
accredit /e'kredit/ *v.* učiniti vjerodostojnim, pripisati
accumulate /e'kju:mju,lejt/ *v.* nagomilati, zgrnuti
accumulation /e,kjumu'lejšn/ *n.* gomila, gomilanje
accuracy /'aekjuresi/ *n.* tačnost, ispravnost, brižnost
accuse /e'kjuz/ *v.* optužiti, okriviti
accustom /e'kastm/ *v.* priviknuti, priučiti
accustomed /e'kastmd/ *adj.* običan, priviknut
ache /ejk/ *n.* bol

ache /ejk/ *v.* boljeti

achieve /e'či:v/ *v.* izvršiti, postići, izvesti

achievement /e'ći:vmnt/ *n.* postignuće, izvanredno dijelo, izvodjenje

acid /'aesid/ *adj.* kiseo; (fig.) mrzovoljan, jedak; *n.* kiselina

acidify /'aesidifai/ *v.* ukiseliti se

acknowledge /ek'nolidj/ *v.* priznati, dopuštati

acknowledgment /aek'nolidjment/ *n.* priznanje, potvrda, izraz

acquaintance /e'kvejntens/ *n.* poznanstvo, znanje, znanac

acquaint /e'kvejnt/ *v.* saopćiti, upoznati sa

acquire /e'kvajer/ *v.* steći (stvar, naviku), naučiti

acre /ejkr/ *n.* američka mjera za duzinu (40 ari)

across /e'kros/ *adv.* preko, sa one strane

act /aekt/ *v.* činiti, ponijeti se, zastupati, djelovati, raditi

action /'aekšn/ *n.* djelovanje, rad, učinak, kretnja, čin

active /'aektiv/ *adj.* djelujući, zaposlen, radin

activity /aek'tiviti/ *n.* djelatnost, radinost, djelokrug

actor /'aekter/ *n.* glumac

actress /'aektris/ *n.* glumica

actual /'aekšuel/ *adj.* stvaran, zbiljski, sadašnji

actually /aek'šjuli/ *adv.* u stvari, faktički

ad /aed/ *n.* oglas, reklama

adapt (adjust) /e'daept/ *v.* prilagoditi, primijeniti, preraditi

add /aed/ *v.* dodati, pridati, zbrojiti

addicted /e'diktid/ *adj.* odan zlu, rob loše navike

addition /e'dišn/ *n.* dodavanje, dodatak, povećanje, zbrajanje

adaptable /e'daeptebl/ *adj.* prilagodljiv, primjenjiv

adept (expert) /e'dept/ *adj.* upucen, vješt

address /e'dres/ *v.* upraviti na, osloviti, obratiti se; *n.* naslov, adresa

adequately /'aedikvitli/ *adv.* dovoljno, primjereno

adhere /ed'hjer/ *v.* prijanjati, lijepiti se

adjacent /e'djejsent/ *adj.* susjedan, pograničan

adjective /'aeddjektiv/ *n.* pridjev

adjust /ed'djast/ *v.* prilagoditi, poravnati, izgladiti
adjustment /ed'djastment/ *n.* prilagodjenje, izravnanje, nagodba
administration /ed'ministrejsn/ *n.* uprava, administracija, sudjenje
admirable /'aedmirbl/ *adj.* divan
admire /ed'majer/ *adj.* diviti se, obožavati
admission /ed'mišn/ *n.* pristup, dopustenje
admission ticket /ed'mišn 'tikit/ *n.* ulaznica
admittance /ed'mitns/ *n.* pristup /no -!, ulaz zabranjen
adopt (take over) /e'dopt/ *v.* posiniti, pokćeriti, prihvatiti (nazor, vjeru)
adorable /e'do:rbl/ *adj.* krasan, vrijedan divljenja
adore /e'do:r/ *v.* obožavati
adult /'aedalt/ *adj.* odrastao, zreo; *n.* odrastao
adultery /e'dalteri/ *n.* preljub
advance /ed'vaens/ *v.* stupiti naprijed, napredovati
advanced /ed'vaensd/ *adj.* napredan, poodmakao
advancement /ed'vaensment/ *n.* unapredjenje, napredovanje
advantage /ed'vaentidj/ *n.* prednost, korist, nadmoć
advertisement /'edvertisment/ *n.* oglas, reklama
advertise /'aedvertaiz/ *v.* obavijestiti, oglasiti
adventure /ed'vence,/ *n.* pustolovina, smion pothvat
advice (suggestion) /ed'vajs/ *n.* savjet
advise (recommend) /ed'vajz/ *v.* savjetovati, obavijestiti, najaviti
advocate /'aedvokejt/ *v.* braniti, zagovarati, zastupati
affair /e'fe,r/ *n.* stvar, posao, briga, prilika
affect /e'fekt/ *v.* utjecati, djelovati, uplivisati
affection /e'fekšn/ *n.* sklonost, ljubav
affidavit /aefi'dejvit/ *n.* iskaz pod zakletvom
affiliate /e'filejt/ *v.* primiti za člana, pripojiti
affirm /e'fe:rm/ *v.* tvrditi, uvjeravati, izjaviti
affix /e'fiks/ *v.* pričvrstiti, pripojiti, dodati na kraju (potpis)
afflict /e'flikt/ *v.* mučiti, ražalostiti
affluent /'aefluent/ *adj.* obilan, imućan
afford /e'fo:rd/ *v.* pružati, davati

affront /e'frant/ *v.* uvrijediti; *n.* uvreda
afraid /e'frejd/ *adj.* uplašen, u strahu, bojati se
after /'a:fte:r/ *adv.* kasnije, poslije, iza
aftermath /'a:ftermat/ *n.* poslije nečega loseg
afternoon /'a:fte:rnu:n/ *n.* poslije podne
afterwards /'a:fte:vodz/ *adv.* poslije, nakon
again /e'gein/ *adv.* opet, nanovo
against /e'geinst/ *prep.* protiv, prema
age /ejdj/ *n.* doba, starost
age /ejdj/ *v.* starjeti, postarjeti
agency /'ejdjensi/ *n.* agencija, posredništvo, djelovanje, učinak
agenda /e'djenda/ *n.* agenda, dnevni red
agent /'ejdjent/ *n.* posrednik, uzročnik
aggravate /'aegrevejt/ *v.* pogoršati, razdražiti, razljutiti
aggression /e'grešn/ *n.* napadaj, agresija
aggressive /e'gresiv/ *adj.* napadački, nasrtljiv
agile /'aedjil/ *adj.* žustar, okretan, hitar, bistar
agitate /'aedjitejt/ *v.* drmati, tresti, uzburkati, agitovati
ago /e'gou/ *adv.* pred nečim, a week - /e vi:k-/ pred nedelju dana
agony /'aegoni/ *n.* bol, smrtne muke
agree /e'gri:/ *v.* slagati se biti u skladu
agreeable /e'gri:ebl/ *adj.* ugodan
agreement /e'gri:ment/ *n.* sporazum, dogovor
agriculture /,aegri'kalčer/ *n.* ratarstvo, poljoprivreda
ahead /e'hed/ *adv.* sprijeda, naprijed
aid /ejd/ *n.* pomoć, potpora, pomoćno sredstvo
AIDS /ejdz/ *n.* SIDA - sindrom smanjenja otpornosti organizma
ailment /'eilmnt/ *n.* lakša bolest
aim /ejm/ *n.* cilj, svrha, namjera, nišan
air /eer/ *n.* zrak
air /eer/ *v.* zračiti, sušiti, provjetriti
airline /'eerlajn/ *n.* zračna (avionska) prometna pruga
airmail /'eermejl/ *n.* zračna (avionska) posta
airplane /'eerplejn/ *n.* avion, aeroplan

airport /'eerpo:rt/ *n.* zračna luka, aerodrom

aisle /ajl/ *n.* prolaz medju sjedalima vlaka, vitrina u samousluzi

alarm /e'la:rm/ *n.* uzbuna, strah, bojazan, zabrinutost

alarm clock /e'la:rm,klok/ *n.* budilica (ura)

alcohol /'aelkehol/ *n.* alkohol

alcoholic /'aelko'holik/ *n.* alkoholičar

alert /e'le:t/ *n.* upozorenje na oprez, spremnost

alias /'ajlies/ *adv.* inače zvan; *n.* krivo ime, pseudonim

alibi /'aelibaj/ *n.* alibi, odsutnost sa mjesta počinjenog zločina

alien /'ejlien/ *adj.* tudj, stran, neprirodjen našoj naravi

align /e'lajn/ *v.* svrtati se u red, poredati se u ravnoj crti

alignment /e'lajnment/ *n.* nova orijentacija, poredak

alike /e'lajk/ *adj.* sličan nekome (nečemu)

alive /e'lajv/ *adj.* živ, žustar

all /o:l/ *adj.* sav, cio, čitav

alleviate /e'li:vjejt/ *v.* ublažiti, olakšati

alley /'aeli/ *n.* aleja, drvored, prolaz

alliance /e'lajens/ *n.* savez, ženidbena veza, srodstvo

allied /e'lajd/ *adj.* srodan, udružen, savezni

allow /e'lau/ *v.* dopustiti, udovoljiti

allowance /e'launs/ *n.* dopuštenje, djeparac

alloy /e'loj/ *n.* legura

alright /o:lrajt/ *adv.* siguran, bezbjedan, u redu

allusion /e'ljuzn/ *n.* aluzija, natucanje, smjeranje na nešto

almond /am'end/ *n.* badem

almost /'ol:moust/ *adv.* malone, gotovo, haman

alone /e'loun/ *adj.* sam

along /e'lo:ng/ *pre.* uzduž, kraj, niz

aloud /e'laud/ *adv.* glasno

alphabet /'aelfebit/ *n.* abeceda, alfabet

already /o:l'redi/ *adv.* već

also /o:lsou/ *adv.* takodjer, osim toga,

alter /'o:lter/ *v.* preudesiti, izmijeniti

alternate /'o:lternejt/ *v.* izmjenjivati, slijediti naizmjenice

alternate /'o:lternejt/ *adj.* izmjeničan

alternating current /ol-ter'nejting karent/ *n.* izmjenična struja

alternation /o:lt,':neišn/ *n.* izmjenjivanje

although /o:ldzou/ *con.* premda, iako, makar

altogether /o:ltu'gedze:r/ *adv.* potpuno, sasvim, u cijelosti

always /'o:lvejz/ *adv.* uvijek, neprestance

am /aem/ *v.* jesam (ja)

amateur /'aemečer:/ *n.* amater

amaze /e'mejz/ *v.* začuditi, zapanjiti

amazing /e'mejzing/ *adj.* zapanjujući, izvanredan

ambassador /aem'baesede:r/ *n.* ambasador, poklisar

ambiguous /aem'bigjues/ *adj.* dvosmislen, dvojben

ambition /aem'bišn/ *n.* ambicija, častohleplje

ambitious /aem'bišs/ *adj.* ambiciozan, častohlepan

ambulance /'aembjulens/ *n.* bolnička kola

ambush /'aembuš/ *n.* zasjeda; *v.* napasti iz zasjede

amend /e'mend/ *v.* popraviti, poboljšati

amendment /e'mendment/ *n.* ispravak, dopuna

Americanism /e'merikenizm/ *n.* američki izraz (riječ)

amiable /'eimjebl/ *adj.* prijazan, ljubazan

amid /e'mid/ *prep.* usred, medju

ammunition /,aemjunišn/ *n.* streljivo, municija

among /e'mang/ *prep.* izmedju, medju

amicable /'aemikbl/ *adj.* prijateljski, susretljiv

amount /e'maunt/ *n.* iznos, svota

ample /'aempl/ *adj.* obilan, prostran, opsežan

amplify /'aemplifaj/ *v.* povećati; pojačati

amusement /e'mju:zment/ *n.* zabava

amusing /e'mju:zing/ *adj.* zabavan

an /en/ *art.* jedan, neki

analysis /e'naelajzis/ *n.* analiza

analyze /e'nelajz/ *v.* analizirati

anatomy /e'naetemi/ *n.* anatomija

ancestor /'aensester/ *n.* predak

anchor /'aenker/ *n.*   sidro, anker
ancient /'ejnšnt/ *adj.*   drevan, starinski, vaktile
and /end/ conj. i
anecdote /'aenik,dout/ *n.*   anegdota
anew /e'nju/ *adv.*   iznova
angel /'ejndjl/ *n.*   andjeo, melek
anger /'enger/ *n.*   gnjev, srdjba
angina /'aen'džain,/ *n.*   angina, grlobolja
angle /'aengl/ *n.*   kut, ugao
angry /aengri/ *adj.*   srdit, gnjevan, ljut
animal /'aeniml/ *n.*   životinja
anguish /'aengviš/ *n.*   tjeskoba, bol
animation /aeni'mejšn/ *n.*   živahnost, bodrost
animosity /,aeni'mositi/ *n.*   neprijateljstvo
ankle /'aenkl/ *n.*   gležanj /sprain -,/sprein -/ uganuti gležanj
anniversary /,aeni've:rseri/ *n.*   obljetnica, godišnjica
announce /e'nauns/ *v.*   najaviti, oglasiti
announcement /e'naunsment/ *n.*   objava, oglas, obznana
annoy /e'noj/ *v.*   dosadjivati, ozlovoljiti
annoyed /e'nojd/ *adj.*   zlovoljan
annual /'aenjuel/ *adj.*   godišnji
annually /'aenjuli/ *adv.*   svake godine
anonym /'aenonim/ *n.*   nepoznata osoba
anonymous /e'nonimes/ *adj.*   anoniman, nepoznat
another /e'nadzer/ *adj.*   drugi, još jedan
answer /'aenser/ *n.*   odgovor
answer /'aenser/ *v.*   odgovoriti
ant /aent/ *n.*   mrav
antagonist /aen'taegonist/ *n.*   protivnik, neprijatelj
anti /'aenti/ *prep.*   ispred, prije
anticipate /aen'tisipejt/ *pre* očekivati, unaprijed odrediti
anticipation /aentisi'pejšn/ *n.*   predvidjanje, predosjećanje
anthem /'aentm/ *n.*   himna
antique /aen'ti:k/ *n.*   starina;   *adj.*   vrijedno zbog starosti

antiquity /aen'tikviti/ *n.* drevna starina
anxiety /'aeng'zajeti/ *n.* zabrinutost, tjeskoba, nemir
anxious /'aenkšz/ *adj.* zabrinut, gorljiv, tjeskoban
any /'eni/ *adv.* iko, itko, isto, ikoji
anybody /'aeni'bodi/ *pro.* iko, itko, ikoji, svako
anyhow /'aenihau/ *adv.* bilo kako, svakako
anyone /'aenivan/ *pro.* iko, itko,ikoji
anything /'eniting/ *pro.* bilo što, što mu drago
anyway /'enivej/ *adv.* bilo kako, ipak, kako god
anywhere /'enive:r/ *adv.* bilo gdje, svuda
apart /e'pa:rt/ *adv.* osobno, odvojeno
apartment /e'pa:rtment/ *n.* stan
apathetic /aepe'tetik/ *adj.* ravnodušan, apatičan
ape /ejp/ *n.* majmun
apex /'ejpeks/ *n.* vršak, vrhunac
apologize /e'poledjajz/ *v.* ispričati se
apology /e'polodji/ *n.* isprika, izvinjenje
apostrophe /e'postrefi/ *n.* apostrof
appalled /e'po:ld/ *adj.* pretstravljen, preneražen
apparatus /aepe'rejt,s/ *n.* aparat, naprava
apparel /e'per,l/ *n.* odjeća
apparent /e'paerent/ *adj.* prividan, naoko
appeal /e'pi:l/ *v.* apelirati, obratiti se s molbom
appear /e'pier/ *v.* pojaviti se, stupiti na
appearance /e'pierens/ *n.* izgled, vanjstina, pojava
append /e'pend/ *v.* pridodati
appendix /e'pendiks/ *n.* dodatak
appetite /'aepitajt/ *n.* apetit, tek
appetizing /'aepitajzing/ *adj.* koji budi apetit / tek
applause /e'plouz/ *n.* pljesak, pljeskanje, odobravanje
apple /'aepl/ *n.* jabuka
appliance /e'plajens/ *n.* primjena, naprava
application /,aepli'kejšn/ *n.* primjena, upotreba
applicant /,aepli'kant/ *n.* molitelj, natjecatelj, podnosilac prijave

apply /e'plaj/ *v.* staviti na, primijeniti
appoint /e'point/ *v.* odrediti, zakazati (sastanak), ustanoviti rok
appreciate /e'pri:šjejt/ *v.* uvažavati, jako cijeniti
appointment /e'pointm,nt/ *n.* sastanak
appraisal /e'preiz,l/ *n.* procjena
apprehend /,aeprihend/ *v.* shvatiti, razumjeti
approach /e'prouč/ *v.* približiti se
appropriate /e'proupriejt/ *adj.* podesan, doličan
approval /e'pru:vl/ *n.* odobravanje, pristanak
approximate /e'proksimit/ *adj.* približan, otprilike
apricot /'eprikot/ *n.* kajsija
April /'ejpril/ *n.* april, travanj
apron /'eipr,n/ *n.* pregača, kecelja
apt /aept/ *adj.* sposoban, dosjetljiv
aptitude /'aeptitju:d/ *n.* sposobnost, podesnost
arbitrary /'a:rbitrari/ *adj.* samovoljan, neopravdan
arbor /'a:rber/ *n.* osovina
arc /a:k/ *n.* luk
arch /a:rč/ *n.* svod, luk
arch /a:rc/ *v.* presvoditi, praviti luk
archeology /a:rki'oledji/ *n.* arheologija
architect /'a:rkitekt/ *n.* arhitekt, graditelj
architecture /a:rkitekčer/ *n.* arhitektura, graditeljstvo
archives /'a:rkvajz/ *n.* arhiva, arhiv
arctic /'a:ktik/ *adj.* arktički, sjeverni
ardent /'a:rdent/ *adj.* žarki, revan
are /a:r/ *v.* si, smo, ste, su
area /'e:rja/ *n.* površina, prostor, područje
argue /'a:rgju:/ *v.* raspravljati, umovati
argument /'a:rgjument/ *n.* dokaz, navodjenje razloga
arise /e'rajz/ *v.* ustati se, dići se, pojaviti se
arm /a:rm/ *n.* ruka
arm /a:rm/ *n.* oružje ; *v.* naoružati
armchair /,a:rm'če:r/ *n.* naslonjać, fotelja

armpit /a:rm-pit/ *n.* pazuh
army /'a:rmi/ *n.* vojska
around /e'raund/ pre naokolo, sa svih strana, oko
arrange /e'rejndj/ *v.* poredati, svrstati
arrangement /e'rejndjment/ *n.* dogovor, sporazum, uredjenje
array /e'rei/ *v.* poredati, nanizati
arrest /e'rest/ *n.* uhapšenje, zatvor
arrival /e'rajvel/ *n.* dolazak, pojava
arrive /e'rajv/ *v.* stići, doći, pojaviti se
arrogant /'aerogent/ *adj.* drzak, nadut, arogantan
arrow /'aerou/ *n.* strijela
arsenal /a:s,nal/ *n.* arsenal
art /a:rt/ *n.* umjetnost, umjeće, vještina
artichoke /'a:rti,ouki/ *n.* artičoka
article /'a:rtikl/ *n.* članak, vrsta robe, clan u ugovoru
artifact /,a:rti'fakt/ *n.* tvorevina ljudske ruke
artificial /a:rti'fišl/ *adj.* umjetan, nenaravan
artist /'a:rtist/ *n.* umjetnik
as /ez/ *adv.* kao
ascend /e'send/ *v.* uspinjati se, ići prema gore
ascent /e'sent/ *n.* uspon, uspinjanje, kosina
ash /aeš/ *n.* pepeo; jasen(drvo)
ashamed /e'šejmd/ *adj.* postidjen, zasramljen
ashtray /'aeštrej/ *n.* pepelnica, pepeljara
ascertain /aes,tein/ *v.* ustanoviti, saznati
ask /ae:sk/ *v.* tražiti, zamoliti, upitati
asleep /e'sli:p/ *adv.* u snu, spavati
aspect /'aespekt/ *n.* izgled, strana, ugao gledanja
aspire /es'pajer/ *v.* težiti za nećim višim
aspiring /ez'paj'ring/ *adj.* častohlepan
ass /aes/ *n.* magarac
assail /e'sejl/ *v.* napasti
assassinate /e'sesinejt/ *v.* ubiti iz potaje
assassination /e,sesi'nejšn/ *n.* umorstvo iz potaje, atentat

assault /e'solt/ *v.* napasti
assembly /e'sembli/ *n.* zbor, skupština
assert /e'se:rt/ *v.* tvrditi, braniti svoje pravo
assessment /e'sesment/ *n.* procjena
assets /'aesets/ *n.* imovina, aktiva, ostavština
assignment /e'sajnment/ *n.* dodjeljenje, prijenos posjeda
assist /e'sist/ *v.* pomagati
assistant /e'sistent/ *n.* pomoćnik, asistent
associate /e'soušjejt/ *adj.* udružen
assortment /e'so:rtment/ *n.* izbor
assume /e'sju:m/ *v.* poprimiti, uzeti za
assumption /e'sampšn/ *n.* predpostavka
assure /e'šu:r/ *v.* uvjeravati, osigurati (policom)
astonish /es'toniš/ *v.* začuditi, iznenaditi
astound /es'taund/ *v.* zapanjiti
astrigent /es'tridjent/ *adj.* koji zatvara (pore, stolicu)
at /aet/ *prep.* kod, prema
athlete /'eatli:t/ *n.* atleta, sportaš, sportista, igrač
attach /e'taeč/ *v.* pripojiti
atrocity /e'trositi/ *n.* grozota, grozno nedjelo
attack /e'taek/ *v.* napasti; *n.* napad, atak
attempt /e'tempt/ *v.* pokušati, *n.* pokušaj
attend /e'tend/ *v.* dvoriti, njegovati, posluživati
attendant /e'tend,nt/ *n.* pohadjač
attention /e'tenš,n/ *n.* pozornost, pažnja
attitude /'aetitju:d/ *n.* položaj, stav, držanje
attract /e'traekt/ *v.* privlačiti, mamiti
attraction /e'traekš,n/ *n.* privlačenje, privlačnost, čar
attractive /e'trektiv/ *adj.* privlačan
attorney /e'to:ni/ *n.* odvjetnik, advokat
auction /'o:kšn/ *n.* dražba, javna licitacija
audience /'o:djens/ *n.* slušateljstvo, slušaoci
audible /'o:dibl/ *adj.* čujan, zamjetljiv sluhom
August /'o:g,st/ *n.* avgust, august, kolovoz

aunt /aent/ *n.* tetka
Australian /o:s'trejljen/ *adj.* australijski, *n.* Australijanac
Austrian /o:'strjen/ *adj.* austrijski, *n.* Austrijanac
authentic /o:'tentik/ *adj.* vjerodostojan, pouzdan, autentičan
author /'o:tor/ *n.* stvaralac, autor, pisac
authority /o:'toriti/ *n.* vlast, upliv, autoritet
automatic /,o:to'maetik/ *adj.* automatski
automation /,o:to'mejšn/ *n.* automatizacija, robotizacija
automobile /'o:tomobil/ *n.* automobil, auto
autumn /'o:t,m/ *n.* jesen
auxiliary /o:'gzilj,ri/ *n.* pomoćnik
available /e'vejl,bl/ *adj.* raspoloživ
avenue /'aevinju/ *n.* aleja, bulevar, široka ulica
average /'aeveridj/ *adj.* prosječan, osrednji,
averse /e've:rs/ *adj.* nesklon, nerad, protivan
avid /'evid/ *adj.* pohlepan, lakom
avoid /e'vojd/ *v.* izbjegavati
avow /e'vau/ *v.* priznati, izjaviti
await /e'vejt/ *v.* čekati, očekivati
awake /e'vejk/ *v.* probuditi se, postati svjestan
award /e'vo:d/ *n.* nagrada, presuda; *v.* nagraditi
aware /e've,/ *adj.* svjestan
away /e'vej/ *adv.* otale, tamo daleko
awful /'o:ful/ *adj.* strašan, grozan
awkward /'o:kv,rd/ *adj.* nespretan, neokretan
axe /aeks/ *n.* sjekira

B

baby /'bejbi/ *n.* beba, djetešce, razmaženko
bachelor /'baečeler/ *n.* neženja
back /baek/ *n.* ledja, zadnja strana; *v.* povući, uzmaći
background /'baekgraund/ *n.* dno, pozadina
backwards /'baekverds/ *adv.* natrag, nazad, naopako
bacon /'bejkn/ *n.* slanina
bad /baed/ *adj.* zao, loš, netačan
badge /baedž/ *n.* značka, znak, bedž
baffle /'baefl/ *v.* zavaravati se, osujetiti
bag /baeg/ *n.* vreća, torba, kesa
bagel /'baegl/ *n.* dževrek, vrsta peciva
baggage /'baegidž/ *n.* prtljag, drska ženska
baggy /'baegi/ *adv.* vrećast
bake /bejk/ *v.* peći
bakery /bejk,ri/ *n.* pekara
balance /'baelens/ *n.* vaga, ravnoteža; *v.* uravnotežiti, balansirati
balcony /'baelk,ni/ *n.* balkon
bald /bo:ld/ *adj.* ćelav, golobrad
balk /bo:lk/ *n.* balvan, greda, prepreka
ball /bo:l/ *n.* lopta
balloon /be'lu:n/ *n.* balon
ballot /'bael,t/ *n.* glasanje (tajno)
balm /ba:m/ *n.* balzam
ban /baen/ *n.* zabrana, prokletstvo; *v.* zabraniti
bang /baeng/ *n.* eksplozija, jak udarac ; *v.* eksplodirati
banish /'baeniš/ *v.* prognati, otjerati
bank /baenk/ *n.* nasip, bedem, obala
bankruptcy /baenkrapsi/ *n.* bankrotstvo
banner /'baener/ *n.* zastava, barjak, steg
bar /ba:r/ *n.* šipka, prečaga, brana
barber /'ba:rber/ *n.* brijač, berber, brico
bare /bae,r/ *adj.* go, nag, nepokriven
barefoot /'bae,fut/ *adj.* bosonog

bargain /'ba:rgin/ *n.* pogodba, pazar barn /ba:rn/ *n.* žitnica, hambar, ambar

barracks /'baereks/ *n.* kasarna, baraka

barrel /'baerel/ *n.* bure; *v.* napuniti bure

barrier /'baerjer/ *n.* prepreka, brana

barter /'ba:rter/ *n.* cjenkati se, pogadjati se; razmjena roba

base /bejs/ *n.* osnova, temelj

basement /'bejsment/ *n.* podrum, suteren

bashful /'baešful/ *adj.* sramežljiv, stidljiv

basic /'bejsik/ *adj.* osnovni

basically (fundamentally) /'bejsik,li/ *adv.* u stvari, u biti

basis /'bejsis/ *n.* osnova, baza, temelj

basket /'ba:skit/ *n.* korpa, košara, koš

bastard /'baesterd/ *n.* kopile, vanbračno dijete

bat /baet/ *n.* slijepi miš; štap za bejzbol

bath /ba:s/ *n.* kada, kupanje (u kadi)

bathe /bejz/ *v.* kupati se (u rijeci)

bathing suit /'bejzing sju:t/ *n.* kupaći kostim, bade kostim

bathroom /ba:zru:m/ *n.* kupatilo, banja (toalet, klozet) Am.

bathtub /'ba:ztab/ *n.* kada, banja

battery /'baeteri/ *n.* baterija, akumulator

battle /'baetl/ *n.* bitka, boj

bay /bej/ *n.* zaliv, lavež ; *v.* lajati

be, was, been /bi:, voz, bi:n/ *v.* biti

beach /bi:č/ *n.* plaža

bead /bi:d/ *n.* zrno, perla

beam /bi:m/ *n.* zrak, greda, balvan; *v.* obasjati, blistati

bean /bi:n/ *n.* pasulj, grah,

bear /be,r/ *n.* medvjed, grubijan, špekulant na berzi

bear, bore, borne /be,r, bo:r, bo:rn/ *v.* nositi, izdržati, podnositi

beard /bierd/ *n.* brada

beast /bi:st/ *n.* životinja, beštija

beat, beat, beaten /bi:t, bi:t, bi:tn/ *v.* tući, udariti, pobijediti

beautiful /'bju:teful/ *adj.* lijep, divan, krasan

beauty /'bju:ti/ *n.* ljepota

because /bi'kouz/ *con.* radi, pošto, zato;   *adv.*   jerbecome,
became, become /bi'kam, bi'kejm, bi'kam/ *v.* postati, slagati se,
pristajati
bed /bed/ *n.* krevet, postelja, ležište; sloj
bedroom /'bedrum/ *n.* spavaća soba
bee /bi:/ *n.* pčela
bee-hive /'bi:haiv/ *n.* košnica
beef /bi:f/ *n.* govedina
beer /bier/ *n.* pivo
beetle /'bi:tl/ *n.* kutljača, varjača
before /bi'fo:r/ *adv.* prije, ranije, naprijed
beg /beg/ *v.* moliti, prositi, tražiti
begin, began, begun /bi'gin, bi'gen, bi'gan/ *v.* početi, nastupiti
beginning /bi'gining/ *n.* početak
behalf /bi'ha:f/ *n.* korist, interes
behave /bi'hejv/ *v.* ponašati se
behaviour /bi'hejv,r/ *n.* ponašanje
behind /bi'hajnd/ *adv.* iza, natrag, pozadi
behold, beheld, beheld /bi'hold, bi'held, bi'held/ *v.*   gledati,
posmatrati
belch /belč/ *v.* povratiti, podrignuti
belief /bi'li:f/ *n.* vjera, uvjerenje, ubjeđenje
believe /bi'li:v/ *v.* vjerovati, smatrati
bell /bel/ *n.* zvono
belly /beli/ *n.* trbuh
belong /bi'long/ *v.* pripadati
belonging /bi'longing/ *n.* svojina
below /bi'lou/ *adv.* niže, ispod
belt /belt/ *n.* pojas, kaiš, opasač
bench /benč/ *n.* klupa
bend, bent, bent /bend, bent, bent/   *n.*   zavoj, krivina, okuka;
v. saviti, presaviti
beneath /bi'ni:s/ *prep.* pod, ispod
beneficial /beni'fišl/ *adj.* koristan, blagotvoran
benefit /'benifit/ *n.* korist, pomoć, povlastica

benevolent /bi'nevolent/ *adj.* dobrotvoran, milosrdan
berry /beri/ *n.* jagoda, bobica
beside /bi'sajd/ *adv.* pokraj, pored
besides /bi'sajds/ pr. uz, osim, pored
best /best/ *adj.* najbolji, najveći
bet /bet/ *n.* opklada; *v.* kladiti se
better /'beter/ *adv.* bolje
between /bi'tvi:n/ *prep.* izmedju
beyond /bi'jond/ *prep.* van, više, iznad
Bible /'bajbl/ *n.* Biblija
bicycle /'bajsikl/ *n.* bicikl
bid /bid/ *n.* ponuda cijene; *v.*   nuditi
big /big/ *adj.* velik, krupan
bike /bajk/ *n.* bicikl
bill /bil/ *n.* račun; novčanica
billion /'bilij,n/ *n.* bilion, milijarda
bind /bajnd/ *v.* vezati, obavezati
bird /b:rd/ *n.* ptica
birth /b:rt/ *n.* rodjenje, porijeklo, porodjaj
birthday /b:rtdej/ *n.* rodjendan
bitch /bič/ *n.* kučka, kuja
bite /bajt/ *n.* komadić; *v.* zagristi
bitter /'bit,r/ *adj.* gorak, zajedljiv
black /laek/ *adj.* crn; *n.* crnac
bladder /'bleder/ *n.* mokraćni mjehur, mokraćna bešika
blade /blejd/ *n.* oštrica, listić, vlat
blame /blejm/ *n.* prijekor; *v.* okriviti, prekoriti
blank /blaenk/ *adj.* prazan, neispisan, čist
blanket /'blaenkit/ *n.* prekrivač, deka, ćebe
blast /bla:st/ *v.* razoriti, dići u vazduh
bleach /bli:č/ *v.* bijeliti, izbjeljivati; *n.* bjelilo
bleed /bli:d/ *v.* krvariti
blemish /'blemiš/ *v.* ružiti, grditi; *n.* grdnja
bless /bles/ *v.* blagosiljati, usrećiti
blind /blajnd/ *adj.* slijep, ćorav; *v.* zaslijepiti

blindness /blindnes/ *n.* sljepoća, sljepilo

blink /blink/ *n.* pogled, tren oka; blinkanje; *v.* brzo pogledati

blizzard /'bliz,rd/ *n.* snježna mećava

block /blok/ *n.* panj, trupac, klada; *v.* blokirati

blonde /blond/ *n.* plavuša, blondinka; *adj.* blond

blood /'blad/ *n.* krv; rod, rasa

blossom /'blos,m/ *n.* behar, cvjetanje voća, cvat

blouse /blauz/ *n.* bluza

blow, blew, blown /blou, blu: , bloun/ *v.* puhati, duvati,

blow /blou/ *n.* udarac, nesreća

blue /blu:/ *adj.* plav, tužan, melanholičan

blunt /blant/ *adj.* tup, bezosjećajan

blush /blaš/ *n.* crvenilo, rumenilo; *v.* pocrveniti, zarumeniti se

board /bo:rd/ *n.* daska, odbor, paluba

boast /boust/ *v.* hvaliti, hvalisati; *n.* hvaljenje; ponos

boat /bout/ *n.* čamac, brod

body /'bodi/ *n.* tijelo, trup

boil /bojl/ *v.* vriti, ključati

bold /bould/ *adj.* smion, drzak, nagao

bond /bond/ *n.* veza, obaveza; priznanica; mjenica; *v.* vezati

bone /boun/ *n.* kost

book /buk/ *n.* knjiga

boot /bu:t/ *n.* obuća, čizma

booth /bu:s/ *n.* tezga, daščara, kiosk

border /'bo:rder/ *n.* granica, medja, ivica; *v.* ograničiti

born /b;:n/ *adj.* rodjen; prirodan

borough /'bar,/ *n.* grad

borrow /'borou/ *v.* pozajmiti, posuditi

boss /bos/ *n.* gazda, šef

both /bous/ *pron.* oba, obje

bother /bodzer/ *n.* dosada; *v.* dosadjivati se

bottle /'botl/ *n.* flaša, boca, šiša

bottom /'bot,m/ *n.* dno, podnožje, temelj

bound /baund/ *v.* ograničiti, omedjiti

boundary /baundry/ *n.* granica, medja

bow /bou/ *n.* luk; poklon, naklon; leptir mašna
bowl /boul/ *n.* kugla; zdjela, ćasa
box /boks/ *n.* kutija, sanduk; *v.* udariti, zatvoriti u kutiju
boy /boj/ *n.* dječak, momak
bra /bra:/ *n.* grudnjak, brushalter, lajb
bracelet /'brejslit/ *n.* narukvica, grivna
braid /brejd/ *n.* pletenica; *v.* plesti, uplitati
brain /brein/ *n.* mozak, um
brake /brejk/ *n.* kočnica
bran /braen/ *n.* mekinje
branch /bra:nč/ *n.* grana, odeljenje; *v.* granati se
brand /braend/ *n.* marka, vrsta
brandy /'braendi/ *n.* rakija; konjak
brass /bra:s/ *n.* bronza, mjed
brat /braet/ *n.* dijete, derište
brave /brejv/ *adj.* hrabar, smion, odvažan, kuražan
bread /bred/ *n.* hljeb, kruh, nimet
break, broke, broken /brejk, broke, broken/ *v.* slomiti, prebiti, prelomiti
breakfast /'brekf,:st/ *n.* doručak
breast /brest/ *n.* grudi, prsa
breath /bres/ *n.* dah, disanje, zadah
breathe /bri:d/ *v.* disati, udisati
breeze /bri:z/ *n.* lahor, povjetarac
brew /bru:/ *n.* vrenje (pivo)
brick /brik/ *n.* cigla, opeka
bridge /bridž/ *n.* most, ćuprija
brief /bri:f/ *adj.* kratak, sažet
bright /brajt/ *adj.* jasan, svijetao, pametan
brilliant /'brilj,nt/ *adj.* sjajan, blistav, briljantan
bring, brought, brought /bring, bro:t, bro:t/ *v.* donijeti, nositi, dovesti
brisk /brisk/ *adj.* živahan, brz, veseo
broad /bro:d/ *adj.* širok, prostran

broadcast /'bro:dka:st/ *n.* širenje na daljinu, razglašavanje
brook /bruk/ *n.* potok
broom /bru:m/ *n.* metla
brother /'badzer/ *n.* brat, burazer
brown /braun/ *adj.* smedj, braon
brush /braš/ *n.* četka, kefa; *v.* četkati
bubble /babl/ *n.* mjehur, pjena
bucket /'bakit/ *n.* vedro, čabar
buckle /'bakl/ *n.* kopča, šnala; *v.* zakopčati
bud /bad/ *n.* pupoljak; *v.* pupati
buffalo /'baf,lou/ *n.* bivo, bizon (divlje goveče)
bug /bag/ *n.* stjenica, insekt
build, built, built /bild, bilt, bilt/ *v.* graditi, zidati
building /bilding/ *n.* zgrada, gradjevina
bull /bul/ *n.* bik; vrsta berzanskih špekulanata; *v.* špekulisati na berzi
bum /bam/ *n.* pijanica, pjandura; neradnik
bump /bamp/ *n.* neravnina (na putu), džomba
bunch /banč/ *n.* kita, buket
bundle /'bandl/ *n.* svježanj, snop; *v.* vezati
burden /'be:rdn/ *n.* opterećenje, teret, odgovornost
burn /be:rn/ *v.* gorjeti, opeći, sjajiti
burst /be:rst/ *n.* prasak, eksplozija; *v.* eksplodirati
bury /'beri/ *v.* sahraniti, ukopati
bus /bas/ *n.* autobus
bush /buš/ *n.* žbun, grm
business /'biznis/ *n.* posao, zanimanje, dužnost
businessman /'biznismen/ *n.* poslovan čovjek, biznismen
busy /bizi/ *adj.* u poslu
but /but/ *adv.* ali
butcher /'buč,:/ *n.* mesar, kasap, kasapin
butter /'bat':r/ *n.* puter, maslac
butterfly /'baterflaj/ *n.* leptir
buttocks /'bat,ks/ *n.* stražnji dio ledja

button /'batn/ *n.* dugme, kopča, puljka; *v.* zakopčati

buy, bought, bought /baj, bo:t, bo:t/ *v.* kupiti

by /baj/ pr. ovdje, blizu; *adv.* od (uz pasiv); pomoću

C

cab /kaeb/ *n.* taksi, fijaker
cabbage /'kaebidž/ *n.* kupus
cabin /'kaebin/ *n.* kabina
cable /'kejbl/ *n.* debelo uže, čelični konop, kabel
cable /'kaejbl/ *v.* telegrafisati, telegrafirati
cafe /'kaefe/ *n.* kafana, bar
cafeteria /'kaefitiria/ *n.* restoran u sklopu ustanove (škole, fabrike)
cage /kejdž/ *n.* kavez, krletka
cake /kejk/ *n.* kolač, komad
calculate /'kaelkjulejt/ *v.* proračunati, obračunati
calendar /'kaelinder/ *n.* kalendar
calf /ka:f/ *n.* tele
call /ko:l/ *v.* zvati, vikati, dozivati; *n.* poziv, posjeta
calm /ka:m/ *adj.* miran, spokojan; *n.* mirnoća, tišina
camel /'kaemel/ *n.* kamila
camera /'kaemera/ *n.* fotografski aparat
camp /kaemp/ *n.* kamp, logor; *v.* logorovati
campaign /kaem'pejn/ *n.* kampanja, borba
campus /'kaempus/ *n.* prostor na kome je škola/ univerzitet
can not/ cannot/ can't /kaen not/'kaenot/ka:nt / *v.* ne moći
can, could /kaen, kud/ *v.* moći, umjeti, znati
canal /ke'nael/ *n.* kanal
cancel /'kaens,l/ *v.* poništiti, izbrisati
cancer /'kaens,r/ *n.* rak, kancer
candidate /'kaendidejt/ *n.* kandidat
candle /'kaendl/ *n.* svijeća
candy /'kaendi/ *n.* slatkiš, karamela, bonbon
cane /kejn/ *n.* štap, trska
canned /'kaend/ *adj.* konzervisan
canvas /kaenv,z/ *n.* platno, platno za slike

cap /kaep/ *n.* kapa, kačket; *v.* pozdraviti

capable /'kejpebl/ *adj.* sposoban, spreman

capital /'kaepitl/ *n.* veliko slovo, prestolnica; *adj.* glavni

captain /'kaeptin/ *n.* kapetan; vodja; *v.* komandovati, upravljati

capture /'kaepč,r/ *v.* zarobiti, uhvatiti, oteti

car /ka:r/ *n.* kola, automobil; vagon

cardboard /ka:dbo:rd/ *n.* karton

card /'ka:rd/ *n.* karta, bilet, posjetnica(business)

cardinal /'ka:rdinl/ *adj.* glavni, prvenstven, osnovni; *n.* kardinal

care /keer/ *n.* briga, oprez, pažnja; *v.* brinuti se

career /ke'rier/ *n.* karijera, tok života

careful /keerful/ *adj.* pažljiv, oprezan

careless /keerles/ *adj.* nemaran, bezbrižan

carpet /'ka:rpit/ *n.* ćilim, tepih

carriage /'kaeridž/ *n.* vagon, prevoz

carrot /'kaeret/ *n.* mrkva, šargarepa

carry /'kaeri/ *v.* nositi, prenositi; *n.* teret

cartoon /ka:tu:n/ *n.* crtani film; karikatura; skica

carve /ka:v/ *v.* rezati, sjeći

case /kejs/ *n.* slučaj; kutija

cash /kaeš/ *n.* gotovina, novac u gotovom, keš

cast /ka:st/ *n.* bacanje, hitac; podjela uloga

castle /'ka:sl/ *n.* zamak

cat /kaet/ *n.* mačka

catch /kaeč/ *v.* uhvatiti, zgrabiti, dohvatiti

cathedral /ke'ti:drel/ *n.* katedrala

cattle /kaetl/ *n.* stoka, marva

cause /ko:z/ *n.* uzrok, povod; *v.* uzrokovati

caution /'ko:š,n/ *n.* predostrožnost, obazrivost; *v.* opomenuti

cave /keiv/ *n.* pećina, špilja;

ceiling /'si:ling/ *n.* plafon, strop, tavanica

celebrate /'selibrejt/ *v.* slaviti, svetkovati

cellular phone /'seljul,/ *n.* celular telefon (bežični telefon)

cemetery /'semitri/ *n.* groblje, mezarje

cent /sent/ *n.* cent (novčana jedinica)

centimeter /'sentimiter/ *n.* centimetar

century /'senčuri/ *n.* vijek, stoljeće

ceremony /'siremoni/ *n.* ceremonija, obred, ritual

certain /'se:rt,n/ *adj.* izvjestan, siguran, odredjen

chain /čejn/ *n.* lanac, okov; *v.* vezati, okovati

chair /če,:r/ *n.* stolica

chalk /čo:k/ *n.* kreda

challenge /'čelindž/ *n.* izazov, megdan; *v.* izazivati, prkositi

camomile /kaem,majl/ *n.* kamilica

chance(opportunity) /ča:ns/ *n.* prilika, šansa

change /čejndž/ *n.* mijenjanje, promjena; *v.* promijeniti, razmijeniti

channel /'čaenel/ *n.* kanal, korito

chapter /'čaepter/ *n.* glava, poglavlje

character /'kaerikt,/ *n.* karakter, znak, slovo

charge /ča:rdž/ *n.* breme, teret, naboj; *v.* opteretiti; zaračunati

charitable /'čaerit,bl/ *adj.* milosrdan, dobrotvoran

charm /ča:rm/ *n.* čar, ljepota; *v.* očarati

charming /ča:rming/ *adj.* čaroban, divan, šarmantan

charter /'ča:t,:/ *v.* iznajmiti; *n.* privilegija, povlastica

chase /čejs/ *v.* juriti, goniti

chat /čaet/ *n.* razgovor, brbljanje; *v.* čavrljati

cheap /či:p/ *adj.* jeftin, beznačajan

cheat /či:t/ *n.* prevara, obmana; *v.* prevariti, obmanuti

check /ček/ *n.* ček, znak; *v.* zaustaviti, spriječiti

check-up /'ček-ap/ *n.* ljekarski pregled (rutinski)

checkbook /'čekbuk/ *n.* čekovna knjižica

cheek /či:k/ *n.* obraz

cheer /či,r/ *v.* klicati, pljeskati

cheerful /'či,ful/ *adj.* veseo

cheerio /'či,riou/ *int.* živjeli!, na zdravlje!

cheese /'či:z/ *n.* sir

chef /šef/ *n.* kuhar

chemical /'kemik,l/ *adj.* hemijski, kemijski

cherish /'čeriš/ *v.* milovati, maziti

cherry (sour) /'čeri/ *n.* višnja

cherry (sweet) /ˈčeri (sviːt)/ *n.* trešnja, ašlama
chess /čes/ *n.* šah
chest /čest/ *n.* prsa, grudi, škrinja
chestnut /ˈčesnat/ *n.* kesten, maron
chew /čuː/ *v.* žvakati
chewing-gum /čuːving-gam/ *n.* žvakača guma
chicken /ˈčik,n/ *n.* pile, piletina; *adj.* pileći
chicken-pox /ˈčik,n-poks/ *n.* male boginje, ospice
chief /čiːf/ *n.* šef, rukovodilac; poglavica plemena
child (pl.children) /čajld (čildrn)/ *n.* dijete (djeca)
childbirth /čajldb,ːrt/ *n.* porodjaj
childish /čajldiš/ *adj.* djetinjast
childhood /čajldhuːd/ *n.* djetinjstvo
chilly /čili/ *adj.* hladno, studeno
chimney /ˈčimni/ *n.* dimnjak, odžak
chin /čin/ *n.* brada, podbradak
china /ˈčajna/ *n.* porcelan (posudje)
chips /čips/ *n.* prženi krompir
chives /čajvz/ *n.* mladi luk
chocolate /ˈčokolit/ *n.* čokolada
choice /čois/ *n.* izbor; *adj.* izabran
choose, chose, chosen /čuːz, čouz, čouz,n/ *v.* birati, izabrati
chop /čop/ *v.* sjeći, prekidati
Christmas /ˈkrism,s/ *n.* Božić
church /čeːrč/ *n.* crkva, bogomolja
circle /ˈs,ːkl/ *n.* kružnica, prsten (površina unutar kruga) *v.* zaokružiti, okretati se
circuit /ˈs,ːkit/ *n.* krug, obim (zatvorena kriva linija)
citizen /ˈsitiz,n/ *n.* gradjanin, gradjanka (punopravni)
city /ˈsiti/ *n.* centar (poslovni dio) grada
civil /ˈsivil/ *adj.* gradjanski
claim /ˈklejm/ *v.* tražiti, zahtijevati
clap /klaep/ *v.* pljeskati
clarify /ˈklaerifaj/ *v.* razjasniti, pročistiti, anlajisati
clash /ˈklaeš/ *n.* sukob, neslaganje; *v.* ne slagati se

class /klaes/ *n.* klasa, lekcija, razred
classic /'klaesik/ *adj.* klasičan; *n.* klasik, uzorno djelo
classify /'klaesifaj/ *v.* svrstavati, sortirati
classmate /'klasmejt/ *n.* školski drug
claw /klo:/ *v.* grepsti, oderati; *n.* kandža, kuka
clay /klej/ *n.* glina, ilovača
clean /kli:n/ *adj.* čist; *v.* čistiti, umivati
clear /kli,/ *adj.* čist, jasan, bistar
clergy /'kle:rdži/ *n.* sveštenstvo, kler
clerk /kla:rk/ *n.* pisar, službenik, činovnik, ćato
clever /'klev,/ *adj.* bistar, pametan, duhovit
client /'klajent/ *n.* klijent, mušterija
cliff /klif/ *n.* stijena, greben, litica
climax /'klajmaeks/ *v.* vrhunac, kulminacija
climb /klajm/ *v.* penjati se, verati se
clock /klok/ *n.* sat, časovnik, sahat
close /klouz/ *v.* zatvoriti, završiti, spojiti; *adv.* blizu
close /klouz/ *adj.* blizak, zatvoren
closet /'klozit/ *n.* ormar u zidu, mala sobica
cloth /klos/ *n.* materijal, štof, tkanina, krpa
clothe /klouz/ *v.* obući(se), odjenuti(se)
clothes /klouz/ *n.* odjeća
clothing /klouzing/ *n.* odjeća
cloud /klaud/ *n.* oblak, tamna mrlja; *v.* naoblačiti se
clown /klaun/ *n.* klovn, komedijaš, pajac
club /klab/ *n.* klub, društvo, palica
clue /klu:/ *n.* klupko, nit(pričanja), zagonetka
clumsy /'klamzi/ *adj.* nezgrapan, netaktičan, nespretan
clutch /klač/ *v.* ščepati, hvatati se, držati se
coach /kouč/ *n.* trener; kola za putnike; *v.* podučavati
coal /koul/ *n.* kameni ugalj, ćumur
coast /koust/ *n.* obala, padina
coat /kout/ *n.* kaput, prekrivač; *v.* prekriti
cock /kok/ *n.* pijetao, horoz, kokot
cockroach /kokrouč/ *n.* buba švabo, žohar

code /koud/ *n.* kod, šifra
coffee /'kofi/ *n.* kafa, kahva, kava
cognition /kog'niš,n/ *n.* razumijevanje, shvatanje
coin /kojn/ *n.* kovani novac
cold /kould/ *n.* zima, hladnoća, nazeb, prehlada; *adj.*   hladno
cole /koul/ *n.* kupus (jedna vrsta)
collaborate /k,'leborejt/ *v.* saradjivati
collar /'koler/ *n.* kragna, okovratnik
collect /'k,'lekt/ *v.* sakupljati, sabirati
collection /'k,'lekš,n/ *n.* zbirka, kolekcija
college /'kolidj/ *n.* fakultet, visoka škola
color, colour /'kal,/ *n.* boja, farba; *v.* bojiti, farbati
comb /koum/ *n.* češalj; *v.* češljati se
come, came, come /kam, kejm, kam/ *v.* doći, pojaviti se
comfort /'kamf,t/ *n.* konfor, udobnost; *v.* tješiti
comfortable /'kamftebl/ *adj.* ugodan, komforan
comforter /'kamf,t,/ *n.* prekrivač, jorgan
command /k,'ma:nd/ *n.* komanda, naredba; *v.* komandovati, upravljati
comment /'koment/ *n.* objašnjenje, komentar, tumačenje
commerce /'kom,:rs/ *n.* trgovina
commercial /'kom,:šl/ *adj.* trgovački, reklama
commit /k,'mit/ *v.* počiniti, izvršiti, obavezati se
committee /k,'miti:/ *n.* odbor, komitet, komisija
common /'komon/ *adj.* običan, jednostavan, prost
commotion /k,'moušn/ *n.* uzbudjenje, uznemirenost, pobuna
community /k'mju:niti/ *n.* zajednica
commute /k,mju:t/ *v.* mijenjati, putovati do posla
compact /'k,mpaekt/ *adj.* složen, zbijen, gust
companion /k,mpaenjen/ *n.* drug, pratilac
comparable /'komp,rbl/ *adj.* uporediv
comparison /k,m'parizon/ *n.* poredjenje, razmjera
compassion /kem'pešn/ *n.* sažaljenje, saučešće
compatible /k,m'paet,bl/ *adj.* odgovarajući
compete /kom'pi:t/ *v.* takmičiti se, natjecati se

competition /,kompi'tišn/ *n.* konkurencija, takmičenje

complain /k,m'plejn/ *v.* žaliti se, tužiti se, optuživati

complete /k,m'pli:t/ *adj.* savršen, dovršen, pun, kompletan; *v.* ispuniti; dovršiti

complicated /'kompli,kejtid/ *adj.* komplikovan, zamršen

complimentary /'kompli'ment,ri/ *adj.* laskav, besplatan

comply /km'pla:j/ *v.* pristati, pokoriti se

compose /k,m'pouz/ *v.* sastaviti, smiriti, komponovati

comprehend /kompri'hend/ *v.* shvatiti, razumjeti, obuhvatiti

comprehensive /kompre'henziv/ *adj.* širok, sveobuhvatan

computation /kompju:'tejšn/ *n.* račun, proračun;

computer /kom'pju:ter/ *n.* računar, kompjuter

comrade /'komrid/ *n.* drug

conceal /k,nsi:l/ *v.* sakrivati

concede /k,nsi:d/ *v.* ustupiti

conceive /k,nsi:v/ *v.* razumjeti, začeti

concentrate /'konsentrejt/ *v.* usresrediti, koncentrisati

concern /kon'se:rn/ *n.* stvar, posao, obzir; *v.* ticati se, odnositi se

concerned /k,n'se:rnd/ *adj.* zainteresovan, zabrinut

concise /k,n'sajz/ *adj.* sažet, zbijen, koncizan

conclude /k,n'klu:d/ *v.* zaključiti, završiti

conclusion /k,n'klu:žn/ *n.* zaključak

concrete /k,n'kri:t/ *n.* beton; *adj.* konkretan

condition /k,n'dišn/ *n.* položaj, stanje, uslov, kondicija

condom /kan'd,m/ *n.* prezervativ, kondom, kurton

confess /k,n'fes/ *v.* priznati, ispovjediti

confession /k,n'fešn/ *n.* vjera, priznanje

confide /k,n'fajd/ *v.* povjeriti, otkriti

confidence /k,n'fidens/ *n.* povjerenje, pouzdanje

confidential /k,n'fidentl/ *adj.* povjerljiv, tajni

confirm /'kon'f,:rm/ *v.* potvrditi, osigurati, posvjedočiti

conflict /'konflikt/ *n.* sudar, sukob

confuse /k,n'fju:z/ *v.* zbuniti, posramiti

congestion /k,n'džeščn/ *n.* nagomilavanje, gomila, priliv krvi

Congress /'kongres/ *n.* Kongres (Parlament SAD)

congress /'kongres/ *n.* kongres
congratulate /k,n'graetju,lejt/ *v.* čestitati, izraziti zadovoljstvo
connect /k,nekt/ *v.* spojiti, sastaviti, povezati
conqueror /'kon,kvaj,r/ *n.* osvajač, pobjednik
conquest /'konkvest/ *n.* pobjeda, osvajanje
conscience /'konš,ns/ *n.* savjest
conscious /'konš,s/ *adj.* svjestan, savjestan, promišljen
consecutive /k,n'sekjutiv/ *adj.* uzastopan, slijedeći, dosljedan
consequence /'konsikv,ns/ *n.* posljedica, konsekvenca
conservative /k,n'se:rvative/ *adj.* zastario, konzervativan
consider /k,n'sider/ *v.* razmisliti, razmotriti
considerable /k,n'siderebl/ *adj.* značajan, važan
considering /k,n'sidering/ *prep.* s obzirom, što se tiče
consist /k,n'sist/ *v.* sastojati se, sačinjavati
consistent /k,n'sistent/ *adj.* dosljedan, postojan
console /k,n'soul/ *n.* podupirač, konzola; *v.*tješiti, ohrabriti
conspicuous /k,nspikju,s/ *adj.* vidan, upadljiv
conspiracy /k,n'spir,si/ *n.* zavjera, urota
constant /'konst,nt/ *adj.* trajan, nepokolebljiv
constitution /konsti'tju:š,n/ *n.* ustav, konstitucija, sklop
construct /k,n'strakt/ *v.* graditi, smisliti, konstruisati
construction /k,n'strakšn/ *n.* gradnja, sklop, sastav
consul /'konsl/ *n.* konzul
consult /k,n'salt/ *v.* savjetovati se, konsultovati se
consume /k,n'sju:m/ *v.* trošiti, konzumirati
consumer /k,n'sju:mer/ *n.* potrošać
contain /k,n'tejn/ *v.* sadržavati
contaminate /k,ntaeminejt/ *v.* uprljati, zaraziti
contemporary /k,ntemp,reri/ *adj.* savremen, moderan
contempt /k,n'tempt/ *n.* preziranje, prkos
content /'kontent/ *n.* sadržina
content /'k,ntent/ *adj.* zadovoljan
contents /'kontents/ *n.* sadržaj u knjizi
contest /k,n'test/ *v.* boriti se, izazivati; *n.* natječaj, konkurs
continual /k,n'tinjuel/ *adj.* neprestalan, neprekidan, stalan

continue /k,n'tinju:/ *v.* nastaviti, produžiti
continuous /k,n'tinju,s/ *adj.* neprekidan, trajan
contract /'k,n'traekt/ *n.* ugovor; *v.* ugovoriti, skratiti
contradict /,kontr,dikt/ *v.* poricati, osporavati
contrary /'kontr,ri/ *adj.* suprotan, protivan
contrast /k,n'tra:st/ *v.* suprotnost, kontrast
contribute /k,n'tribju:t/ *v.* doprinjeti, imati udjela
contribution /k,n'tribjušn/ *n.* doprinos, uplata, prilog
control /k,n'troul/ *n.* nadzor, upravljanje; *v.* upravljati
controversial /kontr,v,šl/ *adj.* sporan, polemičan
convenience /k,n'vi:ni,ns/ *n.* pogodnost, olakšica
convenient /k,n'vi:njent/ *adj.* pogodan, odgovarajući
convention /k,n'venš,n/ *n.* sastanak, dogovor
conversation /,konver'sejšn/ *n.* razgovor
convict /'konvikt/ *n.* osudjenik, kažnjenik; *v.* osuditi, kazniti
cook /kuk/ *n.* kuvar, kuhar; *v.* kuvati, kuhati
cool /ku:l/ *n.* hladnoća, svježina; *adj.* hladnokrvan, ravnodušan
cooperate /kou,ope'rejt/ *v.* saradjivati
cooperation /kou,ope'rejšn/ *n.* saradnja, kooperacija
coordinate /kou'o:rdinejt/ *v.* koordinirati; *n.* koordinata
cope /'koup/ *v.* boriti se, nositi se sa nečim (nekim)
copper /'koper/ *n.* bakar, mjed
copy /'kopi/ *n.* kopija, primjerak; *v.* prepisivati, oponašati
cord /ko:d/ *n.* konopac, uže, štrik, kanafa
cordial /'ko:dj,l/ *adj.* srdačan, iskren, srčan
core /ko:/ *n.* jezgra, srž, srce, sredina
cork /ko:k/ *n.* čep, pluto; *v.* začepiti
corkscrew /'ko:k,skru:/ *n.* vadičep
corn /ko:rn/ *n.* kukuruz, zrno(pšenice), žulj
corner /'ko:rner/ *n.* ugao, kut
corporation /,ko:rpe'rejšn/ *n.* korporacija,udruženje
corpse /ko:rps/ *n.* leš, lešina, truplo
correct /k,'rekt/ *v.* popraviti, ispraviti, kazniti
correspond /'koris'pond/ *v.* slagati se, podudarati, dopisivati se
correspondence /,koris'pondens/ *n.* dopisivanje, korespondencija

corrupt /k,rapt/ *adj.* pokvaren, podmitljiv, truo
corruption /k,rapš,n/ *n.* korupcija, potkupljivost
cost /kost/ *v.* koštati, stajati; *n.* cijena
costume /'kostju:m/ *n.* kostim, nošnja
cosy, cozy /'kouzi/ *adj.* udoban, prijatan
cottage /'kotidj/ *n.* koliba, kućica
cotton /'kotn/ *n.* pamuk; *adj.* pamučni
couch /kauč/ *n.* kauč, divan, kanabe
cough /ko:f/ *v.* kašljati; *n.* kašalj
council /'kaunsil/ *n.* vijeće, sabor, savjet
count /kaunt/ *n.* grof, račun; v.brojati, računati, ići na ruku
countless /'kauntles/ *adj.* bezbrojan
country /'kantri/ *n.* zemlja, domovina, selo
county /'kaunti/ *n.* grofovija, provincija
couple /'kapl/ *n.* par, dvoje
coupon /'ku:pon/ *n.* kupon, karta
courage /'karidž/ *n.* hrabrost, odvažnost
courageous /k,rejdž,s/ *adj.* hrabar, odvažan, smion
courier /'kuri,/ *n.* glasnik, kurir, teklić
course /ko:rs/ *n.* tok, kurs, karijera, jelo
court /ko:rt/ *n.* sud, dvorište; *v.* udvarati se
cousin /kaz,n/ *n.* rodjak, srodnik
cover /'kav,/ *n.* pokrivač, omot; *v.* pokriti, prevući
cow /kau/ *n.* krava; *v.* zaplašiti, obeshrabriti
coward /'kau,rd/ *n.* kukavica, strašljivac
cowboy /'kauboj/ *n.* čuvar krupne stoke, kauboj
crab /kraeb/ *n.* morski rak
crack /kraek/ *n.* pukotina, prasak; *v.* pući, ljuštiti se
cradle /'krejdl/ *n.* koljevka, bešika; *v.* zibati, uspavljivati
craft /kra:ft/ *n.* vještina, zanat
cramp /kraemp/ *n.* grč; *v.* grčiti
crash /kraeš/ *n.* prasak, lom; *v.* prsnuti, raspuknuti se
crazy /'krejzi/ *adj.* lud, oduševljen
cream /kri:m/ *n.* kajmak, krema
create /kri'ːejt/ *v.* stvoriti, kreirati

creation /kri'ejšn/ *n.* kreacija, stvaranje
creature /'kri:č,:/ *n.* stvorenje, biće
credit /'kredit/ *n.* kredit, povjerenje, vjera; *v.* vjerovati
creep /kri:p/ *v.* puzati, gmizati; *n.* jeza, žmarci
crew /kru:/ *n.* posada, momčad, gomila
crime /krajm/ *n.* zločin, kriminal
cripple /kripl/ *n.* bogalj; *v.* osakatiti
crisis /'krajsis/ *n.* kriza
crisp /krisp/ *adj.* kovrdjav, uvijen, hrskav
critic /kritik/ *n.* kritičar
critique /kri'ti:k/ *n.* kritika
criticize /'kritisajz/ *v.* kritikovati
crop /krop/ *n.* žetva; *v.* sakupljati žetvu
cross /kros/ *n.* krst, križ; *adj.* unakrstan, poprečan; *v.*
prekrižiti, prekrstiti
crossing /'krosing/ *n.* raskrsnica, ukrštanje, prelaz
crow /krou/ *n.* vrana; *v.* graktati
crowd /kraud/ *n.* gomila, gužva, svjetina, rulja
crowded /'kraudid/ *adj.* prepun svijeta
crucial /'kru:š,l/ *adj.* kritičan, odlučan (trenutak)
crude /kru:d/ *adj.* grub, neotesan (ponašanje), sirov, neobradjen
cruel /kruel/ *adj.* surov, svirep, okrutan
cruise /kru:z/ *n.* krstarenje; *v.* krstariti, ploviti
crumb /kram/ *n.* mrva, komadić
crunch /kranč/ *v.* krckati, hrskati
crunchy /kranči/ *adj.* hrskav
crusade /kru:'sejd/ *n.* krstaški rat
crush /kraš/ *n.* udarac, sudar, lomljava; *v.* zgnječiti
crust /krast/ *n.* kora, korica, ljuštura, naslaga
cry /kraj/ *v.* plakati, vikati; *n.* plač, krik, uzvik
cube /kju:b/ *n.* kocka, kub (treći stepen)
cucumber /'kju:kamb,r/ *n.* krastavac, krastavica
cuff /kaf/ *n.* manžeta; *v.* boksovati se
cultivate /'kaltivejt/ *v.* gajiti, obradjivati
culture /'kalč,:/ *n.* kultura, gajenje, obrazovanje

cup /kap/ *n.* pehar, šolja, čaša (ne od stakla)

cupboard /kab,d/ *n.* kredenac, orman sa policama

cure /kju,r/ *v.* izliječiti; *n.* lijek, iladj

curiosity /,kju,ri'ositi/ *n.* rijetkost, radoznalost

curious /'kju,ri,s/ *adj.* radoznao

curl /k,:rl/ *n.* uvojak, lokna, kovrdža; *v.* loknati, kovrdžati

currency /'kar,nsi/ *n.* valuta, tekući novac

current /'kar,nt/ *n.* struja, tok; *adj.* tekući

curse /k,:s/ *n.* psovka, kletva; *v.* psovati, proklinjati

curtain /'k,:rtn/ *n.* zavjesa, zastor, firanga; *v.* zastrti

curve /k,:rv/ *n.* okuka, krivina, zavoj; *v.* saviti se, krivudati

custody /'kast,di/ *n.* čuvanje, nadzor, zatvor

custom /'kast,m/ *n.* običaj, navika, carina, kupac

customer /kast,m,r/ *n.* mušterija, klijent, carinik

cut /kat/ *n.* rez, presjek, posjekotina

cut /kat/ *v.* presjeći, odsjeći, skratiti

cute /kju:t/ *adj.* sladak, mio, bistar, oštrouman

cutlery /'katl,ri/ *n.* noževi

cutlet /'katlit/ *n.* kotlet, rebarca

cycle /sajkl/ *n.* ciklus, period vremena

cynic /'sinik/ *n.* cinik; *adj.* ciničan, podrugljiv

D

dad, daddy /daed, daedi/ *n.* tata, babo
dagger /'daeger/ *n.* bodež, kama
daily /'dejli/ *adj.* dnevni, svakodnevan
dairy /'deeri/ *n.* mljekara
daisy /dejzi/ *n.* janja, tratinčica, krasuljak
dam /daem/ *n.* brana, nasip; *v.* zaustaviti, obuzdati
damage /'daemidž/ *n.* šteta, gubitak; *v.* oštetiti
damn /daem/ *v.* osuditi, prokleti
damp /daemp/ *adj.* vlažan; memljiv *n.* vlaga
dance /'da:ns/ *n.* ples, igranka, bal; *v.* plesati
danger /'dejndž,r/ *n.* opasnost, rizik
dangerous /'dejndž,r's/ *adj.* opasan, rizičan
dare /deer/ *v.* usuditi se, smjeti
dark /da:k/ *adj.* taman, mračan; *n.* mrak; neizvjesnost
darkness /'da:knis/ *n.* tama, mrak, tmina
darling /'dar:ling/ *adj.* ljubljen, voljen, omiljen
data /dejta/ *n.* podaci, činjenice
date /dejt/ *n.* datum; *v.* staviti datum; vidjati se, zabavljati se
daughter /'do:t,r/ *n.* kćerka, kći, ćerka
daughter-in-law /'do:t,r-in-lo:/ *n.* snaha
dawn /do:n/ *n.* zora, osvit, sabah; *v.* svitati
day /dej/ *n.* dan, 24 sata
daze /dejz/ *v.* omamiti, ošamutiti, zgranuti
dead /ded/ *adj.* mrtav, bez života; *n.* mrtvi, pokojnici
deadline /'dedlajn/ *n.* rok, termin završetka
deaf /def/ *adj.* gluh, gluv
deal /di:l/ *n.* posao, podjela; *v.* dijeliti, raditi
dean /di:n/ *n.* dekan
dear /di,r/ *adj.* drag, mio
death /des/ *n.* smrt
debate /di'bejt/ *n.* diskusija, debata; *v.* diskutovati
debt /det/ *n.* dug, obaveza
decade /'dekejd/ *n.* dekada, desetljeće

decay /di'kej/ *v.* trunuti, raspadati se; s.trulež
decayed /di'kejd/ *adj.* propao, truo, gnjio
decease /di'si:s/ *n.* bolest, smrt; *v.* umirati
deceive /di'si:v/ *v.* prevariti, obmanti, varati
December / di'semb,r/ *n.* decembar, prosinac
decent /'di:sen/ *adj.* pristojan, prikladan, skroman
decide /di'sajd/ *v.* odlučiti(se), riješiti(se)
decision /di'sižn/ *n.* odluka, rješenje
deck /dek/ *n.* paluba, krov; *v.* pokriti daskom, ukrasiti
declare /di'kle,:r/ *v.* izjaviti, deklarisati (carina)
decline /di'klajn/ *v.* opadati, spuštati se
decorate /'dek,rejt/ *v.* dekorisati, ukrasiti, okititi, odlikovati
decoration /dek'rejš,n/ *n.* odlikovanje, ukras
decrease /'di:kri:s/ *v.* smanjivati, opadati; *n.* smanjenje
decree /di'kri:/ *n.* presuda, rješenje; *v.* odrediti, presuditi
dedicate /'dedikejt/ *v.* posvetiti
deduct /di'dakt/ *v.* odbijati, oduzeti
deed /di:d/ *n.* djelo, dokument o vlasništvu, tapija
deep /di:p/ *adj.* dubok; *adv.* duboko
deer /di,r/ *n.* jelen, srna
defeat /di'fi:t/ *n.* poraz; *v.* poraziti
defect /di'fekt/ *n.* greška, defekt, mana
defense /di'fens/ *n.* odbrana, zaštita
defend /di'fend/ *v.* braniti, štititi
defiance /di'faj,ns/ *n.* prkos, izazivanje (inat) inat=stubborn
define /di'fajn/ *v.* odrediti, definisati, definirati
definite /'definit/ *adj.* odredjen, jasan, definisan, definiran
definition /,defi'niš,n/ *n.* definicija
definitive /di'finitiv/ *adj.* odredjen, jasan, jednoznačan
deflate /di'flejt/ *v.* ispustiti zrak, ispuhati
deform /di'fo:m/ *v.* deformisati, unakaziti, izobličiti
defy /di'faj/ *v.* prkositi,izazivati
degree /di'gri:/ *n.* stepen, stupanj, rang, čin
delay /di'lej/ *v.* odgadjati, zadržavati
deli /deli/ *n.* prodavnica gotove hrane

deliberate /di'liberejt/ *adj.* namjeran, hotimičan, promišljen

delicate /'delikit/ *adj.* delikatan, biran, fin

delicious /di'liš,s/ *adj.* slastan, vrlo ugodan

delight /di'lajt/ *n.* uživanje, radost; *v.* radovati se, uživati

deliver /di'liv,/ *v.* osloboditi, isporučiti, dostaviti

delivery /di'liveri/ *n.* oslobadjanje, isporuka, dostava

delude /di'lju:d/ *v.* obmanuti, varati, namamiti

delusion /di'lju:ž,n/ *n.* obmana, prevara

demand /di'ma:nd/ *n.* traženje, zahtjev, potražnja; *v.* zahtijevati

democracy /di'mokresi/ *n.* demokratija

demolish /di'moliš/ *v.* porušiti, razvaliti, demolirati

demonstrate /dem,nstrejt/ *v.* demonstrirati, pokazati

denounce /di'nauns/ *v.* objaviti, oglasiti

dense /dens/ *adj.* gust, zbijen

density /densiti/ *n.* gustoća, zbijenost

dentist /'dentist/ *n.* zubar

deny /di'nai/ *v.* poricati, ne priznati, poreći

department /di'pa:rtm,nt/ *n.* odeljenje, odsjek, sektor

departure /di'pa:rč,/ *n.* odlazak, udaljavanje

depend /di'pend/ *v.* zavisiti, oslanjati se na

deposit /di'pozit/ *n.* naslaga, talog, ulog u banci

depress /di'pres/ *v.* obeshrabriti, pritisnuti

depth /deps/ *n.* dubina, ponor

deputy /'depjuti/ *adj.* izaslanik, zastupnik, opunomoćenik

descend /di'send/ *v.* sići, spustiti se

descendant /di'send,nt/ *n.* potomak

describe /di'skrajb/ *v.* opisati, prikazati, nazvati

desert /'dez,rt/ *n.* pustinja

desert /di'z,:t/ *n.* zasluga, vrijednost; *v.* napustiti, dezertirati

deserve /di'z,:v/ *v.* zaslužiti, biti dostojan nečeg

design /di'zajn/ *n.* plan, skica; *v.* crtati, planirati

desirable /di'zaj,r,bl/ *adj.* poželjan

desire /dizaj,/ *v.* želja, žudnja

desk /desk/ *n.* pisaći sto

despair /di'spe,r/ *n.* očaj, beznadje; *v.* očajavati

desperate /'desperit/ *adj.* očajan, beznadežan

despise /dis'pajz/ *v.* prezirati

despite (in despite of) /dis'pajt/ *n.* prkos, zloba, preziranje (uprkos)

dessert /di'z,:t/ *n.* desert, posljednji dio jela

destination /desti'nejš,n/ *n.* destinacija, odredište

destiny /'destini/ *n.* sudbina, usud, nafaka

destroy /di'stroj/ *v.* razoriti, uništiti

destruction /dis'trakš,n/ *n.* uništenje, razaranje, destrukcija

detach /di'taeč/ *v.* odvojiti, rastaviti

detail /'di:tejl/ *n.* pojedinost, detalj

detain /di'tejn/ *v.* zadržati, spriječiti

detect /di'tekt/ *v.* otkriti, naći

detergent /di't,:rdžnt/ *n.* deterdžent, sredstvo za čišćenje

deteriorate /di'ti,ri,rejt/ *v.* pogoršati, pokvariti

determine /di'te:rmin/ *v.* odrediti, riješiti se

detest /di'test/ *v.* gaditi se, gnušati se

detour /'di:tu,r/ *n.* obilaznica, skretanje

devastate /'dev,stejt/ *v.* pustošiti, opustošiti

develop /di'velop/ *v.* razviti, proizvesti

development /di'velopm,nt/ *n.* razvoj

device /di'vajs/ *n.* sprava, naprava, sredstvo, nacrt, izum

devil /'devl/ *n.* djavo, vrag, šejtan

devote /di'vout/ *v.* posvetiti, odrediti

dew /dju:/ *n.* rosa, slana

diabetes /,daj,bi:ti:s/ *n.* dijabetis, šećerna bolest

diagnose /'dajeg,nouz/ *v.* dijagnozirati, ustanoviti bolest

diagram /'dajegraem/ *n.* dijagram

dial /'dajel/ *n.* brojčanik, cifarnik, ciferblat

dial /'daj,l/ *v.* okretati brojčanik (telefona), nazivati

dialect /'dajelekt/ *n.* narječje, dijalekt

diamond /'daj,m,nd/ *n.* dijamant

diaper /'daj,per/ *n.* pelena; *v.* poviti dijete

diarrhea /,daj,ri,/ *n.* proljev, proliv, dijareja

diary /'dai,ri/ *n.* dnevnik

dictate /dik'tejt/ *n.* diktat, zapovijed; *v.* diktirati, propisivati

dictionary /dikš,n,ri/ *n.* rječnik

die /daj/ *v.* umrijeti, preminuti

diet /'daj,t/ *n.* dijeta; *v.* staviti na dijetu, pehriziti se

differ /'dif,/ *v.* razlikovati se, ne slagati se

difference /'dif,r,ns/ *n.* razlika

different /'dif,r,nt/ *adj.* različit, drukčiji

dig /dig/ *v.* kopati, riti

digest /di'džest, 'dajdžest/ *v.* probaviti, provariti; *n.* jezgrovit sadržaj

dignified /'dignifajd/ *adj.* dostojanstven, plemenit

dignity /'digniti/ *n.* dostojanstvo, plemenitost

diligent /'dilidž,nt/ *adj.* vrijedan, marljiv, revnostan

dill /dil/ *n.* koper, kopar, mirodjija

dilute /dai'lju:t/ *v.* razrijediti, oslabiti, razblažiti

dim /dim/ *v.* potamniti, zamračiti, zamagliti; *adj.* taman, nejasan

diminish /di'miniš/ *v.* smanjiti, spasti, oslabiti

dine /dajn/ *v.* ručati van kuće, pogostiti

dining room /'dajning ru:m/ *n.* trpezarija

dinner /'din,r/ *n.* glavni objed, glavni obrok (večera/ručak)

direct /di'rekt/ *v.* usmjeriti, pokazati put

direction /di'rekš,n/ *n.* smjer, pravac, adresa

director /di'rekt,/ *n.* režiser, direktor

directory /di'rekt,ri/ *n.* imenik, knjiga adresa, direktorij

dirty /d,:ti/ *adj.* prljav, zamazan; *v.* prljati, blatiti, kaljati

disable /dis'ejbl/ *v.* onesposobiti, osakatiti, lišiti prava

disabled /dis'ejbld/ *n.* invalid; *adj.* nesposoban

disadvantage /dis,d'va:ntidž/ *n.* mana, nedostatak, mahana

disagree /dis,'gri/ *v.* ne slagati se, svadjati se

disappear /,dis,'pi,r/ *v.* izčeznuti, nestati

disappoint /,dis,'point/ *v.* razočarati

disapprove /dis,'pru:v/ *v.* ne slagati se, ne odobravati

disaster /di'za:ster/ *n.* nesreća, katastrofa

discard /dis'ka:rd/ *v.* odbaciti, napustiti, odbaciti kartu

discompose /,disk,m'pouz/ *v.* uznemiriti, uzrujati, uzbuditi

disconnect /'disk,'nekt/ *v.* isključiti, prekinuti spoj/vezu

discontent /'disk,n'tent/ *n.* nezadovoljstvo; *v.* učiniti nezadovoljnim
discount /'diskaunt/ *n.* popust, rabat
discover /dis'kav,/ *v.* otkriti, pronaći, objelodaniti
discuss /dis'kas/ *v.* diskutovati, raspravljati
disease /di'zi:z/ *n.* bolest, zaraza
disgrace /dis'grejs/ *n.* sramota, bruka; *v.* osramotiti
disguise /dis'gajz/ *v.* prerušiti, prikrivati; *n.* maska, krinka
disgust /dis'gast/ *n.* gadjenje, odvratnost, gnušanje; *v.* gaditi se
disgusting /dis'gasting/ *adj.* odvratan, gadan
dish /diš/ *n.* posuda, zdjela, ćasa; jelo
dishwasher /'dišwoš,r/ *n.* mašina za sudje
disintegrate /dis'int,grejt/ *v.* raspasti se na sastojke, raskomadati
dislike /dis'lajk/ *n.* nedopadanje, odvratnost; *v.* ne svidjati se
dismiss /dis'mis/ *v.* otpustiti, otkazati, raspustiti
disorder /dis'o:rd,r/ *n.* nered, pometnja; *v.* poremetiti
display /dis'plej/ *v.* prikazati, izložiti; *n.* prikaz, izložba
disposal /dis'pouz,l/ *n.* raspored, raspolaganje
dispose /dis'pouz/ *v.* rasporediti, raspolagati
dispute /dis'pju:t/ *n.* spor, svadja; *v.* raspravljati, prepirati se
disrupt /dis'rap/ *v.* raskinuti
dissolve /di'zolv/ *v.* rastopiti se, razriješiti
distance /'dist,ns/ *n.* razdaljina, rastojanje
distant /'dist,nt/ *adj.* dalek, uzdržan, udaljen
distinguish /dis'tingviš/ *v.* raspoznavati, jasno opaziti
distract /dis'traekt/ *v.* odvraćati misli, skrenuti pažnju
distressing /dis'tresing/ *adj.* žalostan, mučan
distribute /dis'tribju:t/ *v.* razdijeliti, distribuirati
district /'distrikt/ *n.* okrug, srez, kvart
disturb /dis't,:rb/ *v.* uznemiravati, prekinuti, smetati
ditch /dič/ *n.* jarak, šanac, rov
dive /dajv/ *n.* gnjuranje, ronjenje; *v.* zaroniti
diverse /daj'v,:rs/ *adj.* različit, raznovrstan
divide /di'vajd/ *v.* podjeliti, odvojiti, razdvojiti
divorce /di'vo:rs/ *n.* razvod, rastava braka; *v.* razvesti se

dizziness /'dizinis/ *n.* vrtoglavica

dizzy /'dizi/ *adj.* vrtoglav, zbunjen

do, did, done /du:, did, dan/ *v.* raditi, činiti, obavljati, iskazati

dock /dok/ *n.* dok, optuženička klupa

doctor /'dakt,/ *n.* ljekar, doktor, hećim

dog /dog/ *n.* pas

doll /dol/ *n.* lutka

dome /doum/ *n.* kupola, kube, svod

domestic /d',mestik/ *adj.* domaći, kućni, pitom

dominate /'dominejt/ *v.* vladati, dominirati

donate /dou'nejt/ *v.* pokloniti, darivati

donation /dou'nejš,n/ *n.* poklon, dar, peškeš

donkey /'donki/ *n.* magarac, glupan

doom /du:m/ *n.* zla kob, usud, sudbina, kijamet

door /do:r/ *n.* vrata, kapija

dormitory /'do:rmitri/ *n.* spavaonica

dose /douz/ *n.* doza, propisana količina lijeka

dot /dot/ *n.* tačka, točka; *v.* obilježiti sa tačkom

double /'dabl/ *adj.* dvostruk; *n.* dvostruka količina

doubt /daut/ *n.* sumnja, dvojba, podozrivost; *v.* sumnjati

doubtful /dautful/ *adj.* sumnjičav, podozriv, dvojben

dough /dou/ *n.* tijesto

dove /dav/ *n.* golub(ica)

down /daun/ *adv.* dole, niže, niz

downstairs /'daun'steerz/ *adv.* dolje (u kući), niz stepenice

downtown /'dautaun/ *n.* centar grada; poslovni centar

dozen /dazn/ *n.* dvanaest komada, tuce

draft /dra:ft/ *n.* skica, nacrt; promaja, promaha; *v.* skicirati

drag /draeg/ *v.* vući, tegliti

drain /drejn/ *v.* odvoditi vodu, isušivati; *n.* odvodni kanal, drenaža

drastic /draestik/ *adj.* drastičan, potpun, temeljit

draw, drew, drawn /dro:, dru:, dro:n/ *v.* vući, povući, natezati; *n.* izvlačenje (srećke), podizanje (novca)

drawer /dro:er/ *n.* ladica, fijoka, pretinac,

dreadful /dredful/ *adj.* užasan, strašan

dream, dreamt, dreamt /dri:m, dremt, dremt/ *v.* sanjati;   *n.* san
dress /dres/ *n.* haljina, odijelo; *v.* obući se
dresser /dres,r/ *n.* komoda sa ladicama i ogledalom
dressing /'dresing/ *n.* začin za salatu
drink, drank, drunk /drink, draenk, drank/ *v.* piti, opijati se;
drink /drink/ *n.* piće, napitak, pijanstvo
drip /drip/ *v.* kapati, curiti; *n.* kapanje, curenje
drippings /dripingz/ *n. pl.* mast od pečenja
drive, drove, driven /drajv, drouv, drivn/ *v.* voziti, smjerati, primorati, tjerati
driver's license /drajvers lajs,ns/ *n.* vozačka dozvola
drop /drop/ *n.* kap(lja); *v.* kap(lj)ati, spustiti se
drown /draun/ *v.* utopiti, preplaviti
drowsy /'drauzi/ *adj.* pospan, dremljiv, uspavljujući
drum /dram/ *n.*bubanj, doboš; *v.* bubnjati, dobovati (prstima)
drunk /drank/ *adj.* pijan, napit
dry /draj/ *adj.* suh, suv; *v.* presahnuti, osušiti se
duck /dak/ *n.*patka, plovka; *v.* pognuti se, zagnjuriti
due /dju:/ *adj.* prikladan, odgovarajući, pravovremen
dull /dal/ *adj.* tup, glup, dosadan
dumb /dam/ *adj.* njem, mutav
dummy /'dami/ *n.*lutka za izlog, maneken, statist; *adj.* lažan
dump /damp/ *n.*smetljište, djubrište; *v.* isprazniti, istovariti, istresti
duplicate /'dju:plikit/ *adj.* duplikat, kopija, prepis
durable /'djuerebl/ *adj.* trajan, postojan
during /'dju:ring/ *prep.* za vrijeme, u toku
dust /dast/ *n.* prašina, prah, pepeo
dusty /dasti/ *adj.* prašnjav
duty /'dju:ti/ *n.*dužnost, obaveza, carina
dwarf /dvo:rf/ *n.* kepec, patuljak; *v.* zakržljati
dwell /dvel/ *v.* živjeti, boraviti, stanovati
dye /daj/ *n.* farba, boja; *v.* bojiti, farbati

E

Easter /I:ster/ *n.* Uskrs

each /i:č/ *adj.* ; pron. svaki, svaka, svako

eager /i:g,er/ *adj.* gorljiv, žudan, nestrpljv

eagle /'i:gl/ *n.* orao

ear /ier/ *n.* uho, uvo, sluh

early /'e:rli/ *adv.* rano

earn /e:rn/ *v.* zaraditi, zaslužiti, steći

earnings /'e:rning/ *n.* zarada, dohodak

earth /e:rs/ *n.* Zemlja (planeta), zemlja, svijet

earthquake /'e:rskvejk/ *n.* zemljotres

easily /'i:zili/ *adv.* lako, glatko

east /i:st/ *n.* istok; *adj.* istočni

easy /'i:zi/ *adj.* lak, udoban, spokojan, bezbrižan

eat, ate, eaten /i:t, ajt, i:tn/ *v.* jesti

eccentric /ik'sentrik/ *adj.* nastran čovjek, čudak, tuhaf

echo /'ekou/ *n.* eho, odjek, jeka; *v.* odjekivati

economics /,i:k,nomiks/ *n.* ekonomija

edge /edž/ *n.* ivica, granica, oštrina

edible /'edibl/ *adj.* jestivo; *n.* jelo

edit /'edit/ *v.* izdati, urediti za štampu

educate /'edju:kejt/ *v.* obrazovati, odgajati, učiti

education /,edju'kejš,n/ *n.* obrazovanje, vaspitavanje, podizanje, gajenje

effect /i'fekt/ *n.* rezultat, posljedica, efekat

effective /i'fektiv/ *adj.* djelotvoran, koristan, efektan

efficient /i'fiš,nt/ *adj.* efikasan, sposoban, izvodljiv

effort /'ef,t/ *n.* napor, trud, pokušaj

egg /eg/ *n.* jaje

eight /ejt/ *num.* osam

eighteen /'ejti:n/ *num.* osamnaest

eighty /'ejti/ *num.* osamdeset

either /'ejd,r/ pron oba, i jedan i drugi

elastic /i'laestik/ *adj.* elastičan, rastegljiv
elbow /'elbou/ *n.* lakat, zavoj, okuka
elder /'eld,/ *n.* stariji, viši po činu, zova (bot.)
elect /i'lekt/ *v.* izabrati, birati
election /i'lekš,n/ *n.* izbori
electric(al) /i'lektrik(,l)/ *adj.* električni
electrician /ilek'triš,n/ *n.* električar
electricity /ilek'trisiti/ *n.* elektricitet
elegant /'elig,nt/ *adj.* elegantan, ukusno odjeven
element /'elim,nt/ *n.* osnov, osnovno načelo
elementary /,eliment,ri/ *adj.* elementaran, osnovni, prost
elephant /'elifent/ *n.* slon
elevator /'eli,vejt,r/ *n.* elevator, lift, dizalo
eleven /i'lev,n/ *num.* jedanaest
eliminate /i'liminejt/ *v.* eliminirati, eliminisati, ukloniti
else /els/ *adv.* inače, drukčije, umjesto, pored
embankment /im'baenkm,nt/ *n.* nasip, brana, ustava
embargo /im'ba:gou/ *n.* embargo, prekid trgovine
embark /im'ba:k/ *v.* ukrcati se, uplesti se
embarrass /im'baer,s/ *v.* zbuniti, smetati
embassy /'embesi/ *n.* ambasada
emblem /'emblem/ *n.* amblem, simbol, znak
embrace /im'brejs/ *v.* zagrliti, grliti; *n.* zagrljaj
embroidery /im'brojderi/ *n.* vez, ukrašavanje
emerge /i'me:rdž/ *v.* pojaviti se, izaći, izbiti na površinu
emergency /i'me:rdž,nsi/ *n.* opasnost, hitna potreba
emigrate /'emigrejt/ *v.* emigrirati, iseliti se
emit /i'mit/ *v.* emitovati, širiti se (miris, zvuk)
emotion /i'mouš,n/ *n.* emocija, osjećanje, uzbudjenje
emphasize /'emf,sajz/ *v.* naglasiti, istaći
empire /'empajer/ *n.* carevina, imperija
employ /im'ploj/ *v.* služba, posao; *v.* zaposliti, služiti
employee /,emploj':i/ *n.* zaposleni, službenik
employer /em'plojer/ *n.* poslodavac
employment /em'plojm,nt/ *n.* zaposlenost

empty /'empti/ *adj.* prazan, pust

enable /i'nejbl/ *v.* omogučiti, osposobiti

enclose /in'klouz/ *v.* zatvoriti, ograditi, okružiti

encourage /in'ka:ridž/ *v.* ohrabriti, potstaknuti, okuražiti

end /end/ *n.* kraj; *v.* završiti, prestati

endeavor /in'dev,r/ *n.* nastojanje, napor; *v.* preduzeti, starati se

endure /in'dju,r/ *v.* podnositi, trpiti

enemy /'en,mi/ *n.* neprijatelj, dušman

energetic /,en,:rdžetik/ *adj.* energičan, poduzetan, odrješit

energy /'en,rdži/ *n.* energija, snaga

engage /in'gejdž/ *v.* obavezati se, zaručiti se

engine /'endžin/ *n.* mašina, stroj, motor

engineer /,endži'nier/ *n.* inženjer; *v.* planirati, proračunavati

engrave /in'grejv/ *v.* urezati, gravirati

enigma /e'nigma/ *n.* zagonetka, enigma

enjoy /in'džoj/ *v.* uživati, veseliti se, radovati se

enormous /i'no:rm,s/ *adj.* ogroman, enorman, golem

enough /i'naf/ *adj.* dovoljan; *adv.* dovoljno, dosta

enrage /in'rejdž/ *v.* razdražiti, razjariti

enrich /in'rič/ *v.* obogatiti

enroll /in'roul/ *v.* upisati se

ensure /in'šu,r/ *v.* osigurati, obezbijediti

enter /'ent,r/ *v.* ući, unići, stupiti

enterprise /'ent,prajz/ *n.* preduzeće, smjelost, preduzimljivost

entertain /,ent,r'tejn/ *v.* gostiti, zabavljati

enthusiastic /in'tu:zi'aestik/ *adj.* oduševljen, ushićen

entire /in'taj,r/ *adj.* cio, potpun, savršen

entity /'entiti/ *n.* suština, biće, bitnost

entrance /'entr,ns/ *n.* ulaz, prolaz; *v.* ulaziti

entry /'entri/ *n.* ulaz, unošenje, stavka

envelope /'enviloup/ *n.* omot, koverat

envious /'envi,s/ *adj.* zavidan, zloban

environment /invaj,rnment/ *n.* okolica, okolina, sredina

envy /'envi/ *n.* zavist, zloba; *v.* zavidjeti

episode /'epizoud/ *n.* epizoda, uzgredan dogadjaj

equal /'i:kv,l/ *adj.* jednak
equality /i'kvoliti/ *n.* jednakost
equator /i:'kvejt,/ *n.* ekvator, polutar
equipment /i'kvipm,nt/ *n.* oprema, opremanje
erase /i'rejz/ *v.* izbrisati, pobrisati
erect /i'rekt/ *v.* stajati uspravno; sagraditi; *adj.* uspravan
error /'er,r/ *n.* grijeh, pogreška, zabluda
erupt /i'rapt/ *v.* provaliti (vulkan)
escalator /'esk,lejt,r/ *n.* eskalator, pokretne stepenice
escape /is'kejp/ *v.* pobjeći, umaći, isteći; *n.* bjekstvo
escort /'esko:rt/ *v.* pratiti, provesti; *n.* straža, pratnja
especially /is'peš,li/ *adv.* naročito, posebno, osobito
essay /'esei/ *n.* književni sastav, proba, pokušaj
essence /'es,ns/ *n.* suština, bit, jezgro, esencija
essential /i'senš,l/ *adj.* bitan, osnovni, neophodan
establish /is'taebliš/ *v.* uspostaviti, osnovati, utvrditi
estate /is'tejt/ *n.* imanje, zaostavština, imetak
estimate /'estimejt/ *v.* procijeniti, odrediti vrijednost
eternal /i't,rn,l/ *adj.* vječan, beskonačan
eternity /i't,rniti/ *n.* vječnost, beskonačnost
ethical /'etik,l/ *adj.* etički, moralan
evacuate /i'vaekjuejt/ *v.* napustiti, izbaciti, evakuisati
evade /i'vejd/ *v.* izbjeći, umaći, mimoići
evaluate /i'vaeljuejt/ *v.* procijeniti vrijednost, izračunati
evaporate /i'vaeporejt/ *v.* ispariti, izvjetriti, ishlapiti
even /'i:v,n/ *adj.* ravan, gladak, paran(broj);
evening /'i:vning/ *n.* veče; *adj.* večernji
event /i'vent/ *n.* dogadjaj, rezultat, posljedica
eventual /i'venčuel/ *adj.* moguć, posljedičan, eventualan
ever /'ev,r/ *adv.* uvjek, ikad, uopšte, uopće
every /'evri/ *adj.* svaki, sav, sva sve
everybody /'evribodi/ *pron* svaki,svaka,svako
everyday /'evridej/ *adj.* svakodnevni, običan
everything /'evrising/ *n.* svašta, sve

evidence /'evidens/ *n.* očevidnost, dokaz, jasnost, svedočenje
evil /'i:vl/ *n.* zlo, nevolja
evolution /iv,ljuš,n/ *n.* evolucija, izvlačenje korjena
evolve /i'volv/ *v.* razviti, proširiti
ewe /ju:/ *n.* ovca
exact /ig'zaekt/ *adj.* tačan, pravilan, odredjen
exaggerate /ig'zaedž,rejt/ *v.* pretjerivati, preuveličavati
exam /ig'zaem/ *n.* ispit, pregled (med.), istraga
examination /ig'zaeminejš,n/ *n.* ispit, istraga
examine /ig'zaemin/ *v.* ispitivati, saslušavati
example /ig'za:mpl/ *n.* primjer, uzor, uzorak, slučaj
excavate /'eksk,vejt/ *v.* izbušiti, iskopati, izdubiti
exceed /ik'si:d/ *v.* prevazići, nadvisiti
excel /ik'sel/ *v.* nadvisiti, nadmašiti
excellent /ik's,lent/ *adj.* odličan, izvrstan
except /ik'sept/ *v.* izostaviti, izuzeti, isključiti
exception /ik'sepšš,n/ *n.* izuzetak, prigovor
excessive /ik'sesiv/ *adj.* prekomjeran, neumjeren, pretjeran
exchange /iks'čejndž/ *n.* razmjena; berza; *v.* razmijeniti
excite /ik'sajt/ *v.* potaći, pobuditi, uzbuditi
excitement /ik'sajtm,nt/ *n.* uzbudjenje, uzrujavanje
exciting /ik'sajting/ *adj.* uzbudljiv, napet
exclude /iks'klu:d/ *v.* isključiti, izbaciti, odbiti
excursion /iks'k:ž,n/ *n.* eskurzija, izlet
excuse /iks'kju:z/ *n.* izgovor, izvinjenje; *v.* izvinuti se
execute /'eksikju:t/ *v* pogubiti, kazniti smrću
exercise /'eks,rsajz/ *n.* vježbati, upotrebljavati, izvršavati
exhaust /ig'zo:st/ *v.* iscrpiti, iztrošiti; *n.* iscrpljenost, umor
exhibition /,esi'biš,n/ *n.* izložba, prikazivanje, izlog
exile /'eksajl/ *n.* izgnanstvo, progonstvo; *v.* izgnati, prognati
exist /ig'zist/ *v.* postojati, biti, živjeti
exit /'eksit/ *n.* izlaz, odlazak, smrt
exotic /ig'zotik/ *adj.* čudan, stran, egzotičan
expand /iks'paend/ *v.* proširiti, razviti, rasprostraniti
expect /iks'pekt/ *v.* očekivati, osloniti se, nadati se

expel /iks'pel/ *v.* istjerati, izbaciti
expend /iks'pend/ *v.* potrošiti, trošiti, isplatiti
expense /iks'pens/ *n.* trošak, rashod
expensive /iks'pensiv/ *adj.* skup, skupocjen
experience /iks'pi,ri,ns/ *n.* iskustvo; *v.* iskusiti, osjetiti
experiment /iks'perim,nt/ *n.* pokus, eksperiment; *v.* probati
expert /'eksp,r:t/ *n.* stručnjak, znalac, ekspert
expire /iks'paj,r/ *v.* isteći (vrijeme, rok), umrijeti
explain /iks'plejn/ *v.* objasniti, razjasniti
explanation /ikspl,nejš,n/ *n.* objašnjenje, tumačenje, smisao
explode /iks'ploud/ *v.* rasprsnuti se, raspući se, eksplodirati
explore /iks'plo:r/ *v.* istraživati, ispitivati
expose /iks'pouz/ *v.* izložiti, iznjeti, eksponirati
express /iks'pres/ *v.* izraziti, izreći, objaviti
extend /iks'tend/ *v.* proširiti, produžiti
extent /iks'tent/ *n.* opseg, veličina, stepen
exterior /iks'ti,ri,/ *n.* spoljašnost; *adj.* spoljašnji, spoljni
extinct /iks'tinkt/ *adj.* izumro, ugašen, zastario
extinguish /iks'tinguiš/ *v.* ugasiti, utrnuti, zatrti
extra /'ekstra/ *adj.* dodatni, specijalni, naročit
extract /iks'traekt/ *v.* izvod, ekstrakt; *v.* izvući, izvaditi (zub)
extraordinary /iks'tro:din,ri/ *adj.* izvanredan, neobičan, čudan, rijedak
extreme /iks'tri:m/ *adj.* krajnji, neumjeren
extreme /iks'tri:m/ *n.* krajnost, krajnja granica
extremely /iks'tri:mli/ *adv.* veoma, vrlo
eye /aj/ *n.* oko
eyebrow /'ajbrau/ *n.* obrva
eyelash /'ajlaeš/ *n.* trepavice

F

fable /fejbl/ *n.* bajka
fabric /'faebrik/ *s.* tkanina, materijal, štof
fabricate /'faebrikejt/ *v.* izradjivati, izmišljati, fabrikovati
face /fejs/ *n.* lice, fasada, brojčanik sata, ziferblat
face /fejs/ *v.* okrenuti lice(prema), stajati prema
fact /faekt/ *n.* činjenica, fakat, istina, djelo
faculty /'faek,lti/ *n.* sposobnost, nadarenost, fakultet, profesori
fade /fejd/ *v.* izblijediti, iščeznuti
fail /feil/ *v.* propustiti, izjaloviti se
failure /'fejl,/ *n.* pomanjkanje, nestašica
faint /fejnt/ *n.* nesvjestica, slabost
fair /feer/ *adj.* lijep, ugodan, plavokos; *n.* vašar, sajam, izložba
fairly /'fe,li/ *adv.* prilično, potpuno, pravilno
faith /fejt/ *n.* vjera, povjerenje, pouzdanje, iman
fake /fejk/ *n.* krivotvorina, prevara; *v.* krivotvoriti
falcon /'fo:lk,n/ *n.* soko
fall, fell, fallen /fo:l, fel:,fo:l,n/ *v.* pasti, padati, ispustiti
false /fo:ls/ *adj.* lažan, nepravilan
fame /fejm/ *n.* slava; *v.* proslaviti se
familiar /fe'milj,r/ *adj.* blizak, familijaran
family /'faemili/ *n.* porodica, obitelj, familija, soj
famine /'faemin/ *n.* glad, oskudica, nestašica
famous /'fejm,s/ *adj.* slavan, znamenit, čuven
fan /faen/ *v.* hladiti, raspirivati; *n.* ventilator
fancy /'faensi/ *n.* mašta, fantazija; *v.* maštati, zamišljati
fantastic /faen'taestik/ *adj.* fantastičan, neobičan, hirovit
fantasy /'faent,zi/ *n.* fantazija, mašta, iluzija
far /fa:r/ *adv.* daleko
fare /fe,r/ *n.* vozna karta, vožnja
farm /fa:rm/ *n.* farma, poljoprivredno dobro; *v.* obradjivati zemlju
farmer /'fa:rmer/ *n.* zemljoradnik, farmer
fascinate /'faesinejt/ *v.* očarati, opiniti, fascinirati, hajraniti
fashion /'faeš,n/ *n.* moda, način, običaj; *v.* podesiti

fast /fa:st/ *adj.* brz, čvrst

fasten /'fa:st,n/ *v.* pričvrstiti, prikopčati

fat /faet/ *n.* mast, masnoća; *adj.* debeo, mastan

fate /fejt/ *n.* sudbina, usud, kob, nafaka

father /'fa:dz,r/ *n.* otac, roditelj, tvorac, babo

father-in-law /'fa:dz,r-in-lo:/ *n.* punac, svekar, tast

fatigue /fe'ti:g/ *n.* umor, zamor, malaksalost; *v.* izmoriti

fault /'fo:lt/ *n.* greška, mana, porok

favor /'fejv,r/ *n.* pogodnost, dobrota, naklonost

favorite /'fejv,rit/ *adj.* omiljen, najmiliji; *n.* miljenik

fear /fi,r/ *n.* strah, bojazan; *v.* bojati se, strepiti

feasibility /fi:zi'biliti/ *n.* izvedivost, mogućnost izvedbe

feast /fi:st/ *n.* gozba, praznik; *v.* gostiti

feather /'fedz,r/ *n.* pero, perje; *v.* pokriti perjem

feature /'fi:č,r/ *n.* karakteristika, obilježuje; *v.* ocrtati

February /'febru,ri/ *n.* februar, veljača

fee /fi:/ *n.* naplata, članarina, honorar; *v.* naplatiti

feed, fed, fed /fi:d/ *n.* hrana, jemek; *v.* hraniti

feel, felt, felt /fi:l/ *v.* osjećati, ćutjeti; *n.* osjećaj, opip, čuvstvo

feeling /'fi:ling/ *n.* osjećanje, osjećaj, duša, opip

feet /fi:t/ *n.* stopala, tabani, noge

female /'fi:mejl/ *n.* žena, ženka; *adj.* ženski

feminine /'feminin/ *adj.* ženski, ženskog roda

fence /fens/ *n.* plot, ograda; *v.* ograditi

ferocious /fi'rouš,s/ *adj.* divlji, grub, okrutan

ferry /'feri/ *n.* skela, brod; *v.* prevesti skelom

fertile /'f,:tajl/ *adj.* rodan, plodan, bogat, fertilan

fertilizer /fertilajzer/ *n.* djubre, gnojivo

festive /'festiv/ *adj.* svečan, veseo

fever /'fi:v,r/ *n.* groznica, temperatura, vrućica

few /fju:/ *adj.* malo, rijetko

fiance /fi'a:nsei/ *n.* zaručnik, vjerenik

fiancee /fi'a:nsei/ *n.* zaručnica, vjerenica

fib /fib/ *n.* mala laž, neistina; *v.* lagati

fibre /'fajb,r/ *n.* vlakno, tkivo, osnova am.; eng.=fiber

fickle /'fikl/ *adj.* nestalan, prevrtljiv, mušičav

fiction /'fikš,n/ *n.* izmišljotina, fikcija, beletristika

fidelity /fi'deliti/ *n.* ispravnost, tačnost, vjernost

field /fi:ld/ *n.* polje, livada

fierce /fi,rs/ *adj.* divlji, bjesan, žestok

fig /fig/ *n.* smokva

fight /fajt/ *n.* borba, bitka, tuča, sukob

figure /'fig,r/ *n.* figura, cifra, broj

file /fajl/ *n.* arhiva, turpija; *v.* poredati, registrovati

fill /fil/ *v.* napuniti, puniti, ispunjavati

filling /filing/ *n.* punjenje, plomba

final /'fajn,l/ *adj.* konačan, finalni

find, found, found /fajnd, faund, faund/ *v.* naći, otkriti, utvrditi

fine /fajn/ *n.* novčana kazna, globa

finger /'fing,r/ *n.* prst,

finish /'finiš/ *n.* kraj, konac

fire /'faj,r/ *n.* vatra, požar, plamen; *v.* zapaliti

fireman /'faj,men/ *n.* vatrogasac

firm /f,:rm/ *n.* firma, preduzeće; *adj.* moćan, jak, čvrst

firm /f,:rm/ *v.* učvrstiti, ukrutiti

first /'f,:rst/ *adj.* prvi, najprvi, ponajprije, spočetka

fish /fiš/ *n.* riba; *v.* loviti ribu, ribariti

fist /fist/ *n.* pesnica, šaka; *v.* udariti šakom

fit /fit/ *v.* odgovarati, prilagoditi

fitness /'fitnis/ *n.* prikladost, kondicija

fitting room /fiting ru:m/ *n.* kabina za probanje odjeće

fix /fiks/ *v.* popraviti, pričvrstiti, fiksirati germanizam

flag /flaeg/ *n.* zastava, barjak, steg

flake /flejk/ *n.* pahuljica, tanak istić, flekica

flame /flejm/ *n.* plamen, vatra, žar, strast

flash /fleš/ *n.* sjaj, bljesak

flat /flaet/ *adj.* ravan, pljosnat, tup glup, utučen

flatter /'flaet,r/ *v.* laskati, ulagivati se

flavor /'flejv,r/ *n.* ukus, miris, aroma; *v.* začiniti, dati miris

flea /fli:/ *n.* buva, buha

flee, fled, fled /fli:, fled, fled/ *v.* bježati, pobjeći, uteći

flesh /fleš/ *n.* meso (živo), tijelo

flexible /fl'eksibl/ *adj.* elastičan, savitljiv, gibak

flight /flajt/ *n.* let, bijeg, jato, niz stepenice

flighty /'flajti/ *adj.* lakomislen, brzoplet, smušen

flip /flip/ *n.* lak udarac prstom

flirt /fl,:rt/ *v.* koketa, koketiranje; *v.* koketirati

float /flout/ *v.* ploviti, cirkulisati, pustiti da pliva

flood /flad/ *n.* poplava, potop, bujica; *v.* poplaviti

floor /flo:/ *n.* podloga, dno, pod, patos, sprat

florist /'florist/ *n.* cvjećar

flour /'flau,r/ *n.* brašno

flourish /'flariš/ *v.* cvjetati, razmahivati, uljepšati

flow /flou/ *n.* tok, tećenje, proticanje; *v.* teći, poplaviti

flu /flu:/ *n.* gripa, influenca

fluent /'fluent/ *adj.* tečan, okretan

fluid /'flu:id/ *n.* tečnost, tečan, fluid

fly /flaj/ *n.* muha, let;

fly, flew, flown /flaj, flu, floun/ *v.* letjeti, bježati

foam /foum/ *n.* pjena; *v.* pjeniti se, bjesniti na

focus /'fouk,s/ *n.* žiža, žarište, središte, fokus

fog /fog/ *n.* magla, tmina; *v.* zamagliti, zamutiti

foggy /fogi/ *adj.* maglovit, oblačan

foil /fojl/ *n.* folija, tanak listić metala;

fold /fould/ *v.* saviti, presaviti

folks /fo:ks/ *n.* narod, ljudi

follow /'folou/ *v.* pratiti, slijediti, ići za nekim

fond /fond/ *adj.* naklonjen, sklon, zaljubljen

food /fu:d/ *n.* hrana, jemek

fool /fu:l/ *n.* budala, glupak, luda, smušenjak

foot /fu:t/ *n.* stopalo, taban, noga, mjera za dužinu (30.5cm)

footwear /fu:tve,r/ *n.* obuća

for /fo:/ *prep.* za, zbog, radi, ukoliko, po, u prkos, u ime; *conj.* jer, pošto, budući da

forbid,forbade,forbidden / f,r'bid, f,:r'bejd, f,r'bi dn   *v.* zabraniti, spriječiti

force /fo:s/ *n.* sila, snaga, moć, kuvet; *v.* prisiliti, forsirati

forecast /fo:rka:st/ *n.* prognoza; predvidjanje;v.prognozirati, predvidjeti

foreclosure /fo:klouž,r/ *n.* zapljena, isključenje

forehead /'forid/ *n.* čelo, prednja strana

foreign /'forin/ *adj.* stran, tudj, inostran

foreigner /'forin,r/ *n.* stranac, tudj podanik

forest /forist/ *n.* velika šuma; *v.* pošumiti

forever /f,r'ev,r/ *adv.* vječno, zauvijek

foreword /'fo:v,rd/ *n.* predgovor, uvod

forge /'fo:dž/ *n.* kovačnica; *v.* kovati, krivotvoriti

forgery /'fo:rdž,ri/ *n.* falsifikovanje, prevara

forget, forgot, forgotten /f,rget, f,rgot, f,rgot,n *v.* zaboraviti, ne sjećati se

forgive,forgave,forgiven /f,r'giv, f,r'gejv, f,r' giv, n *v.* oprostiti, izvinuti

fork /fo:k/ *n.* viljuška, vilica

form /fo:m/ *n.* vrsta, oblik, formular, obrazac; *v.* oblikovati

formal /'fo:rm,l/ *adj.* zvaničan, formalan, svečan

former /'fo:rm,r/ *adj.* raniji, bivši, predjašnji

fort /fo:rt/ *n.* tvrdjava, utvrda

forth /fo:rs/ *adv.* dalje, naprijed

fortify /'fo:rtifaj/ *v.* utvrditi, ojačati

fortunate /'fotjunit/ *adj.* srećan, sretan, povoljan

fortunately /'fo:tjunitli/ *adv.* srećom

fortune /'fo:tjun/ *n.* sreća

forward /'fo:rv,rd/ *adj.* prednji,što je naprijed; v.uputiti dalje, poslati

foul /faul/ *adj.* gadan, smrdljiv, blatnjav

foundation /faun'dejš,n/ *n.* temelj, osnivanje, fond, zaklada, fondacija

fountain /fauntin/ *n.* izvor, vrelo, vodoskok, česma, fontana

four /fo:r/ *num.* četiri

fox /foks/ *n.* lisica, lija, prepreden čovjek

fragile /'fraedjajl, 'fraedjil/ *adj.* loman, krt, trošan, nježan

fragment /'fraegm,nt/ *n.* odlomak, komad, fragment, parče
fragrance /'frejgr,ns/ *n.* miris, aroma
frail /frejl/ *adj.* loman, krt, nježan, slab
frame /'frejm/ *n.* ram, okvir, djerdjef, sastav, sklop, struktura
frank /fraenk/ *adj.* iskren, otvoren
fraud /fro:d/ *n.* prevara, obmana
freak /fri:k/ *n.* ćud, hir, kapris, ćeif
freckle /frekl/ *n.* pjega, mrlja na koži *v.* opjegaviti
free /fri:/ *n.* slobodan, nezavisan, besplatan, serbes tur
freedom /'fri:d,m/ *n.* sloboda, oslobodjenje, povlastica, iskrenost
freeze, froze, frozen /fri:z, frouz, frouz,n/ *v.* mrznuti se, lediti se,
zalediti se
freight /frejt/ *n.* tovar, vozarina; *v.* tovariti, voziti
frequent /'fri:kvent/ *adj.* čest, običan, što se često ponavlja
fresh /freš/ *adj.* svjež, nov, prohladan, frišak
Friday / 'frajdi/ *n.* petak
friend /frend/ *n.* prijatelj(ica), ahbab (habab), dost
friendly /'frendli/ *adj.* prijateljski
friendship /'frendšip/ *n.* prijateljstvo
frighten /'frajtn/ *v.* prestrašiti, zaplašiti
frightful /'frajtful/ *adj.* strašan, užasan
frog /frog/ *n.* žaba
from /from/ *prep* od, iz, po
front /frant/ *n.* čelo, fasada zgrade; adj.prednji,
frost /frost/ *n.* mraz, smrzavica
frown /fraun/ *n.* mrštenje, natmuren izgled; *v.* mrštiti se
fruit /fru:t/ *n.* plod, voćka, voće, rod, korist
frustrate /fras'trejt/ *v.* osujetiti, izjaloviti se
frustrate /'frastrit/ *adj.* uzaludan, bezuspješan, frustriran
fry /fraj/ *v.* pržiti, frigati, peći u tavi
fuel /fjuel/ *n.* gorivo
fulfill /ful'fil/ *v.* ispuniti, izvršiti, učiniti obećano
full /ful/ *adj.* pun, potpun
fun /fan/ *n.* zabava, šala
function /'fankš,n/ *n.* dužnost, služba, funkcija; *v.* djelovati, raditi

fund /fand/ *n.* fond, zaliha
funeral /'fju:n,r,l/ *n.* pogreb, sprovod, djenaza
funny /'fani/ *adj.* zabavan, smiješan, komičan, čudan
fur /f,:r/ *n.* krzno, dlaka (na životinji)
furious /'fju:ri,s/ *adj.* bijesan, gnjevan, grub, divlji
furnish /'f,:rniš/ *v.* snabdjeti, opremiti, dobaviti
furniture /'f,:rni,r/ *n.* namještaj, pokućstvo, mebl
further /'f,:rdz,r/ *adv.* dalje; *adj.* krajnji
fuse /fju:z/ *n.* fitilj, osigurač(električni); *v.* rastopiti se
fuss /fas/ *n.* galama, buka
fussy /'fasi/ *adj.* usplahiren, nervozan zbog sitnice
future /'fju:č,r/ *n.* budućnost, buduće vrijeme

G

gadget /'gaedž,t/ *n.* mala mašina, korisna naprava

gain /gejn/ *n.* dobitak, zarada, korist; *v.* dobiti, postići

gall /go:l/ *n.* žuč, jed, gorčina, zloba

gallery /'gaeleri/ *n.* galerija, hodnik

gallon /'gael,n/ *n.* galon (mjera za tečnost, 4.54 l)

gallows /'gaelouz/ *n.* vješala

gamble /'gaembl/ *n.* kockanje, špekulacija; *v.* kockati se, protraćiti

gambler /'gaembl,r/ *n.* kockar

game /gejm/ *n.* igra, zabava, kocka

gang /gaeng/ *n.* grupa, četa, banda

gangster /'gaengst,r/ *n.* gangster, razbojnik

gap /gaep/ *n.* pukotina, jaz, praznina

gape /gejp/ *v.* zjevati, zinuti, buljiti

garage /gaera:dž/ *n.* garaža; *v.* garažirati

garbage /'ga:rbidž/ *n.* otpaci, smeće, bezvrijedna knjiga

garden /'ga:rdn/ *n.* vrt, bašta; bašća; *v.* obradjivati vrt, vrtlariti

gardener /'gardn,r/ *n.* vrtlar, baštovan

garlic /ga:lik/ *n.* bijeli luk, češnjak

garment /'ga:m,nt/ *n.* odjeća, haljina

gas /gaes/ *n.* gas, benzin, plin

gate /gejt/ *n.* kapija, prolaz, otvor

gather /'gaedz,r/ *v.* sakupljati, nabirati

gauge /gejdž/ *n.* mjera, kalibar; *v.* odmjeriti, ocijeniti, baždariti **gay** /gej/ *adj.* veseo, živahan, šaljiv, svijetao; *n.* homoseksualac

gaze /gejz/ *n.* oštar pogled; *v.* piljiti, zuriti

gear /gi,r/ *n.* zupčanik, pribor, alat

gem /dem/ *n.* dragi kamen, nakit; *v.* ukrasiti

general /'džen,r,l/ *n.* general; *adj.* opšti, opći, običan, glavni

generation /'dženerej[,n/ *n.* generacija, pokoljenje

generous /'džen,r,s/ *adj.* velikodušan, plemenit, darežljiv

genius /dži:nj,s/ *n.* genije, darovit čovjek

gentle /'džentl/ *adj.* nježan, otmen, blag
gentleman /'džntlmen/ *n.* gospodin čovjek
genuine /'dženjuin/ *adj.* pravi, originalan, iskren, prirodan, nepatvoren
germ /dž,:rm/ *n.* klica, zametak, mikrob
gesture /'džesč,r/ *n.* pokret
get in /get in/ *v.* ući, unići
get out /get aut/ *v.* izaći
get up /get ap/ *v.* ustati
get, got, gotten /get,got, got,n/ *v.* dobiti, steći, imati, postati, stići
ghost /goust/ *n.* duh, sablast, prikaza
giant /'džaj,nt/ *n.* div, džin, gigant; *adj.* divovski, gigantski
gift /gift/ *n.* poklon, dar, talenat
giggle /gigl/ *n.* kikot; *v.* kikotati se
ginger /'džindž,r/ *n.* džindžer, džumbir
gipsy /'džipsi/ *n.* ciganin, ciganka
girl /g,:rl/ *n.* djevojka, cura, sluškinja
girlfriend /g,:rl'frend/ *n.* prijateljica
give /giv/ *v.* dati, predati, pokloniti, dopustiti
give up /giv ap/ *v.* odustati
glad /glaed/ *adj.* radostan, veseo, zadovoljan
glamorous /'glaem,r,s/ *adj.* blistav, čaroban,
glance /gla:ns/ *n.* brz pogled, pomisao, odbljesak; *v.* pogledati brzo, sjevnuti
gland /glaend/ *n.* žlijezda
glass /gla:s/ *n.* staklo, čaša, prozorsko okno
glasses /gla:sis/ *n.* naočare, naočale, džozluke
glimpse /glimps/ *n.* letimičan pogled, bljesak; *v.* brzo pogledati, sjevnuti
glitter /'glot,r/ *v.* blistati se, svjetlucati; *n.* blještanje, svjetlucanje
globe /gloub/ *n.* globus, kugla zemaljska
gloomy /'glu:mi/ *adj.* mračan, taman, sumoran
glorious /'glo:rj,s/ *adj.* slavan, znamenit, veličanstven
glory /'glo:ri/ *n.* slava, ponos, dika
gloss /glos/ *n.* uglačanost, sjaj, ljepota, ulaštenost, perdah

glossary /'glos,ri/ *n.* rječnik na kraju knjige, slovar
glove /glav/ *n.* rukavica
glow /glou/ *v.* sijati se, žariti, biti uzbudjen; *n.* žar
glue /glu:/ *n.* ljepak, tutkalo; *v.* ljepiti, priljepiti
gnome /noum/ *n.* patuljak, kepec
gnome /noum/ *n.* poslovica, maksima, sentencija
go, went, gone /gou, vent, gon/ *v.* ići, hodati, proći, namjeravati
goal /goul/ *n.* cilj, meta, svrha
goat /gout/ *n.* koza
god /god/ *n.* bog, božanstvo
gold /gould/ *n.* zlato
golden /'gouldn/ *adj.* zlatan
golf /golf/ *n.* golf (sportska igra)
good /gud/ *adj.* dobar *n.* imanje, roba, dobro
good-bye! /,gud'baj/ *int.* zbogom
goose /gu:s/ *n.* guska, budala
gorgeous /'go:rdž,s/ *adj.* veličanstven, sjajan, divan
gossip /'gosip/ *n.* ogovaranje, trač; *v.* ogovarati, tračati
govern /'gav,n/ *v.* vladati, upravljati
government /'gav,rnment/ *n.* vlada, uprava, vladanje
gown /gaun/ *n.* haljina, odjeca, plast
grab /graeb/ *v.* shvatiti, dočepati, zgrabiti
grace /grejs/ *n.* ljepota, milost, vrlina; *v.* ukrasiti
grade /grejd/ *n.* stepen, stupanj, kosina; *v.* redati po veličini
gradual /'graedžuel/ *adj.* postepen
graduate /'graedžuejt/ *n.* diplomirani učenik/student; v.diplomirati
graduation /,graedžu'ejš,n/ *n.* promocija
grain /grejn/ *n.* zrno, tane, sjeme
grand /graend/ *adj.* veliki, odličan, divan, glavni
grandchild /'graen,čajld/ *n.* unuk/unuka
granddaughter /'graen,do:t,r/ *n.* unuka
grandfather /'graend,fa:dzer/ *n.* djed, deda, dedo
grandmother /'graen,madzer/ *n.* baba, baka
grandparents /'graen,paerents/ *n.* baba ili djed, baka ili dedo
grandson /'graensan/ *n.* unuk

grant /gra:nt/ *n.* dar, darivanje, dozvola; *v.* podariti, dozvoliti

grape /grejp/ *n.* grožđe, grozd, vinograd

grapefruit /'grejp-fru:t/ *n.* grejpfrut

graph /graef/ *n.* grafikon, kriva

grasp /gra:sp/ *n.* stisak; shvaćanje; *v.* zgrabiti, sčepati

grass /gra:s/ *n.* trava, pašnjak

grate /grejt/ *n.* rešetka, roštilj; *v.* strugati, grepsti

grateful /'grejtful/ *adj.* zahvalan, prijatan

gratify /'graetifaj/ *v.* zadovoljiti, ugoditi, razveseliti

gratitude /'graetitju:d/ *n.* zahvalnost

grave /'grejv/ *n.* grob, propast; *adj.* ozbiljan, važan

gravy /'grejvi/ *n.* sos, sok od mesa

gray /grej/ *n.* siva boja; *adj.* siv, sjed

grease /gri:s/ *n.* mast, mazivo; *v.* podmazati

great /grejt/ *adj.* velik, silan, značajan

greedy /gri:di/ *adj.* žudan, požudan, pohlepan, lakom

green /gri:n/ *n.* zelena boja; *adj.* zelen, svjež, neiskusan

greet /'gri:t/ *v.* pozdraviti, pozdravljati

greeting /'griting/ *n.* pozdrav, pozdravljanje

grief /gri:f/ *n.* žalost, bol, tuga

grin /grin/ *n.* smješenje, cerenje; *v.* smijati se, ceriti se

grind, ground, ground /grajnd, graund, graund/ *v.* mrviti, mljeti, zdrobiti

grip /grip/ *n.* dohvat rukom, držanje; *v.* dohvatiti, sčepati, zgrabiti

groceries /'grouseris/ *n.* mješovita roba

grocery /'grous,ri/ *n.* trgovina mjesovite robe, granap, bakalnica

gross /grous/ *n.* cjelina, veći dio, masa; bruto

grotesque /grou'tesk/ *adj.* smješan, čudan, groteskan, tuhaf

ground /graund/ *n.* zemlja, tlo, posjed, imanje

group /gru:p/ *n.* grupa, gomila; *v.* sakupljati se, skupiti

grow, grew, grown /grou, gru:, groun/ *v.* rasti, napredovati, povećavati se

grown-up /'groun,ap/ *n.* odrastao čovjek

gruel /gruel/ *n.* kaša (u mlijeku ili vodi)

gruesome /'gru:s,m/ *adj.* užasan, strašan, grozan

grumble /'grambl/ *v.* mumlati, gundjati, prigovarati

guarantee /,gaeren'ti:/ *n.* garancija, jamstvo; *v.* garantovati, garantirati, jamčiti

guard /ga:rd/ *n.* straža, čuvar, zaštita; *v.* čuvati, stramariti

guess /ges/ *n.* nagadjanje, sumnja, zaključak; *v.* nagadjati, sumnjati

guest /gest/ *n.* gost, musafir

guide /gajd/ *n.* vodić, savjetnik; *v.* voditi, upravljati

guilt /gilt/ *n.* krivica, grijeh

guilty /'gilti/ *adj.* kriv/kriva, griješan, kažnjiv

gum /gam/ *n.* desni (oko zuba), ljepilo, guma

gun /gan/ *n.* puška, top, pištolj

gurgle /'g,:rgl/ *n.* žubor, krkljanje; *v.* žuboriti, krkljati

gush /gaš/ *n.* izliv, provala osjećanja; *v.* izliti, provaliti

gutter /gat,r/ *n.* oluk, kanal, žlijeb

guy /gaj/ *n.* uže, konopac, čovjek, stvor (USA)

gymnasium /džim'nejz,m/ *n.* gimnastička sala, sportska hala

gypsum /'džipsum/ *n.* gips

gypsy /'džipsi/ *n.* Cigan/Ciganka, Rom, ciganski jezik

H

habit /'haebit/ *n.* običaj, navika, odijelo, haljina; *v.* obući
hair /he,r/ *n.* kosa, dlaka
hairbrush /'he,rbraš/ *n.* četka za kosu
hairdresser /'he,r,dreser/ *n.* frizer, frizerka, berber
hairy /he,ri/ *adj.* dlakav
half /ha:f/ *n.* polovina; *adj.* polovičan
hall /ho:l/ *n.* hodnik, dvorana
halve /ha:v/ *v.* podijeliti po pola, raspoloviti
ham /haem/ *n.* šunka, bedro, butina, stegno
hamburger /'haemb,:rger/ *n.* hamburger
hammer /'haem,r/ *n.* čekić, malj; *v.* kovati, udarati čekićem
hamper /'haemp,r/ *n.* korpa, košarica, sepet; *v.* zaplesti, smetati
hand /haend/ *n.* ruka, šaka; *v.* dati, uručiti, predati, teslimiti
handbag /'haendbaeg/ *n.* ručna torbica, tašna
handicap /'haendi'kaep/ *n.* prepreka, smetnja; *v.* biti na smetnji, opteretiti
handle /'haendl/ *n.* ručka, drška, ručica; *v.* hvatati, zgrabiti, rukovati
handsome /'haens,m/ *adj.* lijep, prijatan, plemenit
handwriting /haend'rajting/ *n.* rukopis
handy /haendi/ *adj.* priručan, pogodan, vješt, spreman
hang, hung, hung /haeng, hang, hang/ *v.* visiti, objesiti
hangar /'haeng,r/ *n.* hangar
happen /'haep,n/ *v.* dogoditi se, desiti se, trefiti se
happiness /'haepines/ *n.* sreća, radost
happy /'haepi/ *adj.* sretan, srećan, radostan, zadovoljan
harass /'haer,s/ *v.* mučiti, uznemiravati, dodijavati, kinjiti
harbour /'ha:rb,r/ *n.* luka, pristanište; *v.* štititi, zaklanjati
hard /ha:d/ *adj.* tvrd, težak, surov, grub
hardly /'ha:rdli/ *adv.* jedva, s mukom, teško
hardness /ha:dnes/ *n.* tegoba, okorjelost, čvrstina, škrtost
hare /he,r/ *n.* zec
harm /ha:rm/ *n.* šteta, povreda, zlo; *v.* nauditi, naškoditi

harmful /'ha:rmful/ *adj.* štetan, škodljiv

harmless /'ha:rmlis/ *adj.* neškodljiv, bezazlen

harmonious /ha:rmounj,s/ *adj.* skladan, harmoničan

harsh /ha:rš/ *adj.* grub, neprijatan, sirov, uvredljiv

harvest /'ha:rvist/ *n.* žetva, berba, plod, ljetina

hassle /'haes,l/ *n.* svadja, prepirka; *v.* svadjati se, prepirati se

hasty /'hejsti/ *adj.* nagao, nepromišljen, žuran, hitan

hat /haet/ *n.* šešir, klobuk, šapka

hatch /haeč/ *n.* leženje, leglo, nasad; *v.* leći iz jaja, izleći se

hate /hejt/ *n.* mržnja; *v.* mrziti

hatred /'hejtrid/ *n.* mržnja

haughty /'ho:ti/ *adj.* ohol, nadut, ponosit

haul /hol/ *v.* vući, tegliti

haunt /ho:nt/ *v.* stalno posjećivati/boraviti

have, had, had /haev, hed, hed/ *v.* imati, posjedovati, morati, trebati

havoc /'haev,k/ *n.* pustoš, propast; *v.* uništiti, opustošiti

hawk /ho:k/ *n.* soko, jastreb; *v.* prodavati po ulicama, torbariti

hay /hej/ *n.* sjeno

hazardous /'haez,rd,s/ *adj.* rizičan, opasan

hazy /'hejzi/ *adj.* maglovit, zamagljen

he /hi/ *pron.* on

head /hed/ *n.* glava, pamet, vlasnik; *adj.* glavni;*v.*voditi

headache /'haedejk/ *n.* glavobolja

headline /'haedlajn/ *n.* naslov novinskog članka

heal /hi:l/ *v.* liječiti, izliječiti

health /hels/ *n.* zdravlje

healthy /helsi/ *adj.* zdrav

hear, heard, heard /hi,r, h,:rd, h,:rd/ *v.* čuti, slušati, saznati

heart /h,:et/ *n.* srce

hearty /'h,:rti/ *adj.* srdačan, iskren

heat /hi:t/ *n.* toplina, vrelina, uzbudjenost

heat /hi:t/ *v.* ugrijati (se), užariti (se)

heating /'hi:ting/ *n.* zagrijavanje

heaven /'hev,n/ *n.* nebo, nebesa, raj, djenet

heavy /'hevi/ *adj.* težak, sumoran, potišten

heed /hi:d/ *n.* pažnja, briga, obzir; *v.* obratiti pažnju

heel /hi:l/ *n.* peta, kopito

heinous /'hejn,s/ *adj.* gnusan, mrzak, užasan, ogavan

heir /e,r/ *n.* nasljednik, baštinik

hell /hel/ *n.* pakao, djehenem

helmet /'helmit/ *n.* šljem, kaciga

help /help/ *v.* pomagati, pomoći; *n.* pomoć, hizmet

hem /hem/ *n.* obrub (na haljini); *v.* obrubiti, opšiti

hen /hen/ *n.* kvočka, kokoš

hence /hens/ *adv.* odatle, otud, odsada, zato

her /h,:r/ *p.* njen, njezin, nju, nje

herb /h,:rb/ *n.* biljka, trava

herd /h,:rd/ *n.* čopor, stado, krdo, gomila

here /hi,r/ *adv.* ovdje, tu, ovamo, sad

hereafter /hi,ra:ft,/ *adv.* iza, poslije toga

hereditary /hi'redit,ri/ *adv.* nasljedni

herein /'hi,rin/ *adv.* u tome

hereof /'hi,rov/ *adv.* o tome

hereto /'hi,'rtu:/ *adv.* do sada

herewith /'hi,'vid/ *adv.* ovim

heritage /'heritidž/ *n.* nasljedstvo, baština

hero /'hi,rou/ *n.* junak, heroj, gazija

herself /h,:rself/ *p.* njen, njezin, nje, nju

hesitate /'hezitejt/ *v.* oklijevati, skanjivati se

hi /haj/ *excl.* zdravo (am. pozdrav), merhaba

hiccup /'hikap/ *n.* štucanje, štucavica; *v.* štucati

hide, hid, hidden /hajd, hid, hid,n/ *v.* kriti, sakriti, tajiti

high /haj/ *adj.* visok, plemenit, snažan, krajnji

high-fidelity, hi-fi /'haj'faj'deliti, haj'faj *adj.* visoka podudarnost / vjernost (kvalitet zvuka)

highway /'haj'vej/ *n.* glavna saobračajnica, glavni put

high-school /'haj'sku:l/ *n.* srednja škola, gimnazija

hike /hajk/ *n.* planinarenje, dug pješački izlet

hilarious /hi'le,ri,s/ *adj.* veseo, radostan, razdragan

hill /hil/ *n.* brdo, brijeg, humak, tepa

him /him/ *p.* njemu, njega
himself /himself/ *p.* on lično, on sam
hint /hint/ *n.* nagovještaj, mig, aluzija; *v.* nagovjestiti
hip /hip/ *n.* bedro, bok, hiftna
hire /haj,r/ *v.* najmiti, iznajmiti, zakupiti;*n.* najam, zakup
his /hiz/ *p.* njegov
history /'hist,ri/ *n.* istorija, povijest
hit /hit/ *n.* udarac, uspjeh, pogodak; *v.* udariti, lupiti, pogod iti
hitch /hič/ *n.* zastoj, prepreka, zamka, čvor; *v.* pričvrstiti
hitchhike /'hič,hajk/ *n.* autostoper/autostoperka
hithherto /'hid,/ *adv.* do sada
hive /hajv/ *n.* košnica, roj
hobby /'hobi/ *n.* hobi, pasija, razbibriga, omiljena zabava
hog /hog/ *n.* svinja, vepar, brav
hoggish /'hogiš/ *adj.* proždrljiv kao svinja, svinjski
hold, held, held /ho:ld, held, held/ *v.* držati, zadržati; *n.* držanje, zahvat, uporište
hole /houl/ *n.* rupa; *v.* izdupsti, načiniti rupu
holiday /'hol,dej/ *n.* praznik, svetac, blagdan
hollow /'holou/ *n.* udubina, rupa, jama; *adj.* šupalj, prazan, gluv, neiskren
holocaust /'hol,ko:st/ *n.* holokaust, pustošenje ognjem i mačem
holy /'houli/ *adj.* svet, pobožan
home /houm/ *n.* dom, kuća, domovina; *adj.* domaći, kućni
homeless /'houml,s/ *adj.* bez kuće i kućišta, bez krova nad glavom
homely /'houmli/ *adj.* ružan, prost, jednostavan, priprost
homicide /'homisajd/ *n.* ubistvo, ubica
honest /'onist/ *adj.* pošten, čestit, pouzdan
honey /'hani/ *n.* med, dragi, draga
honeymoon /'hani,mu:n/ *n.* medeni mjesec nakon vjenčanja
hono(u)r /'on,r/ *n.* čast, poštovanje, slava; *v.* poštovati
hood /hud/ *n.* kukuljica, kapuljača, poklopac motora, hauba
hoof /hu:f/ *n.* kopito, papak; *v.* ići, pješačiti
hook /huk/ *n.* kuka, udica, čengele
hop /hop/ *n.* skakutanje, poskakivanje; *v.* skakati, poskakivati

hope /houp/ *n.* nada, uzdanica; *v.* nadati se, uzdati se

horizon /h,'rajz,n/ *n.* horizont, vidokrug; *adj.* horizontalan, vodoravan

horn /ho:rn/ *n.* truba, rog, svirala, horna

hornet /'ho:rnit/ *n.* stršljen

horrible /'horibl/ *adj.* užasan, grozan, strahovit

horror /'hor,r/ *n.* užas, grozota, strah

horse /'ho:rs/ *n.* konj, at, konjica

horse-power /'ho:rspau,/ *n.* konjska snaga (mjera)

horseshoe /'ho:rs,šu/ *n.* potkovica, potkova

hose /houz/ *n.* čarapa, nogavica, crijevo za polijevanje, šlauf

hospital /'hospitl/ *n.* bolnica, hastana

hospitality /,hospi'taeliti/ *n.* gostoprimstvo, gostoljublje, gostoljubivost

host /houst/ *n.* domaćin

hostage /'hostidž/ *n.* taoc, talac, zalog, jemstvo

hostel /'hostel/ *n.* dom (djački, radnički)

hostess /'houstis/ *n.* domaćica

hostile /'hostajl/ *adj.* neprijateljski, dušmanski

hostility /hos'tiliti/ *n.* neprijateljstvo, dušmanluk

hot /hot/ *adj.* topao, vruć, vatren, žestok

hour /'au,r/ *n.* sat, čas, ura, sat, sahat

house /haus/ *n.* kuća, dom, domaćinstvo, kućanstvo

housewife /'haus,vajf/ *n.* domaćica, kućanica

how /hau/ *adv.* kako, na koji način

however /hau'ev,r/ *con.* ipak, medjutim, uprkos tome

hug /hag/ *n.* zagrljaj, stisak; *v.* zagrliti

huge /hju:dž/ *adj.* ogroman, golem, silan, divovski

hum /ham/ *n.* zujanje, brujanje, žagor; *v.* zujati, mrmljati

human /'hju:m,n/ *adj.* ljudski, human, čovječan; *n.* ljudsko biće, insan

humble /'hambl/ *adj.* pokoran, ponizan, krotak; *v.* poniziti, ponižavati

humidity /hju'miditi/ *n.* vlažnost, vlaga, mokrina

humorous /'hju:m,r,s/ *adj.* šaljiv, smiješan

hundred /'handrid/ *num.* sto, stotina

hunger /'hang,r/ *n.* glad, žudnja; *v.* gladovati

hungry /'hangri/ *adj.* gladan
hunt /hant/ *n.* lov, hajka, lovište; *v.* loviti
hurricane /'harik,n/ *n.* uragan, hariken, orkan, vihor
hurried /'harid/ *adj.* hitan, brz, žuran
hurry /'hari/ *n.* žurba; *v.* žuriti, hitati
hurt /h,:rt/ *n.* ozlijeda, povreda, šteta; *v.* ozlijediti, raniti
husband /'hazb,nd/ *n.* muž, suprug
hustle /'hasl/ *n.* žurba, gurnjava
hut /hat/ *n.* koliba, daščara, baraka
hygiene /'hajdži:n/ *n.* higijena
hymn /him/ *n.* himna
hyphen /'hajf,n/ *n.* crtica, vezica (-)
hypocrite /'hip,krit/ *n.* licemjer

I

I /aj/ pron. ja

Indian Summer /indj,n 'sam,r/ exp. pozno/kasno ljeto, Miholjsko ljeto

ice /ajs/ n. led; v. zalediti

ice-cream /'ajskri:m/ n. sladoled

icicle /'ajsikl/ n. ledenica

icon /'ajk,n/ n. ikona, lik, kip

idea /aj'di,/ n. ideja, pojam, misao, predodžba

ideal /aj'diel/ n. ideal, oličenje savršenstva; adj. idealan, savršen

identical /aj'dentik,l/ adj. identičan, istovjetan, isti

identification /ajdentifi'kejš,n/ n. identifikacija, identifikovanje, utvrdjivanje

identification card /aj'dentiti ka:rd/ n. lična karta, legitimacija

identity /aj'dentiti/ **n. identitet, istovjetnost**

idiom /'idj,m/ n. idiom, izraz, narječje

idle /'ajdl/ adj. bezposlen, lijen, isprazan

if /if/ conj ako, iako, da li

ignite /ig'najt/ v. zapaliti, paliti

ignoble /ig,noubl/ adj. neplemenit, niskog porijekla, alčak

ignorant /'ign,r,nt/ adj. neuk, neznalački; n. bilmez

ignore /ig'no:r/ v. ignorisati, ignorirati, ne obazirati se

ill /il/ adj. bolestan, zao, koban, loše, hasta

illegal /i'li:g,l/ adj. nelegalan, ilegalan, nezakonit, bezpravan

illicit /i'lisit/ adj. bezpravni, nedopušten, nezakonit

illness /'ilnis/ n. bolest, hastaluk

image /'imidž/ n. slika, lik, imidž

imagine /imaedžin/ v. zamisliti, uobraziti, stvoriti predodžbu

imbecile /'imbisil/ n. maloumnik, budala, ahmak

imitate /'imitejt/ v. imitirati, oponašati, podražavati

immaculate /i'maekjulit/ adj. nevin, bezgrešan, čedan, neporočan

immature /,im'tjuer/ adj. nezreo, nerazvijen, nesavršen

immediately /i'mi:djetli/ adv. odmah, smjesta

immense /i'mens/ *adj.* ogroman, beskrajan
immerse /i'm,:s/ *v.* potopiti, zagnjuriti, umočiti
immigrant /'imigr,nt/ *n.* imigrant, useljenik
impact /'impaekt/ *n.* sudar, dodir, udar
impair /im'pae,r/ *v.* smanjiti, oslabiti, oštetiti
impatient /im'pejš,nt/ *adj.* nestrpljiv, netrpeljiv
imperfect /im'p,:rfekt/ *adj.* nesavršen, nepotpun; *n.* imperfekt
imperial /im'pi,rjel/ *adj.* carski, imperijalni
implacable /im'plaek,b,l/ *adj.* nepomirljiv, neumoljiv
implement /'implim,nt/ *v.* izvršiti, ispuniti ugovor; *n.* alat, orudje, sprava
imply /im'plaj/ *v.* podrazumijevati, uključiti
import /im'po:rt/ *n.* uvoz; *v.* uvoziti
important /im'po:rt,nt/ *adj.* važan, značajan
impossible /im'posibl/ *adj.* nemoguć, nepojmljiv
impotent /im'pot,nt/ *adj.* slab, nejak, nesposoban
impress /im'pres/ *v.* utisnuti, štampati, pritisnuti
impression /im'preš,n/ *n.* žig, znak, utisak, impresija
improper /im'prop,r/ *adj.* nepodesan, neprikladan
improve /im'pru:v/ *v.* popraviti, unaprijediti, poboljšati
impulse /'impals/ *n.* poticaj, potstrek, pobuda, impuls
impressive /im'presiv/ *adj.* upečatljiv, dojmljiv, impresivan
in /in/ *prep* u, po, za, pod, na
inability /,in,'biliti/ *n.* nesposobnost, nemoć
inaccurate /in'aekjurit/ *adj.* netačan, neispravan
inactive /in'aektiv/ *adj.* neaktivan, lijen, trom
inappropriate /,in,'prouprij,t/ *adj.* neprikladan, nepodesan, neumjesan
inborn /in'bo:n/ *adj.* prirodjen, usadjen
incapable /in'kejp,bl/ *adj.* nesposoban
inch /inč/ *n.* mjera za dužinu (2.54 cm); *v.* micati se
incident /'insid,nt/ *n.* slučaj, dogadjaj, okolnost
incline /in'klajn/ *v.* naginjati, biti sklon
include /in'klu:d/ *v.* uključiti, sadržavati
including /in'klu:ding/ *adv.* uključujući
income /in'kam/ *n.* prihod, zarada, dohodak

incomparable /in'komp,r,bl/ *adj.* neuporediv, bez premca

incompatible /ink,m'paetibl/ *adj.* neuporediv, nesaglasan

incompetent /in'kompit,nt/ *adj.* nenadležan, nesposoban, nekompe-
tentan

incorporate /in'ko:rp,rejt/ *v.* spojiti, sjediniti u jedno

incorrect /'ink,'rekt/ *adj.* nepravilan, pogrešan

increase /in'kri:s/ *v.* povećati, proširiti; *n.* porast, povećanje, prirast

incredible /in'kred,bl/ *adj.* nevjerovatan, nevjerojatan

indecent /in'di:s,nt/ *adj.* nepristojan

indecisive /,indi'sajsiv/ *adj.* neodlučan, neizvjestan, kolebljiv

indeed /in'di:d/ *adv.* zaista, odista

indefinite /in'definit/ *adj.* neodredjen, neograničen

independence /indi'pend,ns/ *n.* nezavisnost, samostalnost

independent /,indi'pend,nt/ *adj.* nezavisan, samostalan

indicate /'indikejt/ *v.* nagovjestiti, naznačiti

indifferent /in'difr,nt/ *adj.* ravnodušan, nepristrasan, nemaran,

indignant /in'dign,nt/ *adj.* rasrdjen, ozlojedjen, ogorčen

indirect /,indi'rekt/ *adj.* posredan, zaobilazan

individual /,indi'vidjuel/ *adj.* pojedinačni, poseban, ličan; *n.*
pojedinac

indoors /in'do:rs/ *adj.* unutra, u kući

indulge /in'daldž/ *v.* podnositi, popuštati, ugadjati

indulgence /in'daldž,ns/ *n.* predavanje užicima

industry /'indastri/ *n.* industrija

inertia /i'n,:ršja/ *n.* inercija

inevitable /in'evit,bl/ *adj.* neizbježan, neminovan

infant /'inf,nt/ *n.* dijete

inferior /in'fi,ri,/ *adj.* niži, manji, lošiji

infinite /'infinit/ *adj.* beskonačan, bezgraničan, beskrajan

inflate /in'flejt/ *v.* naduti, naduvati, napuhati

inflict /in'flikt/ *v.* odrediti (kaznu), zadati (bol)

influence /'influ,ns/ *n.* utjecaj, moć, upliv; *v.* utjecati

inform /in'fo:rm/ *v.* obavijestiti, saopštiti

informal /in'fo:m,l/ *adj.* neslužben, neformalan

informer /in'fo:rm,r/ *n.* dostavljač, obavještač

infuriate /in'fju:riejt/ *v.* razbjesniti, pomamiti

ingenious /in'dži:ni,s/ *adj.* duhovit, domišljat, dovitljiv

ingredient /in'gri:djent/ *n.* sastojak smjese

inhale /in'hejl/ *v.* udisati

inherent /in'hi,r,nt/ *adj.* svojstven, prirodjen

inherit /in'herit/ *v.* naslijediti, baštiniti

initial /i'niš,l/ *adj.* početan, prvobitan

inject /in'džekt/ *v.* ubaciti, uštrcati

injection /in'džekš,n/ *n.* inekcija, šprica

injure /'indž,r/ *v.* povrijediti, ozlijediti, oštetiti

injury /'indž,ri/ *n.* povreda, ozljeda

injustice /in'džastis/ *n.* nepravda

ink /ink/ *n.* tinta, mastilo

inn /in/ *n.* gostionica, han, prenoćište

innate /'in'ejt/ *adj.* urodjen, prirodjen

inner /'in,r/ *adj.* unutarnji, unutrašnji, skriven

innocent /'in,sint/ *adj.* nevin, bezazlen

inquire /in'qvaj,r/ *v.* pitati, istraživati

insane /in'sejn/ *adj.* lud, umobolan, nerazuman, mahnit

insert /in's,:rt/ *v.* umetnuti, ubaciti, uvrstiti

inside /'insajd/ *n.* unutrašnjost, nutrina

insight /'insajt/ *n.* uvid, pronicanje u nešto

insist /in'sist/ *v.* insistirati, ne popuštati

inspect /in'spekt/ *v.* ispitivati, pregledati

inspection /in'spekš,n/ *n.* pregledanje, nadziranje, kontrola, inspekcija

instant /'inst,nt/ *adj.* nagli, trenutan, neodložan; *n.* čas, tren

instantly /'inst,ntli/ *adv.* odmah, smjesta

instead /in'staed/ *adv.* umjesto

instinct /'instinkt/ *n.* nagon, pobuda, instinkt

instruct /in'strakt/ *v.* učiti, podučavati, uputiti

insult /'insalt/ *v.* uvrijediti; *n.* uvreda

insurance /in'šu,r,ns/ *n.* osiguranje

intact /in'taekt/ *adj.* nedirnut, netaknut

intellect /'intil,kt/ *n.* razum, intelekt

intelligent /in'tilidž,nt/ *adj.* razuman, inteligentan

intend /in'tend/ *v.* namjeravati, smjerati
intense /in'tens/ *adj.* snažan, intenzivan
intention /in'tenš,n/ *n.* namjera, nakana
intentionally /in'tenš,nli/ *adv.* namjerno, hotimično
intercourse /'int,:ko:s/ *n.* općenje, seksualni snošaj
interest /'intrist/ *n.* pažnja, interesovanje, dobit, interes, kamata
interested /'intristid/ *adj.* zainteresovan, zainteresiran
interesting /'interesting/ *adj.* zanimljiv, privlačan, interesantan
interfere /,inter'fi,r/ *v.* mješati se, uplitati se
interim /'int,rim/ *n.* medjuvrijeme
interior /in'ti,ri,/ *adj.* unutrašnji, unutarnji; *n.* unutrašnjost
intermediate /,inter'mi:dj,t/ *adj.* u sredini, medju; *v.* posredovati
intermission /'inter'miš,n/ *n.* pauza, prekid
internal /'inte:rnal/ *adj.* unutrašnji, unutarnji
international /,inter'naeš,nl/ *adj.* medjunarodni, internacionalni
interpret /in'ter:prit/ *v.* tumačiti, prevoditi, interpretirati
interrogate /in'terogejt/ *v.* pitati, ispitivati
interrupt /,inte'rapt/ *v.* prekinuti, upasti u riječ, spriječiti
interval /,interv,l/ *n.* period, razmak, stanka, interval
intervene /,inter'vi:n/ *v.* umiješati se, intervenisati, intervenirati
interview /'intervju:/ *n.* sastanak, razgovor, intervju
intimacy /'intim,si/ *n.* prisnost, prisna veza, intimnost
intimate /'intimit/ *adj.* prisan, intiman; *v.* natuknuti
intimidate /in'timidejt/ *v.* zaplašiti, zastrašiti
into /'intu:/ prep u, unutra
intolerable /in'tor,l,bl/ *adj.* nepodnošljiv, nesnosan, netrpeljiv
intoxicate /in'toksikejt/ *v.* opiti, napiti
intrepid /in'trepid/ *adj.* neustrašiv
intricate /'intrikit/ *adj.* zamršen, komplikovan
intrigue /in'trig/ *n.* spletka, intriga, smicalica; *v.* spletkariti introduce
/,intr,'dju:s/ *v.* predstaviti, upoznati
introduction /intr'dakš,n/ *n.* uvod, upoznavanje
intrude /in'tru:d/ *v.* nametnuti se, naturiti se
intrusive /in'trusiv/ *adj.* nametljiv
invade /in'vejd/ *v.* navaliti, napasti, izvršiti invaziju

invasion /in'vejž,n/ *n.* invazija, napad
invent /in'vent/ *v.* pronaći, izmisliti, izumiti
invention /in'venš,n/ *n.* pronalazak, izum, ujdurma
invest /in'vest/ *v.* uložiti, investirati
investigate /in'vestigejt/ *v.* istraživati, voditi istragu
invitation /invi'tejš,n/ *n.* poziv, pozivanje
invite /in'vajt/ *v.* pozvati, pozivati
invoice /'invojs/ *n.* faktura, robni račun
invoke /in'vouk/ *v.* pozivati se na, prizivati
involve /in'volv/ *v.* uključiti, uplesti, umotati
iron /'ajr,n/ *n.* željezo, gvožđe, pegla, glačalo
ironic /aj'ronikl/ *adj.* ironičan
ironing /'ajr,ning/ *v.* peglati, glačati
irony /'aj,r,ni/ *n.* ironija
irrational /i'raeš,n,l/ *adj.* nerazuman, iracionalan
irrelevant /i'reliv,nt/ *adj.* beznačajan, irelevantan
irritable /'irit,bl/ *adj.* razdražljiv, iritantan
irritate /'iritejt/ *v.* izazvati, nadražiti, razdražiti
is (to be) /iz/ *v.* je, jeste (biti)
island /'ajl,nd/ *n.* ostrvo, otok
isn't (is not) /'iznt/ *v.* nije
isolated /'ajs,lejtid/ *adj.* usamljen, izolovan, izoliran
issue /'išu:/ *n.* izdanje, izlaženje, spor, pitanje; *v.* izdavati
it /it/ *pron.* ono
itch /'ič/ *n.* svrbež, svrab; *v.* svrbiti
item /'ajt,m/ *n.* pozicija, artikl, stavka
its /its/ *pron.* njegov, svoj
itself /it'self/ *pron.* ono samo, se, sebe
ivory /'ajv,ri/ *n.* slonova kost, slonovača
ivy /'ajvi/ *n.* bršljan

J

jacket /džekit/ *n.* sako, kratak kaput

jail /džejl/ *n.* zatvor, tamnica, haps; *v.* uhapsiti

jam /džaem/ *n.* marmelada, pekmez, navala, gužva; *v.* stisnuti, sabiti

January /'dženju,ri/ *n.* januar, siječanj

jar /dža:r/ *n.* tegla, krčag, kavonoz; *v.* škripati, tresti, drmati

jaw /džo:/ *n.* čeljust, vilica

jay /džej/ *n.* šojka, kreštalica

jealous /'džel,z/ *adj.* ljubomoran, zavidan

jealousy /'džel,si/ *n.* ljubomora, zavist

jelly /'dželi/ *n.* pihtija, sulc, hladetina, žele, almasija

jeopardize /'džep,dajz/ *v.* rizikovati, ugroziti

jerk /'dž,k/ *adj.* nedosljedan, prevrtljiv (am. sleng); *v.* trznuti se

jersey /'dž,:zi/ *n.* žersej, fino vuneno predivo, djemper

jet /džet/ *n.* mlaz, mlazni avion

jet-set /džet-set/ *n.* visoko društvo

jewel /'džu:el/ *n.* dragulj, nakit, dragi kamen, dragocjenost

Jew /džu:/ *n.* Jevrej, Židov, Jehudija

Jewish /'džu:iš/ *adj.* jevrejski, židovski

job /džob/ *n.* posao, rad, namještenje, zaposlenje

jockey /'džoki/ *n.* džokej

jog /džog/ *v.* kaskati, lako udariti, džogirati

join /džoin/ *n.* spajanje, veza; *v.* spojiti, sastaviti

joint /džoint/ *n.* spoj, veza

joint-venture /džoint-venč,r/ *n.* poslovno udruživanje, ortakluk

joke /džouk/ *n.* šala; *v.* šaliti se

jolly /'džoli/ *adj.* veseo, živahan, nasmijan

journal /'dž,:rn,l/ *n.* dnevnik, novine, časopis

journalist /'dž,:rnalist/ *n.* novinar

journey /'dž,:rni/ *n.* putovanje; *v.* putovati

joy /džoj/ n . radost, veselje; *v.* radovati se, veseliti se

joyful /'džojful/ *adj.* radostan, veseo

jubilee /'džu:bili/ *n.* proslava, jubilej, obljetnica
judge /džadž/ *n.* sudija; *v.* suditi, procijeniti
judgment /'džadžm‚nt/ *n.* presuda, ocjena, sud, mišljenje
jug /džag/ *n.* krčag, bokal, vrč
juice /džu:s/ *n.* sok, saft
juicy /'džu:si/ *adj.* sočan, saftan, saftali
July /džu:laj/ *n.* juli, srpanj
jump /džamp/ *n.* skok; *v.* skočiti. skakati
jumper /džamp‚r/ *n.* skakač
June /džu:n/ *n.* juni, lipanj
junction /'džankšin/ *n.* spoj, spajanje, sjedinjavanje, čvorište
jungle /'džangl/ *n.* džungla, prašuma
junior /'džu:nj‚r/ *n.* mladi, junior; *adj.* mladji
jury /'džu:ri/ *n.* žiri, porota
just /džast/ *adv.* upravo, tačno, baš, maločas, pravedan, pošten
justice /'džastis/ *n.* pravda, pravičnost
justify /'džastifaj/ *v.* opravdati, braniti, izvinjavati
juvenile /'džu:vinail/ *adj.* mladalački, mladenački
junk-food /džank-fu:d/ *n.* nezdrava hrana

K

keen /ki:n/ *adj.* oštar, revan, ljut; *v.* naricati
keep away /ki:p ,vej/ *v.* držati se podalje
keep off /ki:p of/ *v.* izostajati, biti udaljen
keep trying /ki:p trajing/ *v.* istrajati
keep, kept, kept /ki:p, kept, kept// *v.* držati, čuvati, voditi(knjige)
keg /keg/ *n.* burence, bačvica
kennel /'kenl/ *n.* pasja kućica, štenara
kernel /'k,:nl/ *n.* zrno, sjeme, srž, jezgra
kettle /'ketl/ *n.* kotao, kazan
key /ki:/ *n.* ključ, dirka, tipka, taster
keyboard /ki:bo:rd/ *n.* klavijatura, tastatura
kick /kik/ *v.* udariti nogom, ritnuti
kid /kid/ *n.* jare, dijete (am.), srndać
kidnap /'kidnaep/ *v.* ukrasti dijete, kidnapovati
kidney /kidni/ *n.* bubreg
kidney-bean /'kidni-bi:n/ *n.* pasulj, grah
kill /kil/ *v.* ubiti, uništiti, zaklati
killer /kil,r/ *n.* ubojica, ubica, katil
kilt /kilt/ *n.* škotska suknja
kin /kin/ *n.* srodstvo, rodjak, rodbina
kind /kajnd/ *n.* vrsta, rod; *adj.* ljubazan, prijazan
kindergarten /'kind,ga:rt,n/ *n.* obdanište, zabavište, vrtić
kindness /'kajndnis/ *n.* ljubaznost, dobrota, prijaznost
king /king/ *n.* kralj
kingdom /kingd,m/ *n.* kraljevstvo
kiss /kis/ *n.* poljubac, pusa; *v.* poljubiti
kit /kit/ *n.* pribor, komplet
kitchen /'kič,n/ *n.* kuhinja
kite /kajt/ *n.* zmaj od papira/hartije
kitten /'kit,n/ *n.* mače
knee /'ni:/ *n.* koljeno
kneel, knelt, knelt /ni:l, nelt, nelt/ *v.* klečati

knickerbockers /nik,bok,rs/   *n.*   pumphozne, duge ženske gaće, Njujorčani (Nicks)

knife /najf/ *n.* nož

knight /najt/ *n.* vitez, borac

knightly /najtli/ *adj.* viteški

knit /nit/ *v.* plesti, štrikati, tijesno sastaviti

knob /nob/ *n.* dugme, puljka, puce

knob /nob/ *n.* ručica na štapu, topuz

knock /nok/ *n.* udarac, kucanje; *v.* kucati

knot /not/ *n.* čvor, morska milja, zamka

know, knew, known /nou, nju:, noun:/   *v.*   znati, poznavati, razumijevati

knowledge /'noulidž/ *n.* znanje, poznavanje

known /noun/ *adj.* izvjestan, poznat

kosher /'kouš,/ *adj.* čist (vjerski, za hranu)

L

label /'lejbl/ *n.* naljepnica, etiketa; *v.* staviti etiketu
labo(u)r /'lejb,r/ *n.* rad, trud, posao, napor; *v.* truditi se
laboratory /lae'bor,t,ri/ *n.* laboratorija
lace /lejs/ *n.* čipka, pertla, šnura; *v.* vezati, šnirati
lack /laek/ *n.* nedostatak, manjak; *v.* nedostajati, manjkati
lad /laed/ *n.* dečko, momče
ladder /'laed,/ *n.* ljestve, lojtre, merdevine
ladle /'lejdl/ *n.* kutljača, velika kašika, kevčija, šeflefel
lady /'lejdi/ *n.* dama, gospodja, hanuma
lag /laeg/ *v.* okljevati, lagano se kretati; *n.* zaostajanje
lake /lejk/ *n.* jezero
lamb /laem/ *n.* jagnje, janje
lame /lejm/ *adj.* šepav, hrom, sakat; *v.* šepati
lament /l,'ment/ *n.* jadikovka; *v.* žaliti se, jadikovati, lamentirati
lamp /laemp/ *n.* lampa, svjetiljka
land /laend/ *n.* zemlja, grunt, kopno; *v.* iskrcati se
landlady /'laend'lejdi/ *n.* gazdarica, kućevlasnica
landlord /'laend'lo:d/ *n.* gazda, kućevlasnik
landmark /'laendma:rk/ *n.* znamenitost, kamen medjaš, značajan dogadjaj
landscape /'laendskejp/ *n.* pejsaž, krajolik
lane /lejn/ *n.* staza, uličica, putanja, trasa, špalir
language /'laengvidž/ *n.* jezik, govor, način izražavanja
languish /'laengviš/ *v.* slabiti, malaksati, opadati, venuti
lanky /'laenki/ *adj.* tanak, suv, mršav, gladak (za kosu)
lantern /'laent,rn/ *n.* fenjer, ulična svjetiljka, laterna
lap /laep/ *n.* krilo, skut, okrilje; *v.* oplakivati (more)
lapel /l,'pel/ *n.* rever
large /la:dž/ *adj.* velik, opsežan, krupan
lark /la:k/ *n.* šala, lakrdija
lash /laeš/ *n.* trepavica, bič, korbač, šiba; *v.* šibati, ismijavati
last /la:st/ *adj.* posljednji, prošli, krajnji; *n.* kalup

lastly /laestli/ *adv.* najzad, konačno

latch /laeč/ *n.* kvaka, zasun, mandal; *v.* zaključati vrata

late /lejt/ *adj.* kasni, prijašnji; pokojni, rahmetli

lately /lejtli/ *adv.* u posljednje vrijeme

latent /'lejt,nt/ *adj.* neprimjetan, skriven, latentan

latitude /'laetitju:d/ *n.* geografska širina

latter /'laeter/ *adj.* posljednji, skorašnji

laugh /la:f/ *n.* smijeh; *v.* smijati se

laughter /'a:ft,r/ *n.* smijeh

launch /lo:nč/ *n.* spuštanje, porinuće; *v.* porinuti, lansirati

laundry /'lo:ndri/ *n.* praonica, večeraj, veš za pranje

lavatory /'laev,t,ri/ *n.* umivaonik, lavabo, javni zahod, hala

lavish /laeviš/ *adj.* izdašan, rasipan, neobuzdan; *v.* rasipati, harčiti

law /lo:/ *n.* zakon, pravo, pravilo

lawn /lo:n/ *n.* proplanak, travnjak ispred kuće (am.)

lawyer /'lo:j,r/ *n.* advokat, odvjetnik, pravnik, fiškal

lay, laid, laid /lej, lejd, lejd/ *v.* položiti, metnuti, staviti; *n.* položaj

layer /'lejer/ *n.* sloj, naslaga; kat; šihta

layer cake /lejer kejk/ *n.* torta (am.)

lazy /lejzi/ *adj.* lijen, dembel

lead /led/ *n.* olovo, kuršum

lead, led, led /li:d, led, led/ *v.* voditi; rukovoditi

leader /'li:d,r/ *n.* vodja, rukovodilac, lider

leaf, *pl.* **leaves** /li:f, *pl.* li:vz/ *n.* list

leak /li:k/ *n.* pukotina, rupa, curenje; *v.* curiti, propuštati

lean /li:n/ *adj.* mršav, posan, krt; *v.* oslanjati se (na nešto)

leap, leapt, leapt /li:p, lept, lept/ *v.* skočiti, skakati; *n.* skok

leap-year /li:p-je,r/ *n.* prestupna godina

learn, learnt, learnt /l,:n, l,:nt, l,:nt/ *v.* učiti, saznati, saopštiti

lease /li:s/ *n.* iznajmljivanje, zakupnina, lizing; *v.* iznajmiti

least /li:st/ *adj.* najmanji; at a least: barem

leather /'ledz,r/ *n.* koža (štavljena); *v.* presvući kožom

leave, left, left /li:v, left, left/ *v.* ostaviti, napustiti

lecture /'lekč,r/ *n.* predavanje, lekcija, propovjed; *v.* predavati, pridikovati

leek /li:k/ *n.* praziluk, prasa, poriluk
left /left/ *adv.* na lijevo; *n.* lijeva strana
leg /leg/ *n.* noga, but, plećka, batak
legal /'li:g,l/ *adj.* zakonit, pravovaljan, legalan
legend /'ledž,nd/ *n.* legenda, priča, zapis
leggings /'leginz/ *n.* sare, kožne dokoljenice, čarape sa gaćicama bez stopala (am.)
legible /'ledž,bl/ *adj.* čitak, čitljiv
legislation /,ledžis'lejš,n/ *n.* zakonodavstvo
leisure /'li:ž,r, 'le:ž,r/ *n.* dokolica, slobodno vrijeme, rahatluk
lemon /lem,n/ *n.* limun
lend, lent, lent /lend, lent, lent/ *v.* posuditi, pozajmiti, pružiti pomoć
length /lengs/ *n.* dužina, trajanje, daljina, rastojanje
lens /lens/ *n.* sočivo, objektiv, lupa, leća
less /les/ *adv.* manje; *adj.* manji, neznatniji
lesson /lesn/ *n.* lekcija, zadaća, čas, zadatak
let /let/ *v.* pustiti, dopustiti (let us go!: hajdemo!)
lethal /'li:dh,l/ *adj.* smrtonosan, letalan
letter /'let,r/ *n.* pismo, slovo
lettuce /'letis/ *n.* salata (zelena)
level /'levl/ *n.* nivo, razina, ravan; *v.* poravniti, izjednačiti
lever /'li:v,/ *n.* poluga, opruga
liability /laj,'biliti/ *n.* odgovornost, pasiva dugovanja
liable /'laj,bl/ *adj.* odgovoran, obavezan
liaison /li'jzo:n/ *n.* veza, spona
liar /'laj,r/ *n.* lažov, lažljivac
libel /'lajbl/ *n.* kleveta, optužba
liberate /'lib,rejt/ *v.* osloboditi, izbaviti, kutarisati
liberty /'liberti/ *n.* sloboda, oslobodjenje
librarian /laj'brerij,n/ *n.* bibliotekar
library /lajbr,ri/ *n.* biblioteka, knjižnica
license (licence) /'lajs,ns/ *n.* dozvola, ovlaštenje, pravo (driving licence) vozač ka dozvola; *v.* dozvoliti
lick /lik/ *v.* lizati, oblizati
lid /lid/ *n.* poklopac, kapak (očni)

lie, lay, lain /laj, lej, lejn/ *v.* ležati; *n.* položaj, laž
lie, lied, lied /laj, lajd, lajd/ *v.* lagati
life *pl.* **lives** /lajf/ *n.* život
lift /lift/ *n.* lift, dizalo, podiznje; *v.* dizati, ukrasti
light, lid, lid /lajt, lid, lid/ *v.* zapaliti, osvijetliti; *n.* svjetlost; *adj.* svijetao, lagan, plavokos
lighter /'lajter/ *n.* upaljač, fajerzajg
lighthouse /'lajthaus/ *n.* svjetionik
lightminded /'lajtmajndid/ *adj.* bezbrižan, lakomislen
lightning /'lajt,ning/ *n.* munja (lightning-conductor/rod: gromobran
like /lajk/ *v.* voljeti, svidjati se; *adj.* sličan; *adv.* kao, slično
likely /'lajkli/ *adj.* vjerovatan, moguć, očevidan, zgodan, lijep
likelihood /'lajklihu:d/ *n.* vjerovatnoća, izgled, mogučnost
lilac /'lajlek/ *n.* jorgovan, ljubičasta boja, lila boja
limb /lim/ *n.* udo, grana
lime /lajm/ *n.* kreč, vapno, lipa, citrus
lime-decease /lajm -di'si:s/ *n.* teško oboljenje od ujeda krpelja
lime-light /lajm-lajt/ *n.* pozorišna svjetlost (biti u centru pažnje)
limit /'limit/ *n.* granica, prepreka; *v.* ograničiti, limitirati
limp /limp/ *v.* zastajati, hramati, šepati; *adj.* opušten, mlitav
line /lajn/ *n.* linija, crta, red, vod, žica, sura; *v.* poredati
linen /'linin/ *n.* rublje, veš, bjelina, laneno platno; *adj.* platnen
linger /'ling,r/ *v.* okljevati, vuči se (bolest)
lingerie /'l,:nž,ri/ *n.* žensko donje rublje
lingering /'ling,ring/ *adj.* dugotrajan
lining /'lajning/ *n.* postava
link /link/ *n.* veza, spona, karika, omča; *v.* povezati, spregnuti
lion /lajon/ *n.* lav
lip /lip/ *n.* usna, usnica; *v.* doticati usnama
lipstick /'lipstik/ *n.* ruž za usne, karmin
liquid /'likvid/ *n.* tečnost, tekućina; *adj.* tečan, tekući, lak
liquor /'lik,r/ *n.* alkoholni napitak, alkoholno piće
lisp /lisp/ *v.* šuškati (loše izgovarati "s")
listen /'lis,n/ *v.* slušati
listless /'listlis/ *adj.* bezvoljan, ravnodušan

literacy /'liter,si/ *n.* pismenost
literal /'liter,l/ *adj.* bukvalan, doslovan
literary /'liter,ri/ *adj.* književni, literarni
literature /'litr,čr/ *n.* književnost, literatura
litter /'lit,r/ *n.* smeće
little /'litl/ *adj.* mali, niski, mališan; *adv.* malo
live /liv/ *v.* živjeti, postojati, biti u životu
live (alive) /lajv (,lajv)/ *adj.* živ, svjež, živahan, nov
livelihood /'lajvlihu:d/ *n.* izdržavanje, zarada za život
lively /'lavli/ *adj.* živahan
liver /'liv/ *n.* jetra, džigerica
livestock /'lajvstok/ *n.* živi inventar, stoka
lizard /'liz,d/ *n.* gušter
load /loud/ *n.* tovar, teret, naboj; *v.* tovariti, napuniti (pušku)
loaf *pl.* **loaves** /louf/ *n.* okrugli hljeb, *v.* besposličiti
loan /loun/ *n.* zajam, pozajmnica; *v.* pozajmiti
lobby /'lobi/ *n.* predvorje, hol, foaje, forcimer
lobbying /'lobing/ *n.* lobiranje:pokušaj utjecaja na glasove članova
zakonodavnih tijela
lobster /'lobst,/ *n.* morski rak, jastog
local /'louk,l/ *adj.* lokalni, mjesni
locate /'loukejt/ *v.* smjestiti, naći mjesto
location /'loukejš,n/ *n.* mjesto, položaj, lokacija
lock /lok/ *n.* brava, ključaonica, lokna, uvojak; *v.* zaključati
locker /'lok,r/ *n.* ladica/ormarić koji se zaključava am.
lodge /lodž/ *n.* koliba, kućica, loža; v.stanovati, primiti na stan
loft /loft/ *n.* potkrovlje
log /log/ *n.* deblo, panj, glupak (fig.)
logical /'lodžik,l/ *adj.* logičan
loiter /'lojt,/ *v.* klatiti se, dangubiti
lonely /'lounli/ *adj.* usamljen, pust, sam
long /long/ *adj.* dug, dugačak, dugoročan
long-distance call /long-dist,ns ko:l/ *n.* medjugradski poziv (tel.)
longing /'longing/ *n.* čežnja
longwise/longways /longvajz/ *adv.* uzduž, po dužini

look /luk/ *n.* pogled, izgled, vanjština; *v.* gledati
look after /luk a:ft,/ *v.* brinuti se za
look at /luk et/ *v.* pripaziti
look for /luk fo:/ *v.* tražiti
look forward to /luk 'fo:v,d tu/ *v.* unaprijed se radovati
look out(!) /luk aut/ *v.* izabrati, pazi!
loop /lu:p/ *n.* omča, petlja; *v.* pričvrstiti petljom
loose /lu:z/ *adj.* labav, klimav, raspušten
loot /lu:t/ *v.* pljačkati, opljačkati, oplindrati, opelješiti, ujagmiti
lord /lo:rd/ *n.* gospodin, lord, bog
lose, lost, lost /lu:z, lost, lost/ *v.* gubiti, izgubiti, lišiti
loss /los/ *n.* gubitak, šteta
lost /lost/ *adj.* izgubljen, propao, upropašten
lot /lot/ *n.* parcela, žrijeb, kocka, velika količina
lottery /'lot,ri/ *n.* lutrija, loza
loud /laud/ *adj.* glasan, bučan
lounge /laundž/ *v.* besposličariti, lješkariti; *n.* sofa, divan, loža
louse *pl.* **lice** /lauz *pl.* lis/ *n.* vaška, uš
lousy /lauzi/ *adj.* mizeran, bijedan
love /lav/ *n.* ljubav, naklonost, sevdah; *v.* voljeti
lovely /'lavli/ *adj.* divan, privlačan, dražestan
lover /'lav,/ *n.* ljubavnik, gelibter
loving /laving/ *adj.* ljubeći, voleći, blagonaklon
low /lau/ *adj.* nizak, dubok, tiho; *adv.* nisko, prosto, bajagi
lower /'lau,r/ *adj.* niži, donji; *v.* spustiti, prigušiti
loyal /loj,l/ *adj.* vjeran, odan, privržen, lojalan
lozenge /'lozindž/ *n.* bonbona, tableta, pastila
lubricate /'lu:brikejt/ *v.* podmazati, nauljiti
lucid /'lu:sid/ *adj.* bistar, jasan, lucidan
luck /lak/ *n.* sreća (sretan slučaj), tref
luckily /'lakili/ *adv.* srećom, na sreću
lucky /'laki/ *adj.* srećan, sretan, povoljan, uspješan
luggage /'lagidž/ *n.* prtljag, gepek, bagaža
lumber /'lamb,/ *n.* drvena gradja, starudija
luminous /'lju:min,s/ *adj.* svijetao, sjajan, jasan

lump /lamp/ *n.* gomila, hrpa, gruda, grumen **lunacy** /'lu:n,si/ *n.* ludilo, poremećenost uma

lunatic /'lu:n,tik/ *n.* ludak; *adj.* lud, ludački

lunch /lanč/ *n.* ručak, objed; *v.* ručati'

lungs /langz/ *n.* pluća

lure /lju,r/ *n.* mamac; *v.* mamiti, privlačiti

lurk /l,k/ *v.* vrebati, ležati u zasjedi

luxurious /lag'žju,rj,s/ *adj.* raskošan, bujan, preobilan

luxury /'lakš,ri/ *n.* luksuz, obilje, bogatstvo

M

machine /m,'ši:n/ *n.* mašina, stroj, mehanizam, sprava
mackerel /'maekr,l/ *n.* skuša, lokarda
mackintosh /'maekintoš/ *n.* kabanica, kišni ogrtač, regenmantil
mad /maed/ *adj.* lud, ljut, mahnit, bijesan
madam /'maed,m/ *n.* gospodja, hanuma
madden /'maed,n/ *v.* pobjesniti, pomamiti se
madman /'maedm,n/ *n.* ludjak, manijak, furija
madness /'maednis/ *n.* ludilo, umna poremećenost
magazine /maeg,zi:n/ *n.* magacin, skladište, depo; časopis
magic /'maedžik/ *n.* madjija, čarolija, sihir; *adj.* madjijski, volšeban
magician /'maedžiš,n/ *n.* madjioničar, čarobnjak
magnificent /maeg'nifis,nt/ *adj.* veličanstven, sjajan, divan
magnify /'maegnifaj/ *v.* uvećati, povećati, pretjerati
maid /mejd/ *n.* djevojka, cura, sluškinja
mail /mejl/ *n.* pošta; *v.* poslati poštom
mailman /mejlmen/ *n.* poštar, pismonoša
maim /mejm/ *v.* osakatiti
main /'mejn/ *adj.* glavni, najvažniji
mainly /'mejnli/ *adv.* uglavnom
maintain /men'tejn/ *v.* održavati, držati u redu, podržavati
maintenance /'mejnt,n,ns/ *n.* održavanje, podržavanje, izdržavanje
majestic /m,'džestik/ *adj.* veličanstven, dostojanstven, uzvišen
major /'mejdž,r/ *adj.* glavni, dur (muz.), glavni predmet studija
majority /m,'džoriti/ *n.* većina
make, made, made /mejk, mejd, mejd/ *v.* praviti, učiniti, proizvoditi
make-up /mejk-ap/ *v.* sastaviti, našminkati se; *n.* nadoknada
make-up for /mejk-ap fo:/ *v.* nadoknaditi (propušteno)
malady /'mael,di/ *n.* bolest, hastaluk
male /mejl/ *n.* muškarac, mužjak; *adj.* muški
malevolent /m,'lev,l,nt/ *adj.* zloban, pakostan

malice /'maelis/ *n.* zloba, pakost; *adj.* zloban, pakostan, maliciozan

malignant /m,'lign,nt/ *adj.* zloban, podmukao, opasan, koban, maligan

mall /mo:l/ *n.* mol(prostor sa mnogo prodavnica) am.

malnutrition /'maelnju'triš,n/ *n.* neishranjenost

mammal /m,'ma:l/ *n.* sisar

man *pl.* **men** /maen *n.* čovjek, insan, *pl.* ljudi

manage /'maenidž/ *v.* rukovati, upravaljati, služiti se, rukovoditi

management /'maenidžm,nt/ *n.* rukovodstvo, uprava, upravljanje

manager /'maenidž,r/ *n.* rukovodilac, direktor, menedžer

mane /mejn/ *n.* griva

manful /'maenful/ *adj.* muževan, srčan

manipulate /me'nipjulejt/ *v.* rukovati, manipulirati

mankind /'maenkajnd/ *n.* čovječanstvo, ljudska vrsta, ljudski rod

manner /'maen,r/ *n.* način, manir

manor /'maen,r/ *n.* plemićki/gospodski posjed

mansion /'maenš,n/ *n.* velika kuća, konak

manual /'maenjuel/ *adj.* ručni; *n.* priručnik

manufacture /'maenju'fekč,r/ *v.* proizvoditi, izradjivati

many /meni/ *adj.* mnogo

map /maep/ *n.* mapa, plan, geografska karta; *v.* izraditi nacrt

maple /'mejpl/ *n.* javor

marble /'ma:bl/ *n.* mramor, mermer

march /ma:rč/ *v.* marširati; *n.* marš

March / ma:rč/ *n.* mart, ožujak

margin /'ma:džin/ *n.* rub, prostor za manevrisanje, marža

marine /m,'ri:n/ *adj.* morski, pomorski; *n.* mornarica

mark /ma:k/ *n.* marka, znak, biljeg, išaret; *v.* označiti,

market /'ma:kit/ *n.* pijaca, tržište, tržnica, čaršija, pazar *v.* prodavati/kupovati na tržištu

marriage /'maeridž/ *n.* ženidba, udaja, svadba, vjenčanje

married /'maerid/ *adj.* oženjen, udata

marry /'maeri/ *v.* oženiti se, udati se

martial /'ma:š,l/ *adj.* ratnički, ratni

martial law /'ma:š,l lo:/ *n.* prijeki sud, vanredno stanje

marvelous /'ma:rvil,s/ *adj.* divan, čudesan

masculine /'maeskjulin/ *adj.* muški, muževan

mash /maeš/ *n.* kaša

mashed potatoes /maešd p,'tejtos/ *n.* pire krompir

mask /maesk/ *n.* maska, obrazina; *v.* maskirati, prikriti

mason /'mejsn/ *n.* zidar, klesar

mass /maes/ *n.* masa, komadina

massacre /'maes,k,r/ *n.* masakr, pokolj; *v.* masakrirati

massage /'maesa:ž/ *n.* masaža, masiranje; masirati

massive /'maesiv/ *adj.* masivan, težak, glomazan, čvrst

master /'ma:st,r/ *n.* gospodar, majstor, magistar (ak.stepen), umjetnik; *v.* savladati, poraziti

mat /maet/ *n.* mat, bez sjaja

match /maeč/ *n.* šibica, žigica, utakmica; *v.* pristajati nečemu, slagati se

mate /mejt/ *n.* kolega, drug, kamerad, suprug(a)

material /m,'ti,rjal/ *n.* materijal(sukno), gradja, gradivo

maternity /m,'t,:rniti/ *n.* majčinstvo

mathematics /,maeti'maetiks/ *n.* matematika

matter /'maet,r/ *n.* stvar, predmet, sadržaj, činjenica

mattress /'maetris/ *n.* dušek, madrac, šilte

mature /m,'tju,r/ *adj.* zreo, sazreo; *v.* sazreti, dospjeti(mjenica)

may, might /mej, majt/ *v.* smjeti, moći

May /mej/ *n.* maj, svibanj

maybe /'mejbi:/ *adv.* može biti

mayor /medž,/ *n.* gradonačelnik

me /mi:/ *pron.* mene, me; meni, mi; mnom; ja(sleng)

meadow /'medou/ *n.* livada

meager /'mi:g,r/ *adj.* mršav, štur

meal /mi:l/ *n.* obrok, jelo, jemek, brašno

mean, meant, meant /mi:n, ment, ment/ *v.* namjeravati, misliti; *adj.* podao, bijedan; *n.* sredina, srednji put

meaning /'mi:ning/ *n.* značenje, namjera, smisao

meantime /mi:ntajm/ *n.* medjuvrijeme

meanwhile /mi:nvajl/ *adv.* medjutim, u medjuvremenu

measles /'mi:zlz/ *n.* ospice, boginje, krzamak

measure /'mež,r/ *n.* mjera, takt

measurement /'mež,rment/ *n.* mjera, mjerenje

meat /mi:t/ *n.* meso

mechanical /mi'kaenikl/ *adj.* mehanički; *n.* mehaničar, obrtnik

mediate /'mi:dj,t/ *v.* posredovati, miriti

medical /'medikl/ *adj.* ljekarski, medicinski

medicine /'medisin/ *n.* lijek, medicina, iladj

medieval /,medi'i:vl/ *adj.* srednjovjekovni

mediocrity /'mi:dioukriti/ *n.* osrednjost, čovjek osrednjih sposobnosti

meditate /'meditejt/ *v.* razmišljati; snivati

medium /'mi:dj,m/ *n.* sredina, sredstvo, medijum; *adj.* srednji, prosječni

meek /mi:k/ *adj.* krotak, ponizan, nenametljiv

meet /mi:t/ *v.* sresti, sastati se, upoznati se

meeting /mi:ting/ *n.* sastanak, zasjedanje

melancholy /'m,l,nk,li/ *n.* melankolija, karasevdah; *adj.* melan-holičan

mellow /'melou/ *adj.* zreo, mekan, blag; *v.* smekšati

melodious /mi'loudj,s/ *adj.* melodičan, harmoničan

melon /'mel,n/ *n.* dinja

melt /melt/ *v.* topiti (se), rastopiti(se)

member /'memb,r/ *n.* član

membership /'memb,ršip/ *n.* članstvo

memorial /mi"mo:ri,l/ *n.* spomenik

memorize /'mem,rajz/ *v.* zapamtiti, memorisati

memory /'mem,ri/ *n.* memorija, sjećanje, pamćenje, uspomena

menace /'men,s/ *n.* prijetnja, opasnost; *v.* prijetiti, ugrožavati

mend /mend/ *v.* popraviti, poboljšati

mental /'mentl/ *adj.* duševni, intelektualni, umni

mention /'menš,n/ *n.* spominjanje; *v.* spomenuti

menu /'menju:/ *n.* jelovnik

merchandise /'m,:rč,ndajz/ *n.* trgovačka roba

merchant /'m,:rč,nt/ *n.* trgovac
merciful /'m,:rsiful/ *adj.* milostiv, milosrdan, merhametli
mercy /'m,:rsi/ *n.* milost, milosrdje, merhamet
mere /mi,/ *adv.* puki, tek, samo
merge /m,:dž/ *v.* stopiti (se)
merit /'merit/ *n.* zasluga, prednost; *v.* zaslužiti, biti zaslužan
merry /'meri/ *adj.* veseo, radostan
mess /mes/ *n.* zbrka, nered; *v.* pobrkati
message /'mesidž/ *n.* poruka, vijest, haber
messenger /'mesindž,r/ *n.* glasnik, kurir
messy /'mesi/ *adj.* neuredan, zbrkan am.
meticulous /mi'tikjul,s/ *adj.* isuviše pedantan/kritičan
metropolitan /,metr,'polit,n/ *adj.* gradski(glavnog grada)
microphone /'majkr,foun/ *n.* mikrofon
middle /'midl/ *adj.* srednji, u sredini; *n.* sredina, središte
middling /'midling/ *adj.* osrednji
midget /'midžit/ *n.* mušica, minijatura; *adj.* minijaturan
midnight /'midnajt/ *n.* ponoć; *adj.* ponoćni
might /'majt/ *n.* moć, sila, snaga, kuvet
mighty /'majti/ *adj.* moćan, snažan
migrate /'maj,grejt/ *v.* seliti se, lutati okolo
mild /majld/ *adj.* blag, nježan, lagodan
mildew /'mildju:/ *n.* plijesan, snijet, kukolj
mile /majl/ *n.* milja (1,609 m)
military /'milit,ri/ *adj.* vojni, vojnički; *n.* vojska
milk /milk/ *n.* mlijeko; *v.* musti
mill /mil/ *n.* mlin, fabrika; *v.* mljeti
mince /mins/ *v.* sjeckati, kosati, faširati,govoriti kroz zube
minced-meat /mins,d-mi:t/ *n.* mljeveno meso, faširano meso
mind /majnd/ *n.* um, pamet, duh, mišljenje; *v.* pamtiti, paziti
mine /majn/ *pron.* moj; *n.* rudnik, mina; *v.* rovati
miner /'majn,r/ *n.* rudar
mingle /'mingl/ *v.* miješati(se), pačati(se)
minister /'minist,/ *n.* sveštenik, ministar; *v.* pomagati
mink /mink/ *n.* nerc, vizon, krzno kanadske kune

minor /'majn,r/ *adj.* manji, nevažan; *n.* mol(muz.), sporedan predmet studija

minority /maj'noriti/ *n.* manjina, maloljetnost

mint /mint/ *n.* nana, menta, metvica; *v.* kovati novac

minute /'minit/ *n.* minuta, tren, čas; zapisnik

miracle /'mir,kl/ *n.* čudo

mirage /'mira:dž/ *n.* fatamorgana, prividjenje

mirror /'mir,r/ *n.* ogledalo, špigla, zrcalo; *v.* ogledati se

miscarriage /mis'kaeridž/ *n.* pobačaj, gubitak(pošiljke)

miscellaneous /misi'leinj,s/ *adj.* raznovrstan, mješovit, svestran

mischief /'misči:f/ *n.* zlo, inat, pakost

miser /'majz,/ *n.* škrtac, tvrdica

miserable /'miz,r,bl/ *adj.* jadan, bijedan, mizeran, nesrećan,

misfortune /mis'fo:č,n/ *n.* nesreća, peh, belaj

misprint /misprint/ *n.* štamparska greška

Miss /mis/ *n.* gospodjica, frajlica

miss /mis/ *v.* propustiti, promašiti, neuspjeti; *n.* promašaj

missing /'mising/ *adj.* odsutan, nedostajući

mist /mist/ *n.* magla, izmaglica

mistake /mis'tejk/ *n.* greška, nesporazum, zabuna

mistress /'mistris/ *n.* gospodarica, gospodja, ljubavnica

mistrust /mis'trast/ *v.* sumnjati, nevjerovati; *n.* nepovjerenje

Mister /'mist,r/ *n.* gospodin

misunderstanding /'misand,:'stending/ *n.* nesporazum

mitten /'mit,n/ *n.* rukavica sa jednim prstom

mix /miks/ *v.* miješati, pomiješati, družiti se; *n.* mješavina

moan /moun/ *n.* oplakivanje, jecanje, stenjanje; *v.* oplakivati

mob /mob/ *n.* gomila, rulja, banda, mafija; *v.* nasrnuti u gomili

mobile /'moubajl/ *adj.* pokretan; mobilan *n.* viseća apstraktna kompozicija (umj.)

mock /mok/ *v.* rugati se, ismijavati

mockery /'mok,ri/ *n.* ruganje, sprdnja, podrugivanje

moderate /'mod,rit/ *adj.* umjeren, srednji

moderate /'mod,rejt/ *v.* ublažiti, popustiti

modest /'modist/ *adj.* skroman, pristojan, umjeren

modification /modifi'kejš,n/ *n.* prepravka, preinačenje
modify /'modifaj/ *v.* preinačiti, ublažiti, modifikovati
moist /mojst/ *adj.* vlažan, memljiv
moisture /'mojšč,r/ *n.* vlaga, vlažnost, mem
mole /moul/ *n.* krtica; mladež; brana, ustava, bedem, molo
molest /mou'lest/ *v.* gnjaviti, kinjiti, dodijavati
mold /mould/ *n.* pljesan, budž; zemlja crnica; kalup, oblik,
monastery /'mon,st,ri/ *n.* manastir, samostan, kloster
Monday/'mandi/ *n.* ponedeljak
money /'mani/ *n.* novac, pare
monk /mank/ *n.* kaludjer, monah, redovnik
monkey /manki/ *n.* majmun
monotonous /m,'not,ns/ *adj.* jednoličan, dosadan, monoton
monster /'monst,r/ *n.* čudovište, neman, monstrum
month /mants/ *n.* mjesec (kalendarski)
monthly /mantli/ *adj.* mjesečni
mood /mu:d/ *n.* raspoloženje, ćud, štimung
moon /mu:n/ *n.* mjecec (nebesko tijelo)
moonlight /mu:nlajt/ *n.* mjesećina
mop /mop/ *n.* otirač, krpa za pranje poda; *v.* obrisati krpom
morbid /'mo:rbid/ *adj.* nezdrav, bolestan, morbidan
more /mo:r/ *adv.* više, još
morever /mo:rouv,/ *adv.* osim toga, čak, čak šta više, obaška
morning /'mo:rning/ *n.* jutro, prije podne
mortal /'mo:t,l/ *adj.* smrtan, smrtonosan
mortar /'mo:tl/ *n.* malter; minobacać
mortgage /'mo:gidž/ *n.* hipoteka, zajam za kuću ; *v.* založiti
mosquito /m,s'ki:tou/ *n.* komarac
moss /mos/ *n.* mahovina, treset
most /moust/ *adj.* najviše, većina (sup. od much i many)
mostly /moustli/ *adv.* većinom, uglavnom
moth /mos/ *n.* moljac, noćni leptir
mother /madz,r/ *n.* majka
mother-in-law /'madz,r in lo:/ *n.* punica, tašta; svekrva
motion /'mouš,n/ *n.* kretanje, pokret, zamah; stolica (med.)

motivate /'moutivejt/ *v.* nadahnuti, motivirati, imati/dati povoda

mountain /'mauntin/ *n.* planina, brdo

mourn /mo:rn/ *v.* oplakivati, žaliti

mouse *pl.* **mice** /maus *pl.* majs/ *n.* miš *pl.* miševi

moustache /mos'ta:š/ *n.* brk

mouth /mauts/ *n.* usta, njuška; ušće

move /mu:v/ *v.* maknuti se, poticati, ganuti

movement /mu:vm,nt/ *n.* pokret, pobuda, kretanje

movies /'mu:viz/ *n.* kino, bioskop, film

mow /mou/ *v.* kositi

mower /mouv,r/ *n.* kosilica za travu am.

much /mač/ *adj.* mnogo, daleko (više), neusporedivo

mud /mad/ *n.* blato, prljavština

muddy /madi/ *adj.* blatnjav, prljav

mug /mag/ *n.* krčag, šolja, vrč, bardak

multiply /'maltiplaj/ *v.* umnožavati, razmnožavati(se)

multitude /'maltitju:d/ *n.* mnoštvo, gomila

mumps /mamps/ *n.* zaušnjaci

munch /manč/ *n.* glasno žvakanje, mljackanje

mural /'mju,r,l/ *n.* freska; *adj.* zidni

murder /'m,:rd,r/ *n.* ubistvo, umorstvo; *v.* ubiti, umoriti

murderer /'m,:rd,r,r/ *n.* ubica, katil

murmur /'m,:m,r/ *n.* mrmljanje, žamor, gundjanje; *v.* mrmljati

muscle /'masl/ *n.* mišić, mišica

mushroom /'mašru:m/ *n.* gljiva, pećurka, šampinjon; *v.* brati gljive

music /'mju:zik/ *n.* muzika, glazba, melodija

musician /'mju:ziš,n/ *n.* muzičar, svirač

must /mast/ *v.* morati;

mustard /'mast,rd/ *n.* senf, gorčica

mute /mju:t/ *adj.* nijem

mutilate /'mju:tilejt/ *v.* osakatiti, okrnjiti

mutiny /'mju:tini/ *n.* pobuna, bunt; *v.* pobuniti se

mutter /'mat,r/ *v.* gundjati, mrmljati

my /maj/ *pron.* moj, moja, moje

myself /maj'self/ pron. ja sam, sebi, sebe, meni, mene
mysterious /mis'ti,rj,s/ *adj.* tajanstven, misteriozan
mystify /mistifaj/ *v.* varati, obmanjivati, blefirati

N

nag /naeg/ v. zanovijetati, izazivati, bockati; n. mali jahaći konj

nail /nejl/ n. nokat; ekser, čavao, čivija; v. zabiti, prikovati

naive /na'i:v/ adj. naivan, prostodušan, bezazlen

naked /'nejkid/ adj. gol, nag, obnažen

name /nejm/ n. ime, naziv; v. nazvati, imenovati, navesti

nap /naep/ v. odrijemati; n. kratak san

napkin /'naepkin/ n. ubrus, salveta, servijeta

narrate /nae'rejt/ v. pričati, pripovijedati

narrator /nae'rejt,r/ n. pripovjedač

narrow /'naerou/ adj. uzak, tijesan, ograničen; v. oduzimati

narrow-minded /'naerou'majndid/ adj. ograničen, koji usko gleda

nasty /'na:sti/ adj. neugodan, gadan, ružan

nation /'nejš,n/ n. nacija, narod

native /'nejtiv/ adj. domaći, prirodjen, urodjen; n. urodjenik,
domorodac

natural /'naečr,l/ adj. prirodan, naturalan

nature /'nejč,r/ n. priroda, narav, ćud, tabijat

naughty /no:ti/ adj. nepristojan, neodgojen, freh

nausea /'no:si,/ n. muka, morska bolest

naval /'nejv,l/ adj. pomorski, mornarički

navel /'nejv,l/ n. pupak

navigate /'naevigejt/ v. ploviti, upravljati brodom

navy /'nejvi/ n. ratna mornarica

near /ni,r/ adj. blizak, srodan, prisan

nearly /'ni,rli/ adv. skoro, umalo ne

neat /ni:t/ adj. uredan, skladan, čist

necessary /'nesis,ri/ adj. potreban, obavezan

necessity /ni'sesiti/ n. potreba, nužda

neck /nek/ n. vrat, šija

neck-tie /'nektaj/ n. kravata;

necklace /'neklis/ n. ogrlica, djerdan

need /ni:d/ n. potreba, nužda; v. trebati

needle /'nidl/ *n.* igla
neglect /ni'glekt/ *v.* zanemariti, zapustiti; *n.* nepažnja
negligent /'neglidž,nt/ *adj.* nemaran, ravnodušan
negotiate /ni'goušjejt/ *v.* pregovarati, ugovarati
neighbo(u)r /'nejb,r/ *n.* susjed, komšija
neighbo(u)rhood /'nejb,rhu:d/ *n.* susjedstvo, komšiluk
neither /'ni:dz,r/ *pron.* & *adj.* nijedan (od dva)
nephew /'nefju:/ *n.* sestrić, bratić, nećak
nerve /n,:v/ *n.* nerv, živac, snaga, hrabrost
nervous /'n,:rv,s/ *adj.* nervozan, razdražljiv
nest /nest/ *n.* gnjijezdo, leglo; *v.* gnijezditi se
net /net/ *n.* mreža, zamka; neto, čist; *v.* plesti mrežu
neutral /'nju:tr,l/ *adj.* neutralan, nepristrasan, neodredjen
never /'nev,r/ *adv.* nikada, nijednom
nevertheless /,nev,rtil,s/ *adv.* ipak, uprkos tome
new /nju:/ *adj.* nov; svjež, taze, frišak; moderan
news /nju:z/ *n.* vijest(i), novost(i), haber
next /nekst/ *adj.* slijedeći, najbliži, susjedni
nibble /'nibl/ *v.* grickati; prigovarati
nice /najs/ *adj.* lijep, fin, ugodan, simpatičan
nickel /'nikl/ *n.* nikl; kovani novac od 5 centi (SAD); *v.* poniklovati
nickname /'niknejm/ *n.* nadimak
niece /ni:s/ *n.* sestričina, nećakinja
nightgown /'najtgaun/ *n.* spavaćica
night /najt/ *n.* noć, veče
nightmare /'najtme:r/ *n.* noćna mora
nil /nil/ *n.* nula, ništica
nine /najn/ *num.* devet
nipple /'nipl/ *n.* bradavica (na sisi); ispupčina
no /nou/ *adv.* ne; *adj.* nijedan, nikakav
noble /noubl/ *adj.* plemenit, otmjen
nobody /'noub,di/ *n.* niko, nitko; čovjek bez položaja
nod /nod/ *v.* klimnuti(glavom); namignuti; *n.* klimanje; mig
noise /'nojz/ *n.* buka, galama, larma
noisy /'nojzi/ *adj.* bučan, glasan; napadan (odijelo)

nominate /'nominejt/ *v.* imenovati; *n.* naimenovanje
nonsense /'nons,ns/ *n.* glupost, apsurd
noodle /'nu:dl/ *n.* rezanac, nudla; budala
noon /nu:n/ *n.* podne
north /no:rt/ *n.* sjever; *adj.* sjeverni
nose /nouz/ *n.* nos, njuška; *v.* njušiti, šnjuflati
nostril /'nostril/ *n.* nosnica, nozdrva
not /not/ *adv.* ne
notable /'nout,bl/ *adj.* značajan
notary /'nout,ri/ *n.* javni bilježnik,
note /nout/ *n.* znak, oznaka, pisamce; *v.* zabilježiti
nothing /'nating/ *n.* ništa, nikako
notice /'noutis/ *n.* bilješka, obavijest; *v.* primijetiti, opaziti
notion /'nouš,n/ *n.* pojam, predodjba
nourish /'nariš/ *v.* hraniti
November /novem'b,r/ *n.* novembar, studeni
now /nau/ *adv.* sada
nowhere /'nouv,r/ *adv.* nigdje
nude /nju:d/ *adj.* go, nag, neodjeven
nuisance /'nju:sns/ *n.* smetnja, muka
numb /namb/ *adj.* ukočen, obamro
number /'namb,/ *n.* broj, brojka; *v.* brojati
nun /nan/ *n.* kaludjerica, opatica
nurse /n,:s/ *n.* medicinska sestra, bolničarka; rasadnik; v.dojiti, njegovati
nut /nat/ *n.* orah; matica šarafa
nutritious /nju'triš,s/ *adj.* hranjiv

O

oak /ouk/ *n.* hrast, hrastovina

oar /o:r/ *n.* veslo; *v.* veslati

oat /out/ *n.* zob

oath /out/ *n.* zakletva, prisega

obedient /,'bi:djnt/ *adj.* poslušan

obey /,bej/ *v.* slušati, biti poslušan

object /'obdžikt/ *n.* predmet, stvar, objekt; cilj, namjera

objection /,bdžekš,n/ *n.* prigovor

objective /,bdžektiv/ *n.* nepristrasan, istinit, stvaran

obligation /obli'gejš,n/ *n.* obaveza, dužnost, zahvalnost, obveznica

oblique /o'bli:k/ *adj.* kos, nagnut; neiskren (figurativno)

oblivion /,'blivjn/ *n.* zaborav, pomilovanje

oblivious /o'blivij,s/ *adj.* zaboravan, nesvjestan

oblong /'oblong/ *adj.* duguljast; *n.* pravougaonik

obscene /ob'si:n/ *adj.* nepristojan, bestidan, obscen

obscure /,b'skju,r/ *adj.* nejasan, zamagljen, mračan; *v.* prikriti, zamračiti

observe /,b'z,:rv/ *v.* opažati, primijetiti; slaviti

observer /ob's,rv,r/ *n.* posmatrač

obsess /,b'ses/ *v.* opsjedati, proganjati

obsolete /'obsoli:t/ *adj.* staromodan, zastario, suvišan, nekoristan

obstacle /'obst,kl/ *n.* smetnja, teškoća, zapreka

obstinate /'obstinit/ *adj.* tvrdoglav, nepopustljiv

obstruct /,b'strakt/ *v.* zakrčiti, smetati, osujećivati

obtain /,b'tejn/ *v.* dobiti, nabaviti; postići

obvious /'obvjs/ *adj.* očigledan, očit, jasan

occasion /,'kejž,n/ *n.* prilika, povod, razlog; *v.* prouzrokovati

occasional /,'kejž,nl/ *adj.* povremen

occupation /,oku'pejš,n/ *n.* zauzeće, okupacija; zanimanje;

occur /,'k:r/ *v.* dogoditi se, pasti na pamet

ocean /'ouš,n/ *n.* okean, ocean

October /ok'toub,r/ *n.* oktobar, listopad

odd /od/ *adj.* neparan; prekobrojan; pojedinačan; čudan

odor /'oud,r/ *n.* miris, zadah

of /ov/ *prep.* od, iz, zbog, s obzirom na

off /of/ *prep.* od, iz, odatle; dolje; dalje; izvan

off-spring /of'spring/ *n.* potomak, potomstvo

offend /,'fend/ *v.* vrijedjati, povrijediti, razljutiti

offensive /,'fenziv/ *n.* ofenziva; *adj.* neugodan, ofenzivan

offer /'of,r/ *n.* ponuda, prijedlog; *v.* ponuditi

office /'ofis/ *n.* kancelarija, ured, biro, ofis, služba

officer /'ofis,r/ *n.* službenik, činovnik, oficir

official /,fiš,l/ *adj.* služben, zvaničan, javan, oficijelan

often /'o:f,n/ *adv.* često

oil /ojl/ *n.* ulje, zejtin; *v.* mazati uljem

ointment /'ojntm,nt/ *n.* mast za rane

okay /'ou'kej/ *adv.* u redu, dobro (Am.)

old /oold/ *adj.* star

old-fashioned /'ould-faeš,nd/ *adj.* staromodan

olive /'oliv/ *n.* maslina

omen /'oum,n/ *n.* loš predznak

ominous /'ouminij,s/ *adj.* zloslutan

omit /ou'mit/ *v.* propustiti, izostaviti

on /on/ *prep.* na, nad, u, kod, o, uz

once /uans/ *adv.* jedanput, jednom, nekada

one /uan/ *num.* jedan; *adj.* jedini, neki

oneself /uan'self/ pron. se, sebe

onion /'anj,n/ *n.* luk (crni), zvibel, sogan

only /'ounli/ *adj.* jedini; *adv.* samo, jedino

open /'oup,n/ *adj.* otvoren, slobodan, javan; *v.* otvoriti

opening /'oup,ning/ *n.* otvaranje, otvor

operate /'op,rejt/ *v.* djelovati, funkcionisati, operirati

opinion /,'pinj,n/ *n.* mišljenje, uvjerenje, nazor

opponent /,'poun,nt/ *n.* protivnik; *adj.* protivnički; *adv.* protivan

opportune /'op,tju:n/ *adj.* podesan, pravovremen, pravodoban

opportunity /op,tju:niti/ *n.* prilika

opposite /',p,zit/ *adj.* suprotan, oprečan; *adv.* nasuprot

oppress /,'pres/ *v.* tištati, tlačiti, ugnjetavati
optician /op'tiš,n/ *n.* optičar, okulista
option /'opš,n/ *n.* slobodan izbor, opcija
or /o:r/ conj. ili, inače
oral /'o:r,l/ *adj.* usmen
orange /'orindž/ *n.* narandža, pomoranča; *adj.* narandžast
orchard /o:č,rd/ *n.* voćnjak, bašča
orchestra /'o:kistr,/ *n.* orkestar
order /'o:rd,r/ *n.* red, poredak; zapovjed, nalog; narudjba; stalež,či
n; *v.* narediti; poredati
ordinary /'o:din,ri/ *adj.* običan, prost
organ /'o:rg,n/ *n.* organ; orgulje; novine
organize /'o:rg,najz/ *v.* organizovati, organizirati
origin /'oridžin/ *n.* porijeklo, početak, loza, izvor
original /,'ridžin/ *adj.* originalan, izvoran
originally /'oridžinali/ *adv.* izvorno, prvobitno
ornament /'o:nam,nt/ *n.* ukras, nakit
orphan /'o:rf,n/ *n.* siroče
other /'adz,r/ pron. drugi, drukčiji, različit
otherwise /'adz,rvajz/ *adv.* inače, drugačije
ought /o:t/ *v.* morati, trebati
our /'aur/ *adj.* naš
ourselves /au,'selvz/ pron. mi (sami)
out /aut/ *adv.* izvan, napolje
outbalance /'autbalans/ *v.* pretegnuti
outcast /'autka:st/ *adj.* izbačen iz društva, izopčen
outcome /'autkam/ *n.* posljedica, konsekvenca
outer /'aut,r/ *adj.* spoljnji
outfit /'autfit/ *n.* oprema, pribor, mondura
outlet /'autlet/ *n.* izlaz, otvor
outline /'autlajn/ *n.* nacrt, skica, obris
outrage /'autrejdž/ *n.* uvreda, zločin, nasilje, zulum; *v.* povrijediti,
zlostavljati
outside /'autsajd/ *adj.* spoljašnji, krajnji, površan
outskirts /'autsk,rts/ *n.* predgradje, rub

outspoken /'autspouk,n/ *adj.* iskren, otvoren
outstanding /'autstending/ *adj.* istaknut, izvanredan
oval /'ouvl/ *adj.* ovalan, elipsastog oblika
oven /'ov,n/ *n.* rerna, pećnica, furuna
over /'ouv,r/ *prep.* preko, iznad; *adj.* odviše
overcoat /'ouv,kout/ *n.* ogrtač
overcome /,ouverkam/ *v.* savladati
overdo /ov,'du:/ *v.* pretjerati
overdue /'ouv,'dju:/ *adj.* zakasnio, prekoračio rok plaćanja
overlook /,ouv,'luk/ *v.* ne opaziti; nadzirati; oprostiti
overseas /'ouv,r'si:z/ *adv.* preko mora; *adj.* preko morski
oversleep /'ouv,sli:p/ *v.* prespavati
overwhelm /,ouv,r'velm/ *v.* obasuti; uništiti; savladati
owe /ou/ *v.* dugovati, biti obavezan
owl /aul/ *n.* sova
own /oun/ *v.* posjedovati; *adj.* vlastit, sopstven
owner /oun,r/ *n.* vlasnik
ox /oks/ *n.* vol, govedo
oxygen /'oksidž,n/ *n.* kisik
oyster /'ojst,/ *n.* ostriga

P

pace /pejs/ *n.* korak, mjera, tempo, takt; *v.* koračati, stupati

pack /paeck/ *n.* svježanj, zavežljaj, bala; *v.* upakovati, spakovati

package /'paekidž/ *n.* zavežljaj, paket, svježanj

packing /'paeking/ *n.* pakovanje, zamotavanje

pact /paekt/ *n.* ugovor, pakt

pad /paed/ *n.* jastuk; notes; *v.* podložiti, tapecirati

paddle /'paedl/ *n.* krato veslo; *v.* veslati kratkim veslom

page /pejdž/ *n.* stranica (knjige); paž; *v.* paginirati, pozivati

pain /pejn/ *n.* bol, patnja, kazna; *v.* mučiti

painful /'pejnful/ *adj.* bolan, mučan, zahmetli

paint /pejnt/ *n.* boja, farba, ličilo, šminka; *v.* bojiti, farbati

painting /'pejnting/ *n.* slikarstvo, slikanje, slika, maleraj

pair /peer/ *n.* par, bračni par; *v.* spariti, pariti se

pajamas /p,'dža:m,z/ *n.* pidjama am.

palace /'paelis/ *n.* palača, palata

pale /pejl/ *adj.* blijed, svijetao; *v.* problijediti; *n.* kolac

paleness /pejln,s/ *n.* blijedilo

palette /'paelit/ *n.* paleta

palm /pa:m/ *n.* palma, dlan

palpable /'paelp,bl/ *adj.* opipljiv, očigledan (fig.)

paltry /'po:ltri/ *adj.* jadan, bezvrijedan

pamphlet /'paemflit/ *n.* pamflet, brošura

pan /paen/ *n.* tava, tiganj

pancake /'paen,kejk/ *n.* palačinka

pane /pein/ *n.* prozorsko staklo

pants /paents/ *n.* pantalone, hlače (am.)

paper /'pejp,r/ *n.* papir, hartija

paprika /p,pri'k,/ *n.* crvena(mljevena)paprika, aleva paprika

parachute /'paer,šu:t/ *n.* padobran

paradise /'paer,dajz/ *n.* raj, nebo, djenet
parcel /'pa:rsl/ *n.* parcela, čestica(zemlje); pošiljka, paket
parent /'peerent/ *n.* roditelj
parliament /'pa:l,m,nt/ *n.* parlament
parrot /'paer,t/ *n.* papagaj, papiga; *v.* mehanički govoriti
parsley /'pa:rsli/ *n.* peršin
part /pa:t/ *n.* dio, komad, parče; kraj, strana svijeta; *v.* podijeliti
partial /'pa:š,l/ *adj.* djelomičan
participate /pa:r'tisipejt/ *v.* učestvovati, sudjelovati
pass /pa:s/ *v.* proći, proteći; *n.* propusnica
pass away /pa:s ,vej/ *v.* umrijeti, preminuti
passenger /'paes,ndž,r/ *n.* putnik
passion /'paešin/ *n.* strast, pasja; gnjev, srdžba
passport /'pa:sport/ *n.* pasoš, putna isprava
past /pa:st/ *adj.* istekao, prošao
paste /pejst/ *n.* tijesto; pašteta; ljepilo *v.* zalijepiti
pastry /'pejstri/ *n.* kolači, torte, paštete, poslastice
pat /paet/ *n.* tapšanje; kućni mjezimci; *v.* tapšati
patch /paeč/ *n.* zakrpa; mrlja, fleka; *v.* krpati
path /pa:s/ *n.* staza, put, putanja
pathetic /p,'tetik/ *adj.* žalostan, dirljiv, patetičan
patience /'pejš,ns/ *n.* strpljenje, istrajnost, sabur
patient /'pejš,nt/ *n.* pacijent; *adj.* strpljiv, istrajan, marljiv
patron /'p,jtr,n/ *n.* zaštitnik, mušterija, patron
pattern /'paet,n/ *n.* uzorak, šablon, kalup, mustra
pavement /'pejvm,nt/ *n.* pločnik, trotoar
paw /po:/ *n.* šapa, pandja
pawn /po:n/ *n.* zalog; *v.* založiti
pay, paid, paid /pej, pejd, pejd/ *v.* platiti; iskazati postovanje
payment /'pejm,nt/ *n.* plata, isplata
pea /pi:/ *n.* grašak
peace /pi:s/ *n.* mir, spokoj
peaceful /'pi:sful/ *adj.* miran, tih
peach /pi:č/ *n.* breskva, šeftelija
peacock /'pi:k,k/ *n.* paun

peak /pi:k/ *n.* vrh, šiljak, špic, tepa; vrhunac

peal /pi:l/ *n.* zvonjava, tutnjava; *v.* zvoniti, brujati, oriti se

peanut /'pi:n,t/ *n.* kiki-riki

peanut butter /'pi:n,t bat,r/ *n.* puter sa kiki rikijem

pear /pe,r/ *n.* kruška

pearl /p,:rl/ *n.* biser, perla

peasant /'pez,nt/ *n.* seljak; *adj.* seljački

peck /pek/ *v.* kljucati, zanovjetati; *n.* obilje (fig.)

peculiar /pi'kju:li,/ *adj.* čudan, neobičan, tuhaf; svojstven, naročit

pedestal /'pedistl/ *n.* podnožje stuba, temelj, sokla, pijedestal

pedestrian /pi'destri,n/ *n.* pješak; *adj.* pješački

peek /'pi:k/ *v.* viriti

peel /pi:l/ *n.* kora, ljuska; *v.* guliti, ljuštiti

peep /'pi:p/ *v.* viriti; *n.* kradomičan pogled, virenje

peer /pi,/ *n.* plemstvo, plemić; *v.* zuriti, buljiti

peg /peg/ *n.* kolac, klin, kuka, kvaka, čivija

pelvis /'pelvis/ *n.* karlica

pen /pen/ *n.* penkalo, hemijska olovka,pero (književno), pisac

penalty /'penlti/ *n.* kazna, globa, penal

pencil /'pensl/ *n.* olovka (grafitna)

pendant /'pend,nt/ *n.* privjesak, ukras

pending /'pending/ *adj.* viseći, u toku

penetrate /'peni,trejt/ *v.* probiti, prodrijeti, prozreti

peninsula /pi'ninsjul,/ *n.* poluotok, poluostrvo

penitence /'penit,ns/ *n.* kajanje

penitent /'penit,nt/ *n.* pokajnik; *adj.* pokajnički, pišman

penny *pl.* **pence** /peni *pl.* pens/ *n.* novčić, peni

pension /'penš,n/ *n.* penzija, mirovina

pensive /'pensiv/ *adj.* zamišljen

people /'pi:pl/ *n.* narod, ljudi, svijet, rodjaci

pepper /'pep,r/ *n.* paprika; biber; papar; *v.* papriti, biberiti

per /per/ *prep.* po, prema, na

perceive /p,'si:v/ *v.* opaziti, primijetiti, razumjeti

percent /per's,nt/ *n.* posto, odsto

percentage /p,'sentidž/ *n.* postotak, procenat, provizija

perception /per'sepš,n/ *n.* opažanje, spoznaja, percepcija

perennial /p,'reni,l/ *adj.* višegodišnji, trajan

perfect /'p,:fikt/ *adj.* savršen, potpun, tačan; *v.* usavršiti, dotjerati

perform /per'fo:m/ *v.* izvršiti, izvesti, obaviti

performance /per'fo:m,ns/ *n.* predstava, izvedba

perfume /'p,:fjum/ *n.* parfem, miris; *v.* namirisati

perhaps /p,'haeps/ *adv.* možda

period /'pi,ri,d/ *n.* period, doba; menstruacija; tačka (interpunkcija)

perish /'periš/ *v.* uginuti, propasti, pokvariti se

perishable /'periš,bl/ *adj.* pokvarljiv

perjury /'p,:dž,ri/ *n.* krivokletstvo

perm /p,:rm/ *n.* trajna ondulacija, trajna am.

permanent /'p,:rm,n,nt/ *adj.* trajan, postojan, stalan

permission /per'miš,n/ *n.* dozvola, dopuštenje

permit /per'mit/ *v.* dozvoliti, dopustiti

pernicious /p,:rniš,z/ *adj.* štetan, ubitačan

perpendicular /,p,:rp,n'dikjul,r/ *adj.* okomit, pod 90 stepeni

perpetual /p,r'petj,l/ *adj.* stalan, vječan

persecute /'p,:sikju:t/ *v.* proganjati, mučiti, dodijavati

persecution /'p,s.kjuš,n/ *n.* proganjanje, zulum

persist /p,'rsist/ *v.* istrajati, ne popustiti

person /'p,:rson/ *n.* osoba, ličnost, čovjek

personally /'p,:s,nali/ *adv.* lično, osobno

personnel /,p,:s,'nel/ *n.* osoblje, personal

perspire /,p,:r'spaj,r/ *v.* znojiti se

persuade /p,:svejd/ *v.* nagovoriti, ubijediti

pest /pest/ *n.* zaraza, pošast, kuga, pokora

pet /pet/ *n.* kućni ljubimac

petal /'petl/ *n.* latica

petition /pi'tiš,n/ *n.* peticija, molba (pismena), podnesak

petty /peti/ *adj.* tričav, neznatan (novac)

pharmacy /'fa:rm,si/ *n.* apoteka, farmacija

phase /fejz/ *n.* faza, stepen razvoja

pheasant /'fez,nt/ *n.* fazan

physician /'fiziš,n/ *n.* ljekar, doktor, lječnik

phone /foun/ *n.* telefon

phrase /frejz/ *n.* fraza, izraz, stil

physical /'fizikl/ *adj.* fizički, fizikalan

physicist /'fizisist/ *n.* fizičar

piano /'pjaenou/ *n.* klavir, glasovir

pick /pik/ *v.* glodati;kljucati; odabirati; brati, kidati

pickle /'pikl/ *n.* turšija, rasol, salamura; *v.* ukiseliti

picture /'pikč,r/ *n.* slika, crtež, prizor, kino; *v.* slikati, opisivati pie /paj/ *n.* pita, pašteta; svraka

piece /pi:s/ *n.* komad, parče; *v.* sastaviti

pierce /pi,rs/ *v.* probosti, probušiti, probiti

pig /pig/ *n.* svinja, prase

pigeon /'pidžin/ *n.* golub, gugutka

pile /pajl/ *n.* hrpa, gomila, štos

pilgrim /'pilgrim/ *n.* hodočasnik, hadjija

pill /pil/ *n.* tableta, pilula

pillow /'pilou/ *n.* jastuk

pillowcase /'pilou,kejs/ *n.* jastučnica

pilot /'pajl,t/ *n.* pilot, kormilar, vodič; *v.* pilotirati, voditi

pimple /'pimpl/ *n.* bubuljica, akna, priština, pikna

pin /pin/ *n.* igla, špenadla, pribadača; *v.* pričvrstiti (iglom)
zašpendlati

pineapple /'pajnepl/ *n.* ananas

pinch /pinč/ *v.* štipati, uštinuti; *n.* uštipak, mala količina

pine /pajn/ *n.* bor, omorika, borovina; *v.* ginuti, čeznuti

pink /pink/ *n.* karanfil; adj.roza, ružičast

pint /pajnt/ *n.* američka mjera za tekućinu (0.47 l ; 1/8 galona)

pipe /pajp/ *n.* cijev, rora), lula; svirala; *v.* zviždati

pirate /'pajr,t/ *n.* gusar, pirat

pit /pit/ *n.* jama, rudnik; grob; ponor

pitch /pič/ *n.* smola; nagib; v.mazati smolom; smjestiti se

pitcher /'pič,r/ *n.* vrč za vodu; bacać lopte u bejzbolu am.

pitiful /'pitiful/ *adj.* samilostan, merhametli

pity /'piti/ *n.* sažaljenje, samilost; šteta

place /plejs/ *v.* postaviti, metnuti, uložiti, smjestiti

place /plejs/ *n.* mjesto, plac, mejdan, položaj

placid /'plesid/ *adj.* miran, spokojan, blag

plague /plejg/ *n.* kuga, pomor; *v.* mučiti, dodijavati

plain /plejn/ *adj.* jednostavan, priprost, skroman; jednobojan

plaintiff /'plejntif/ *n.* tužilac, tužitelj

plan /plaen/ *n.* plan, nacrt; *v.* planirati, zamisliti

plane /plejn/ *adj.* ravan, plosnat, flah, gladak; *n.* avion

plank /plaenk/ *n.*   daska; politička platforma (SAD);v.pokriti daskama

plant /'pla:nt/ *n.* biljka; postrojenje, fabrika; *v.* posaditi

plaster /'pla:st‚r/ *n.* flaster; žbuka, malter; *v.* staviti flaster, žbukati

plate /plejt/ *n.* ploča, tacna, tabak, tanjir; *v.* popločati, obložiti ;

play /plej/ *n.* igra, zabava; predstava, drama; *v.* igrati; svirati

playground /plejgraund/ *n.* igralište

plea /pli:/ *n.* odbrana, izgovor, isprika; molba, apel

pleasant /'plez‚nt/ *adj.* prijatan, prijazan

please /pli:z/ *v.* svidjati se, biti drag; goditi, zadovoljiti; izvoliti

pleasure /'plež‚r/ *n.* zadovoljstvo, svidjanje, uživanje

pleat /pli:t/ *n.* nabor, faltna, plise

pledge /pledž/ *n.* zalog, svečano obećanje; *v.* založiti, nazdraviti

plentiful /plentiful/ *adj.* obilan, izobiljan

plenty /plenti/ *n.* obilje, bogatstvo

plot /plot/ *n.* zaplet (drame), spletka; osnova; parcela; *v.* spletkariti

plough /plau/ *n.* plug; *v.* orati

pluck /plak/ *v.* čupati, perušati

plug /plag/ *n.* klin, čep, plomba; el.utikač *v.* začepiti, zatrpati

plum /plam/ *n.* šljiva; grožđjica, rozina

plumb /plam/ *n.* plomba; teg od olova; *adj.* okomito

plumber /'plam‚r/ *n.* vodoinstalater, limar

plunge /plandž/ *v.* ronjenje; skok u dubinu; ritnuti se; strovaliti se

plush /plaš/ *n.* pliš: *adj.* plišani

pod /pod/ *n.* mahuna, čaura, komuška

poem /'pouim/ *n.* pjesma

poetry /'pouitri/ *n.* poezija, pjesništvo

point /point/ *n.* šiljak, špic; tačka; stepen, stupanj; srž, smisao; *v.* naoštriti

poise /poiz/ *n.* poza, nacin drzanja glave; *v.* uravnotežiti

poison /'pojz,n/ *n.* otrov; *v.* otrovati

pole /poul/ *n.* motka, ruda, direk, štanga; jarbol ;

police /p,'li:s/ *n.* policija; *v.* upravljati pomoću policije

polish /'poliš/ *n.* sjaj; krema za cipele; *v.* (u)glancati, (u)laštiti

polite /p,'lajt/ *adj.* ugladjen, učtiv, uljudan

poll /poul/ *n.* anketa, brojanje glasova

pollute /p.'lju:t/ *v.* zagadjivati, ukaljati

pollution /p,'lju:šin/ *n.* zagadjenje

pond /pond/ *n.* ribnjak

ponder /'pond,/ *v.* razmišljati, zadubiti se u misli

pool /pu:l/ *n.* lokva; bazen(swimming pool); ulog u igri

poor /pu,r/ *adj.* siromašan, oskudan, bijedan

pope /poup/ *n.* papa, Sveti Otac

poppy /'popi/ *n.* mak

popular /'popjul,r/ *adj.* narodni; popularan

population /'popjulejš,n/ *n.* stanovnišvo

porch /po:č/ *n.* trijem; veranda

pork /po:k/ *n.* svinjetina

porridge /'poridž/ *n.* zobena kaša

port /po:t/ *n.* luka, pristaniše; vrata

portable /'po:rt,bl/ *adj.* lako prenosiv

porter /'po:t,/ *n.* nosač, vratar

portfolio /po:t'fouljou/ *n.* mapa; ministarski portfelj; rezultat istraživanja

portion /'po:ršn/ *n.* dio, parče; obrok, porcija; miraz;

position /p,'zišn/ *n.* položaj; služba; gledište

positive /'pozitiv/ *adj.* siguran, pozitivan

possess /p,'zes/ *v.* posjedovati, imati

possession /p,'zešn/ *n.* vlasnišvo
possibility /pos,biliti/ *n.* mogučost, vjerovatnoća
possible /'posibl/ *adj.* moguć, vjerovatan
post /poust/ *n.* pošta; stup, direk , kolac
postage /'poustidž/ *n.* poštarina
postcard /'poust,ka:d/ *n.* dopisnica
poster /'poust,/ *n.* poster, veliki plakat
postpone /poust'poun/ *v.* odgoditi, odložiti
posture /postč,/ *n.* drzanje tijela; položaj
pot /pot/ *n.* lonac
pot-hole /pot-houl/ *n.* rupa, ulegnuće
potato /p,'tejtou/ *n.* krompir, krumpir
pouch /pauč/ *n.* kesa, vrećica, mala torbica koja se nosi oko pasa
poultry /'poultri/ *n.* perad, pernata živina
pound /paund/ *n.* funta (mjera za težinu 454 gr.); *v.* udarati, tucati
pour /po:/ *v.* lijevati, sipati, natočiti piće
poverty /'pov,ti/ *n.* siromaštvo, oskudica, kokuzluk
powder /'paud,/ *n.* prah, puder; *v.* smrviti u prah
power /'pau,/ *n.* snaga, sposobnost, moć
power station (plant)/'pau, stejš,n(plaent)/ *n.* elektricna centrala,
elektrana
powerful /'pau,ful/ *adj.* močan, snažan, silan
practice /'praektis/ *n.* vježba, praksa; *v.* vježbati
practitioner /praek'tišn,/ *n.* ljekar opšte prakse
praise /preiz/ *n.* pohvala, hvaljenje; *v.* hvaliti
pray /prej/ *v.* moliti, prositi; zaklinjati
prayer /'prej,r/ *n.* moitva, zaklinjanje
preach /pri:č/ *v.* propovijedati, pridikovati
precaution /pri'ko:š,n/ *n.* oprez, mjera predostroznosti
precede /pri:'si:d/ *v.* predhoditi, prednjačiti
precious /'preš,z/ *adj.* dragocjen, plemenit
precise /pri'sajz/ *adj.* tačan, odredjen, jasan
precision /pri'sižin/ *n.* tačnost, jasnoća
predecessor /'pri:dises,/ *n.* predhodnik

predict /pri'dikt/ *v.* proreći
prefer /pri'f,:r/ *v.* više voljeti, davati prednost
pregnant /'pregn,nt/ *adj.* trudna; pun značenja, zbijen
prejudice /'predžudis/ *n.* predrasuda, šteta
prepare /pri'pe,r/ *v.* pripremiti, pripraviti
prescribe /pris'krajb/ *v.* propisati, odrediti, zapovijediti
prescription /pri'skripšin/ *n.* recept, propis, pravilo
presence /'prez,ns/ *n.* prisutnost, pojava
present /'prez,nt/ *adj.* prisutan, sadašnji, današnji; *v.* predstaviti (se); prikazati
preserve /pri'z,:rv/ *v.* čuvati, održati, ukuhati, konzervirati
preside /pri'zajd/ *v.* predsjedavati
president /'prezid,nt/ *n.* predsjednik
press /pres/ *n.* štampa; presa; gužva; *v.* štampati, pritiskati, gnječiti
pressure /'preš,r/ *n.* pritisak, tlak; nužda
prestige /pres'ti:dž/ *n.* ugled, prestiž
presume /pri'zju:m/ *v.* predpostaviti; usuditi se, drznuti se
presumption /pri'zampš,n/ *n.* predpostavka; drskost
pretend /pri'tend/ *v.* pretvarati se, praviti se;usuditi se, pretendovati
pretty /'priti/ *adj.* zgodan, dražestan; *adv.* prilično
prevail /pri,vejl/ *v.* preovladati, pobijediti, postići svrhu
prevent /pri'vent/ *v.* spriječiti, preduprijediti
previous /'pri:vj,s/ *adj.* predhodni, raniji, predjašnji
prey /prej/ *n.* plijen, žrtva, pljačka; *v.* vrebati, pljačkati
price /prajs/ *n.* cijena, vrijednost
priceless /prajsl,s/ *adj.* neprocjenjiv, vrlo vrijedan
pride /prajd/ *n.* ponos, oholost, taština
priest /pri:st/ *n.* sveštenik
primacy /'prajm,si/ *n.* primat, prvenstvo
prime /'prajm/ *adj.* osnovni, najvažniji
primer /'prajm,r/ *n.* početnica
principal /'prins,p,l/ *adj.* glavni, najvažniji; *n.* direktor škole,
principle /'prins,p,l/ *n.* načelo, princip

print /print/ *n.* otisak, štampa, fotografija; *v.* štampati, drukati

prior /'praj,r/ *adj.* predjašnji, raniji; *n.* nastojnik samostana

priority /'praj'oriti/ *n.* prioritet, prvenstvo

prison /'prizn/ *n.* zatvor, tamnica, haps

prisoner /'prizner/ *n.* hapšenik, zatvorenik, sužanj

privacy /'prajv,si/ *n.* privatnost, povučenost, skrovito mjesto

private /'praj'vit/ *adj.* privatan, osoban; povjerljiv; nezavisan; neslužben

prize /prajz/ *n.* nagrada, premija, plijen; *v.* cijeniti

probable /'prob,bl/ *adj.* vjerovatan, vjerojatan, moguć

probe /proub/ *n.* sonda; *v.* sondirati

proceed /pr,'si:d/ *v.* poći dalje, nastaviti

proclaim /pr,'klejm/ *v.* proglasiti, najaviti, proklamovati, proklamirati

produce /'prodju:s/ *n.* plod, proizvod(poljoprivredni), prinos

produce /pr,'dju:s/ *v.* proizvesti, prouzrokovati

product /'pr,dakt/ *n.* proizvod, produkt

profession /pr,'fešin/ *n.* zvanje, profesija

professional /pr,'feš,nl/ *adj.* profesionalan; *n.* stručnjak, profesionalac

proficiency /pr,'fiš,nsi/ *n.* vještina, znanje, napredak

profile /'profi:l/ *n.* profil, lice sa strane, slika sa strane

profit /'profit/ *n.* koris, dobitak, dohodak

profound /pr,'faund/ *adj.* iskren; dubok, temeljit

progress /'prougres/ *v.* napredak, tok, razvoj

progress /pr,'gres/ *v.* napredovati

prohibit /pro'hibit/ *v.* zabraniti, spriječiti

project /'prodžekt/ *n.* projekat, plan

project /pro'džekt/ *v.* baciti; zasnovati, planirati, projektovati

prolong /prou'long/ *v.* produžiti

prominent /'prominent/ *adj.* istaknut, važan

promise /'promis/ *n.* obećanje, očekivanje; *v.* obećati, davati nade

prompt /prompt/ *adj.* brz, hitar, okretan; *v.* nagnati

prong /prong/ *n.* šiljak; vile

pronounce /pr,'nauns/   *v.*   izgovarati; svečano izreći

pronunciation /pra,nansi'ejšin/   *n.*   izgovor, fonetski zapis

proof /pru:f/   *n.*   dokaz; proba, pokus;   *adj.*   otporan, čvrst

propagate /'prop,'gejt/   *v.*   širiti(se), množiti(se)

propel /'pr,'pel/   *v.*   tjerati, pokretati

proper /'prop,/   *adj.*   svojstve; umjestan; prav, tačan,

properly /'prop,li/   *adv.*   tačno, ispravno

property /'prop,rti/   *n.*   imanje, vlasništvo; svojstvo

prophet /'profit/   *n.*   prorok

proportion /pr,'po:rš,n/   *n.*   omjer, razmjera

proposal /pr,'pouz,l/   *n.*   prijedlog, ponuda(bračna)

propose /pr,'pouz/   *v.*   predložiti; namjeravati

proprietor /pr,'praj,t,r/   *n.*   vlasnik, gospodar

prosecute /'prosikju:t/   *v.*   progoniti

prospect /'prospekt/   *n.*   izgled

prosper /'prosp,/   *v.*   napredovati, uspijevati

protect /pr,'tekt/   *v.*   zaštititi

protection /pr,'tekšn/   *n.*   zaštita

protest /'proutest/   *v.*   protestvovati, negodovati;   uvjeravati

protest /pr,'test/   *n.*   protest

protrude /pr,'tru:d/   *v.*   ispružiti(se); stršiti

proud /praud/   *adj.*   ponosan, ohol, dostojanstven, drzak

provide /pr,'vajd/   *v.*   pribaviti, pobrinuti se za

provoke /pr,'vouk/   *v.*   izazvati, uzbuditi

proximate /'proksimit/   *adj.*   najbliži

prudence /'pru:d,ns/   *n.*   razboritost, bistrina

prune /pru:n/   *n.*   šljiva

pseudonym /'sju:d,nim/   *n.*   pseudonim, drugo ime

psychiatrist /saj'kajetrist/   *n.*   psihijatar

pub /pab/   *n.*   krčma, birtija

puberty /'pju:b,rti/   *n.*   pubertet

public /'pablik/   *adj.*   javan, opšti, opći

publish /'pabliš/   *v.*   izdati knjigu

publisher /'pabliš,r/   *n.*   izdavač

pull /pul/   *v.*   vući, tegliti

pulp /palp/ *n.* meso (voća, ploda), pulpa
pulpit /'pulpit/ *n.* propovjedaonica
pulse /pals/ *v.* kucati, pulsirati; *n.* puls, bilo
pump /pamp/ *v.* pumpati; *n.* pumpa; cipela za ples
pumpkin /pampkin/ *n.* tikva, bundeva
pun /pan/ *n.* igra riječi; *v.* igrati se riječima
punch /panč/ *v.* udariti; probušiti; *n.* udarac; snaga
punctual /'panktjuel/ *adj.* tačan, točan
puncture /'pankč,r/ *n.* gumi defekt; *v.* probušiti se
punish /'paniš/ *v.* kazniti
pupil /'pju:pl/ *n.* zjenica; učenik, djak, štićenik
puppy /'papi/ *n.* štene
purchase /'p,:č,s/ *n.* kupovina, kupljena roba; *v.* kupiti, nabaviti
pure /pju,/ *adj.* čist, nepatvoren, čistokrvan
purge /p,:dž/ *n.* čistka; *v.* očistiti, istrijebiti
purple /'p,:pl/ *n.* ljubičasta boja; *adj.* ljubičast
purpose /'p,:p,s/ *n.* namjera, nakana, svrha
purse /p,:s/ *n.* ženska torbica, tašna
pursue /p,r'sju:/ *v.* baviti se, slijediti
pursuit /p,r'sju:t/ *n.* bavljenje, zanimanje; progon
push /puš/ *n.* guranje, potstrek; *v.* gurati, poticati
put, put, put /put, put, put/ *v.* staviti, metnuti, položiti
putty /'pati/ *n.* kit za pričvršćenje stakla
puzzle /'pazl/ *n.* zagonetka, zabuna, zbrka; *v.* zbuniti
pyjamas /p,'dža:m,s/ *n.* pidjama

Q

quack /kvaek/ *n.* gakanje; nadriljekar; šarlatan; *v.* gakati
quadrangular /kvo'draeng,l,r/ *adj.* četverougaoni
quadrant /'kvodr,nt/ *n.* kvadrant, četvrtina kruga
quagmire /'kwaegmaj,/ *n.* močvara, močvarno tlo
quaint /kvejnt/ *adj.* čudnovat, stran, neobičan
qualified /'kvolifajd/ *adj.* kvalifikovan, kvalificiran
quality /'kvoliti/ *n.* svojstvo, kakvoća, kvalitet
qualm /kvo:m/ *n.* tegoba, griža
quantity /'kvontiti/ *n.* količina, množina, kvantitet
quarrel /'kvo:r,l/ *n.* svadja, prepirka; *v.* svadjati se, prepirati se
quart /kvo:t/ *n.* mjera za tekućinu 1,136 l
quarter /'kvo:t,r/ *n.* četvrtina; frtalj, čejrek
quay /ki:/ *n.* zidana obala, pristanište, kej
queen /kvi:n/ *n.* kraljica
quench /kvenč/ *v.* ugasiti (vatru, žedj), zatomiti; savladati
query /'kvi,ri/ *n.* pitanje, ispitivanje; *v.* ispitivati, pitati
question /'kvešč,n/ *n.* pitanje; *v.* postaviti pitanje, upitati, ispitivati
queue /kju:/ *n.* red, niz; *v.* poredjati se u red
quick /kvik/ *adj.* brz, žustar, okretan
quicken /kvik,n/ *v.* ubrzati; oživjeti
quiet /'kvaj,t/ *adj.* tih, miran, spokojan; *v.* smiriti se
quilt /kvilt/ *n.* pokrivač, jorgan, štep deka; *v.* postaviti vatom
quince /kvins/ *n.* dunja
quit /kvit/ *adj.* riješen, slobodan, ostavljen, serbes; *v.* otići
quite /kvajt/ *adj.* sasvim, potpuno, taman
quotation /kvoutejš,n/ *n.* citat; navedena cijena, kvotacija; *v.* citirati

R

rabbit /'raebit/ *n.* kunić
raccoon /ra'ku:n/ *n.* rakun
race /rejs/ *n.* trka; rasa, pasmina, pleme, soj; *v.* trčati, juriti
rack /raek/ *n.* stalak, vješalica; raf; gepek; mučilište; *v.* mučiti
racket /'raekit/ *n.* reket; buka, graja, larma
racketeer /'raekiti:r/ *n.* ucjenjivač
radiant /'reidi,nt/ *adj.* sjajan, blistav
radiate /'reidijejt/ *v.* isijavati, zračiti
radish /'raediš/ *n.* rotkvica
rag /raeg/ *n.* krpa, dronjak, prnja; *v.* praviti "neslane" šale
rag-time /raegtajm/ *n.* muzički stil u Americi (1890-1920)
rage /rejdž/ *v.* bjesniti, goropaditi se; *n.* bijes, gnjev, žestina
ragged /'raegid/ *adj.* pocjepan, poderan; grub; rutav; nazubljen
raid /reid/ *n.* provala, iznenadan napad, racija
rail /rejl/ *n.* šina, tračnica; štanga, gelender; v.ružiti, grditi
railroad/railway /'rejlroud/'rejlvej/ *n.* željeznička pruga
rain /rejn/ *n.* kiša; *v.* kišiti, pada kiša
rainbow /'rejn,bou/ *n.* duga
raincoat /'rejn,kout/ *n.* kabanica, kišni kaput, regenmantil
raise /rejz/ *v.* podići; uzdići; naglasiti;uzbuditi; započeti
raisin /'rejzin/ *n.* grožđžica, rozina, suho grožđje
rake /rejk/ *n.* grablje; nagib; razvratnik; *v.* grabljati
rally /'raeli/ *n.* zbor; *v.* okupiti (se)
ramp /raemp/ *n.* rampa
rampage /'raempidž/ *n.* bijes, uzbuna; *v.* bjesniti
rampant /'raemp,nt/ *adj.* neobuzdan, žestok
ranch /raenč/ *n.* ranč, stočarska farma
random /'raend,m/ *adj.* besciljan, nasumice
range /rejndž/ *n.* djelokrug; opseg, skala; područje; *v.* redjati
rank /raenk/ *n.* red, čin, rang, položaj; *v.* poredjati, rangirati
rap /raep/ *n.* kucanje; stil u muzici u SAD 70-tih; *v.* kucati
rape /rejp/ *n.* silovanje, otmica; *v.* silovati

rare /re,r/ *adj.* rijedak, dragocjen, izvanredan

rash /raeš/ *n.* osip; *adj.* nagao

raspberry /ra:zb,ri/ *n.* malina

raspberry juice /ra:zb,ri djus/ *n.* himber, malinovac

rat /raet/ *n.* pacov, štakor; *v.* nanjušiti opasnost

rate /rejt/ *n.* omjer, cijena, tarif brzina, stopa, procenat

rather /'ra:dz,r/ *adv.* radije, više; prilično

ratio /'rejšiou/ *n.* srazmjer, odnos, proporcija

rational /'raeš,nl/ *adj.* racionalan, razuman, pametan

rattle /'raetl/ *v.* brbljati, klepetati; *n.* brbljanje

raven /'rejv,n/ *n.* gavran; *v.* proždirati, pljačkati

raw /ro:/ *adj.* sirov, prijesan; neobrađen; neiskusan

ray /rej/ *n.* zraka (svjetla)

rayon /'rei,n/ *n.* umjetna svila

razor /'rejz,r/ *n.* britva, razir

reach /ri:č/ *v.* dohvatiti, doseći; *n.* domet, opseg

react /ri'aekt/ *v.* reagovati, reagirati

read, read, read /ri:d, red, red/ *v.* čitati; glasiti

readable/legible /ri:d,bl/'ledž,bl/ *adj.* čitak, čitljiv

ready /'redi/ *adj.* spreman, gotov; voljan; sklon

real /ri,l/ *adj.* stvaran, realan

reality /ri'aeliti/ *n.* realnost, stvarnost

realize /'ri:,lajz/ *v.* ostvariti; shvatiti; anlaisati; zamisliti

really /'ri,li/ *adv.* zaista, stvarno

realm /relm/ *n.* kraljevstvo

realtor /'ri,lt,/ *n.* posrednik u prodaji nekretnina

rear /ri,r/ *n.* pozadina; *v.* uzgojiti; graditi

reason /'ri:z,n/ *n.* razum; razlog, povod

reasonable /'ri:zn,bl/ *adj.* opravdan; razborit, umjeren

rebel /'reb,l/ *n.* buntovnik, pobunjenik; *v.* buniti se

rebound /ri'baund/ *v.* odskočiti, odbiti se, skok pod košem

recall /ri'ko:l/ *v.* opozvati; sjetiti se

receipt /ri'si:t/ *n.* potvrda, račun

receive /ri'si:v/ *v.* primiti, dobiti, uzeti, prihvatiti, kabuliti

recent /'ri:s,nt/ *adj.* nov, nedavni

reception /ri'sepš,n/ *n.* primanje, (radio)prijem

recess /ri'ses/ *n.* pauza (školska), odmor, ferije

recipe /'risipi/ *n.* recept(kuharski)

reckless /'reklis/ *adj.* bezobziran; nesmotren

reckon /'rek,n/ *v.* računati, misliti

recognize /'rek,g,najz/ *v.* prepoznati, priznati, biti zahvalan

recommend /rek,mend/ *v.* preporučiti

recommendation /,rek,men'dejš,n/ *n.* preporuka

reconcile /'rek,nsajl/ *v.* izgladiti, pomiriti, uskladiti

record /ri'ko:d/ *v.* bilježiti, registrirati

record /'riko:d/ *n.* zapis, bilježenje, protokol; gramofonska ploča

recover /ri'kav,r/ *v.* oporaviti se, povratiti se, nadoknaditi

recreation /,rekri'ejš,n/ *n.* osvježenje, oporavak; zabava

rectangle /'rektaengle/ *n.* pravougaonik, pravokutnik

rectify /'rektifaj/ *v.* ispraviti, poboljšati

recycle /,ri'sajkl/ *v.* preradjivati po drugi put

red /red/ *adj.* crven; *n.* crvena boja

reduce /ri'dju:s/ *v.* svesti, smanjiti, reducirati; prisiliti

reed /ri:d/ *n.* trska, šaša

reel /ri:l/ *n.* kalem, čaura, rola, špula

refer /ri'f,:r/ *v.* uputiti na, odnositi se

reference /'refr,ns/ *n.* preporuka, referenca ; *v.* upućivanje na
preporuku

refill /'ri'fil/ *n.* uložak; *v.* ponovo napuniti, dopuniti

refine /ri'fajn/ *v.* (pro)čistiti, oplemeniti, rafinirati

reflect /ri'flekt/ *v.* odbijati; odražavati

reflection /ri'flekš,n/ *n.* odraz, odbijanje, refleks; misao; primjedba

reform /ri'fo:m/ *n.* poboljšanje, reforma; *v.* poboljšati, reformirati

refrain /ri'frejn/ *v.* obuzdati(se), uzdržati(se); *n.* refren, napjev

refresh /ri'freš/ *v.* osvježiti

refreshment /ri'frešm,nt/ *n.* osvježenje

refrigerator /ri'fridž,rejt,r/ *n.* frižider, hladnjak

refugee /,refju'dži:/ *n.* izbjeglica, muhadjir

refund /ri'fand/ *v.* vratiti novac, nadoknaditi, refundirati

refuse /ri'fju:z/ *v.* odbiti, reći ne; *n.* odpadak, smeće, rinfuza

regard /ri'ga:d/ *n.* obzir, poštovanje, pozdrav; *v.* smatrati, ticati se
regarding /ri'ga:ding/ *prep.* što se tiče, u vezi sa
regime /ri'ži:m/ *n.* režim, način života
regret /ri'gret/ *n.* žaljenje, kajanje, tuga; *v.* žaliti, požaliti
regulation /,regju'lejš,n/ *n.* propis, pravilo
rehearsal /ri'h,:sal/ *n.* proba(glume), pokus
rehearse /ri'h,:s/ *v.* probati, uvježbavati, ponavljati
reimburse /ri:im'b,:s/ *v.* nadoknaditi, obeštetiti
reject /ri'džekt/ *v.* odbiti, odbaciti
rejuvenate /ri'džu:vinejt/ *v.* podmladiti(se)
relation /ri'lejš,n/ *n.* odnos, veza; rodjak; pripovjetka
relationship /ri'lejš,nšip/ *n.* srodstvo; odnos
relative /ri'lejtiv/ *adj.* srodan, koji se odnosi; *n.* rodjak
relax /ri'laeks/ *v.* opustiti se, relaksirati se; olabaviti
release /ri'li:z/ *v.* osloboditi(se), kutarisati(se); *n.* oslobadjanje
relevant /'reliv,nt/ *adj.* primjenjiv, u vezi, relevantan
reliable /ri'laj,bl/ *adj.* pouzdan, siguran
reliance /ri'laj,ns/ *n.* pouzdanje, oslonac
relic /'relik/ *n.* relikvija; ostatak
relief /ri'li:f/ *n.* olakšanje; pomoć; oslobodjenje; reljef
religion /ri'lid,n/ *n.* religija, vjera, pobožnost, din
relinquish /ri'lingviš/ *v.* napustiti(pomisao), odreći se, odstupiti
reluctant /ri'lakt,nt/ *adj.* nesklon, nerad, koji okljeva
rely on /ri'laj on/ *v.* osloniti se, uzdati se
remain /ri'mejn/ *v.* preostati
remark /ri'ma:k/ *n.* primjedba; *v.* primijetiti
remarkable /ri'ma:k,bl/ *adj.* značajan, osobit
remedy /'remidi/ *n.* lijek, pomoć; *v.* liječiti, pomoći
remember /ri'memb,/ *v.* sjetiti se; podsjetiti; pamtiti, zapamtiti
remembrance /ri'membr,ns/ *n.* sjećanje, uspomena
remind /ri'majnd/ *v.* podsjetiti
reminder /ri'majnd,/ *n.* opomena
remit /ri'mit/ *v.* doznačiti, poslati novac
remittance /ri'mit,ns/ *n.* novčana doznaka
remorse /ri'mo:s/ *n.* grižnja savjesti, skrupula

remote /ri'mout/ *adj.* dalek, udaljen

remove /ri'mu:v/ *v.* ukloniti, udaljiti, otpustiti

rend, rent, rent /rend, rent, rent/ *v.* cijepati, kidati, raspuknuti se

rent /rent/ *n.* najam, zakupnina, kirija; *v.* iznajmiti, zakupiti

repair /ri'pe,/ *v.* popraviti, obnoviti, reparirati

repay /ri'pej/ *v.* vratiti dug (pare)

repeat /ri'pi:t/ *v.* ponoviti; *n.* ponavljanje

replace /ri'plejs/ *v.* zamijeniti, vratiti na staro mjesto

reply /ri'plaj/ *n.* odgovor; *v.* odgovoriti

report /ri'po:t/ *v.* izvještaj, svjedožba; svjedočanstvo *v.* izvjestiti, javiti

reporter /ri'po:t,/ *n.* izvještač, novinar, reporter

represent /,repri'z,nt/ *v.* predstavljati

representative /,repri'zent,tiv/ *n.* predstavnik; *adj.* reprezentativan, tipičan

reproach /ri'prouch/ *n.* prijekor, ukor; sramota; *v.* prekoriti, prebaciti

reptile /'reptajl/ *n.* gmizavac

reputable /'repjut,bl/ *adj.* ugledan, čestit

request /ri'kvest/ *n.* molba, potražnja; *v.* zamoliti, zatražiti

require /ri'kvaj,/ *v.* tražiti, zahtjevati, pozvati

requirement /ri'kvaj,me,nt/ *n.* potražnja, zahtjev

rescue /'reskju:/ *v.* spasiti, osloboditi; *n.* spasenje, oslobodjenje

research /ri's,:č/ *v.* istraživati; *n.* naučno istraživanje

resemble /rizembl/ *v.* sličiti, biti nalik na

resemblance /ri'zembl,ns/ *n.* sličnost

resent /ri'zent/ *v.* zamjeriti, biti uvrijedjen

resentful /ri'zentful/ *adj.* uvredljiv, kivan

reserve /ri'z,:rv/ *n.* zaliha, rezerva; ograničenje; *v.* zadržati, sačuvati

residence /'rezidens/ *n.* mjesto stanovanja, prebivalište

residue /'rezidju:/ *n.* ostatak, resto

resign /ri'zajn/ *v.* napustiti, odreći se, dati ostavku

resist /ri'zist/ *v.* odupirati se, odoljevati

resolute /'res,lju:t/ *adj.* nepopustljiv, odlučan, postojan

resolve /ri'zolv/ *v.* riješiti; rastvoriti

resort /ri'zo:t/ *n.* utočište; *v.* često pohađati

resource /ri'so:s/ *n.* izvor, vrelo, resurs; pomoćno sredstvo

respect /ris'pekt/ *n.* poštovanje, respekt; veza, odnos; *v.* poštovati, cijeniti

respectable /ri'spekt,bl/ *adj.* ugledan, čestit, uvažavan

respectful /ri'spektf,l/ *adj.* učtiv, pun poštovanja

respective /ris'pektiv/ *adj.* odnosan, svaki pojedini

respond /ris'pond/ *v.* odgovoriti, reagirati, reagovati

rest /rest/ *n.* odmor, počinak, rahatluk; *v.* odmarati se

restful /restful/ *adj.* opušten, smiren, spokojan, rahat

restless /'restlis/ *adj.* uznemiren, nespokojan

restore /ris'to:r/ *v.* obnoviti, rekonstruisati; uspostaviti

restrict /ris'trikt/ *v.* ograničiti, stegnuti

restroom /'restru:m/ *n.* toalet, javni klozet/zahod

result /ri'zalt/ *n.* rezultat, son

resume /'reizju:mei/ *n.* sažetak; curriculum vitae, kretanje u karijeri

resurrection /rez,rekš,n/ *n.* uskrsnuće

retain /ri'tejn/ *v.* zadržati, sačuvati, zapamtiti

retire /ri'taj,r/ *v.* povući (se); penzionisati(se)

retreat /ri'tri:t/ *v.* povući se, uzmaći, odstupiti; *n.* utočište

retrieve /ri'tri:v/ *v.* dozvati; ponovo dobiti

retrospect /'retrspekt/ *n.* osvrt na prošlost, retrospektiva

return /ri't,:rn/ *v.* vratiti(se); odgovoriti; zahvaliti; *n.* povratak

reveal /ri'vi:l/ *v.* otkriti, odati, raskrinkati

revenge /ri'vendž/ *n.* osveta; revanš; *v.* osvetiti se

reverse /ri'v,:s/ *adj.* naličje v. obrnuti; *adj.* obratan, suprotan

review /ri'vju:/ *v.* pregledati, pisati prikaz; *n.* pregled; kritika

revise /ri'vajz/ *v.* pregledati, ispravljati, revidirati

revival /ri'vajv,l/ *n.* oživljavanje, preporod

reward /ri'vo:d/ *n.* nagrada

rhyme /rajm/ *n.* stih, rima; praviti stihove

rib /rib/ *n.* rebro

ribbon /rib,n/ *n.* vrpca, traka

rice /rajs/ *n.* riža, pirinač

rich /ri^/ *adj.* bogat, imućan; obilat

rid, rid, ridded /rid, rid, 'ridid/ *v.* osloboditi (se), riješiti se

riddle /'ridl/ *n.* zagonetka; grubo sito; *v.* odgonetati

ride, rode, ridden /rajd, roud, 'ridn/ *v.* jahati, voziti se; *n.* jahanje, vožnja

ridiculous /ri'dikju:l,s/ *adj.* smiješan

rifle /rajfl/ *n.* puška; *v.* opljačkati

right /rajt/ *adv.* pràvo, pravično, ispravno; na desno; *n.* prâvo; *adj.* prav

rigid /ridžid/ *adj.* ukočen, krut, strog

rigorous /'rig,r,s/ *adj.* oštar, strog, nepopustljiv

rim /rim/ *n.* ivica, rub, rand; *v.* oivičiti

rind /rajnd/ *n.* kora, lupina; *v.* guliti koru

ring /ring/ *n.* prsten; kolut, halka; arena

ring, rang, rung /ring, raeng, rang/ *v.* zvoniti; okružiti; staviti prsten

rink /rink/ *n.* klizalište (vještačko)

rinse /rins/ *v.* ispirati, oplakivati; *n.* ispiranje, oplakivanje

riot /'rajot/ *n.* galama; nered; buna, kraval; *v.* činiti izgrede

rip /rip/ *v.* rasporiti, oporiti, parati

ripe /rajp/ *adj.* zreo, izrastao, razvijen

rise, rose, risen /rajz, rouz, 'riz,n/ *v.* podići(se), ustati, pobuniti

risk /risk/ *n.* rizik, opasnost; *v.* rizikovati, riskirati

risky /riski/ *adj.* riskantan, opasan

river /'riv,r/ *n.* rijeka

road /roud/ *n.* cesta, put, staza

roar /ro:r/ *v.* rikati, urlati, tutnjati; *n.* rika, grmljavina

roast /roust/ *v.* peći, pržiti; *n.* pećenje, pećenka

rob /rob/ *v.* pljačkati, orobiti

robber /'rob,r/ *n.* razbojnik, rauber, hrsuz

robe /roub/ *n.* haljina, nošnja; *v.* obući se, odjenuti se

robust /ro'bast/ *adj.* krepak, snažan

rock /rok/ *n.* stijena, litica, hrid; *v.* ljujlati se, njihati se

rocket /'rokit/ *n.* raketa

rod /rod/ *n.* šipka, prut, motka, štanga

roll /rol/ *v.* kotrljati, valjati, (za)motati; *n.* zamotuljak; kifla

roller-skates /'roul,r-skejt/ *n.* koturaljke, rolšue
roof /ru:f/ *n.* krov; *v.* pokriti krovom
room /ru:m/ *n.* soba, prostor, mjesto; mogućnost
room-mate /ru:m,mejt/ *n.* sobni kolega, cimer
rooster /ru:st,/ *n.* pijetao, pijevac, horoz
root /ru:t/ *n.* korjen, temelj; *v.* ukorijeniti, usaditi
rope /roup/ *n.* konopac, uže,konop, štrik
rose /rouz/ *n.* ruža, djul
rot /rot/ *n.* trulež, raspadanje; *v.* trunuti, propadati
rotate /'routejt/ *v.* okretati (se)
rotten /'rot,n/ *adj.* truo, gnjio, pokvaren, odvratan
rough /raf/ *adj.* hrapav, buran (more), opor, grub
round /raund/ *adj.* okrugao, pun; *v.* obilaziti, okružiti
route /ru:t/ *n.* put, cesta, trasa, maršuta
routine /ru:'ti:n/ *n.* izvježbanost, rutina; tok
row /rou/ *n.* niz, red; veslanje; *v.* veslati
row /rau/ *v.* galamiti, grditi, ružiti; *n.* svadja, gungula
royal /'roj,l/ *adj.* kraljevski, dostojanstven
royalty /'roj,lti/ *n.* autorski honorar, tantijema
rub /rab/ *n.* trenje, trljanje; neprilika; *v.* trljati, strugati
rubber /'rab,r/ *n.* guma,lastika; kaučuk
rubbish /rabiš/ *n.* smeće, otpaci, šund
rude /ru:d/ *adj.* grub, sirov, neotesan
rug /rag/ *n.* ćilim, sag
ruin /,rujn/ *n.* ruševina, ruina, harabatija *v.* uništiti, upropasti
rule /ru:l/ *n.* pravilo, propis, načelo; vlast; *v.* vladati
ruler /'ru:l,r/ *n.* vladar; ravnalo, linijar
rumor /'ru:m,r/ *n.* glasina, govorkanje; *v.* širiti glasine
run, ran, ran /ran, raen, raen/ *v.* trčati, juriti; biti u pogonu; *n.* trka
rural /'ru,rl/ *adj.* seoski, ruralan
rush /raš/ *v.* žuriti(se), navaliti; *n.* navala, potražnja
rust /rast/ *n.* rdja; *v.* rdjati, propadati
rusty /rasti/ *adj.* rdjav
ruthless /'ru:tlis/ *adj.* nemilosrdan
rye /raj/ *n.* raž

S

sack /saek/   *n.* vreća; torba; pljačkanje;   *v.* pljačkati

sacred /'sejkrid/   *adj.* svet, posvećen, crkven

sacrifice /'saekrifajs/   *n.* žrtva;   *v.* žrtvovati, posvetiti

sad /saed/   *adj.* žalostan, tužan, nepovoljan, jadan

saddle /'saedl/   *n.* sedlo; sarač, sedlar

safe /sejf/   *adj.* siguran, zaštićen, pouzdan;   *n.* sef, kasa

safety /'sejfti/   *n.* sigurnost

sag /saeg/   *v.* ulegnuti se, spustiti se

sail /sejl/   *n.* jedro, jedrenjak;   *v.* jedriti, ploviti

sailor /'sejlor/   *n.* mornar

saint /sejnt/   *n.* svetac;   *adj.* svet

salad /'sael,d/   *n.* salata

salary /'sael,ri/   *n.* plata

sale /sejl/   *n.* rasprodaja

salesman /'sejlsmen/   *n.* prodavac

saliva /s,'lajva/   *n.* pljuvačka, slina

salmon /'saem,n/   *n.* losos, som

salt /so:lt/   *n.* so, sol

salute /s,'lju:t/   *v.* pozdraviti;   *n.* pozdrav, selam

salvation /sael'vejš,n/   *n.* spas, spasenje

same /sejm/   *adj.* isti, nepromijenjen

sample /'sa:mpl/   *n.* uzorak, mustra

sanction /'saenkš,n/   *n.* sankcija, potvrda, odobrenje;   *v.* odobriti

sand /saend/   *n.* pijesak;   *v.* brusiti, šmirglati

sane /sein/   *adj.* razborit, zdrave pameti

sanitary /'saenit,ri/   *adj.* higijenski, zdravstveni, sanitaran

satire /'saetaj,r/   *n.* satira

satisfaction /,saetis'faekšin/   *n.* satisfakcija, zadovoljenje

satisfactory /'saetis'faektori/   *adj.* zadovoljavajući

satisfy /'saetis,fai/   *v.* zadovoljiti, udovoljiti, uvjeriti

Saturday /'saet,rdi/   *n.* subota

sauce /so:s/   *n.* saft, sos, umak

saucepan /'so:spaen/   *n.* lonac

saucer /so:s,r/   *n.* tanjirić
sausage /'sosidž/   *n.* kobasica, sudjuka (govedja kobasica)
savage /'saevidž/   *adj.* divlji;   *n.* divljak
save /sejv/   *v.* spasiti, sačuvati, izbaviti; uštediti
savior /'sejvj,r/   *n.* spasilac
savor /'sejv,r/   *n.* okus, tek;   *v.* imati okus
saw /so:/   *n.* pila, testera;   *v.* pilati, testerisati
say /sej/   *v.* reći, kazati
scale /skejl/   *n.* vaga, terazije; ljuska(ribe); mjerilo, razmjer
scar /ska:r/   *n.* ožiljak, brazgotina; ljaga; litica;   *v.* ostaviti br
scarce /ske,rs/   *adj.* rijedak, oskudan
scarcely /ske,sli/   *adv.* jedva
scare /ske,r/   *v.* preplašiti, prepasti
scarecrow /ske,rkro:/   *n.* strašilo za ptice
scarf /ska:f/   *n.* marama, šal, ešarpa
scatter /'skaet,r/   *v.* rasuti, raširiti; raštrkati
scene /si:n/   *n.* prizor, scena; mjesto radnje, pozornica
scent /sent/   *n.* miris, parfem, trag;   *v.* namirisati; nanjušiti
schedule /'skedžul/'šedju:l/ *n.* raspored, popis, tabela;   *v.* upisati, napraviti raspored
scheme /ski:m/ *n.* pregled, plan, program, šema;   *v.* planirati
scholar /'skol,r/   *n.* naučnik; učenik, stipendista
scholarship /'skol,ršip/   *n.* stipendija; naobrazba
school /sku:l/   *n.* škola
science /'saj,ns/ *n.* nauka, znanost (prirodna), sistematizirano znanje
scissors /'siz,z/   *n.* makaze, škare, nožice
scoop /sku:p/   *n.* kutljača, šefkel, kevčija;   *v.* izdubiti
scope /skoup/   *n.* djelokrug, vidokrug, područje
score /sko:r/   *n.* račun, dug; trag; ogrebotina;   *v.* pobijediti
scorn /sko:n/   *n.* prezir;   *v.* prezirati
scornful /sko:nful/   *adj.* prezriv
scout /skaut/   *n.* izvidjač, uhoda;   *v.* izvidjati
scramble /'skrembl/ *n.* žurba, gužva; *v.* pržiti jaja; verati se, otimati
scrap /skraep/   *n.* komadić, izrezak iz novina, staro gvoždje

scrape /skrejp/   *n.* struganje, grebanje, neprilika;   *v.* strugati

scratch /skraeč/   *n.* ogrebotina, laka rana;   *v.* izgrepsti

scream /skri:m/   *n.* vrisak;   *v.* vrisnuti

screen /skri:n/   *n.* zaslon, platno, perde

screw /skru:/   *n.* šaraf, vijak, zavrtanj;   *v.* zašarafiti, zavrnuti

screwdriver /skru:‚drajver/   *n.* šarafziger, odvijač

scribble /skribl/   *v.* šarati, črčkati

scrub /skrab/   *n.* grmlje, šiblje

scrutinize /'skru:tinajz/   *v.* istraživati, pregledati

sculpture /'skalpč‚r/ *n.* kip, skulptura; kiparstvo, vajarstvo

sea /si:/   *n.* more

seafood /si:fu:d/   *n.* hrana iz mora (ribe, školjke)

seal /si:l/   *n.* pečat, žig, muhur; tuljan;   *v.* zapečatiti

seam /si:m/   *n.* rub, šav, nat;   *v.* sašiti, spojiti šavom

seamstress /'semstris/   *n.* krojačica, švelja, šnajderica

search /s‚:rč/ *n.* traženje, pretraživanje;   *v.* pretraživati, ispitivati

seaside /'si:'sajd/   *n.* primorje, obalno područje

season /'si:z‚n/   *n.* godišnje doba, sezona;   *v.* začiniti

seasoned /'si:z‚nd/   *adj.* dozreo, suv

seasoning /'si:z‚ning/   *n.* začin, isušivanje

seat /si:t/   *n.* sjedište, mjesto; članstvo; boravište

seclude /si'klu:d/   *v.* odijeliti(se), odvojiti(se)

second /'sek‚nd/   *adj.* drugi, slijedeći;   *n.* sekunda

secondhand /'sek‚nd‚haend/   *adj.* upotrebljavan, rabljen, antikvaran

secret /si:krit/   *n.* tajna;   *adj.* tajni; šutljiv

secretary /'sekr‚tri/   *n.* sekretarica, tajnica

secrete /si'kri:t/   *v.* izlučivati; sakriti

section /'sekšin/   *n.* presjek; odsječak, paragraf

secular /'sekjul‚/   *adj.* svjetovni; stoljetni; laički

secure /si'kju‚r/   *adj.* siguran;   *v.* osigurati, zaštititi

security /si'kju‚riti/   *n.* sigurnost, bezbrižnost; kaucija

sedentary /'sednt‚ri/   *adj.* sjedečki (način života)

seduce /si'dju:s/   *v.* zavesti, namamiti

see, saw, seen /si:, so:, si:n/   *v.* vidjeti, shvatiti, razumjeti
seed /si:d/   *v.* sijati;   *n.* sjeme, klica
seek, sought /si:k, so:t/   *v.* čeznuti; tražiti; nastojati
seem /si:m/   *v.* učiniti se, izgledati
seep /si:p/   *v.* curiti, cijediti se
seize /si:z/   *v.* zgrabiti; prisvojiti; oteti
seldom /'seld,m/   *adv.* rijetko
select /si'lekt/   *v.* odabrati, izabrati
self, selves (pl.) /self, selvz/   *n.* sam, sami (pl)
self-defense /selfdifens/   *n.* samoodbrana
selfish /selfiš/   *adj.* sebičan
sell, sold, sold /sel, sold, sold/   *v.* prodavati, prodati
send, sent, sent /send, sent, sent/   *v.* poslati
sender /'send,r/   *n.* pošiljalac
senior /'si:nj,r/   *adj.* stariji;   *n.* stariji čovjek
sense /sens/   *n.* smisao; osjetilo, čulo; razum, svijest
senseless /'sensl,s/   *adj.* besmislen
sensible /'sensibl/   *adj.* osjetljiv; pametan; znatan
sensitive /'sensitiv/   *adj.* osjetljiv, lako uvredljiv; nj=ežan
sentence /'sent,ns/   *n.* rečenica; presuda, kazna;   *v.* osuditi
sentiment /'sentim,nt/   *n.* osjećanje, osjećaj; njeênost
separate /'sep,rejt/   *v.* odijeliti, rastaviti
separate /'seprit/   *adj.* odijeljen, poseban, obaška
September / sep'temb,r/   *n.* septembar, rujan
sequence /'si:kv,ns/   *n.* poredak, niz; tok dogadjaja
serene /si'ri:n/   *adj.* vedar, miran, ravnodušan, bezbrižan
serious /'si,rj,s/   *adj.* ozbiljan, važan; težak; opasan
servant /'s,:rv,nt/   *n.* sluga, sluškinja, hizmećar
serve /s,:rv/   *v.* služiti, posluživati, dobavljati
service /'s,:rvis/   *n.* usluga, servis; služba;
session /'seš,n/   *n.* sjednica, zasjedanje
set, set, set /set, set, set/   *v.* postaviti, metnuti, položiti, udesiti
setting /'seting/   *n.* postavljanje; zalazak
settle /'setl/   *v.* ustanoviti, nastaniti, smjestiti(se)
seven /'sevn/   *num.* sedam

seventeen /'sevn'ti:n/ *num.* sedamnaest

seventy /'sevnti/ *num.* sedamdeset

several /'sevr,l/ *adj.* nekoliko; više njih

severe /si'vi,r/ *adj.* surov, strog, oštar

sew, sewed, sewn /sou, soud, soun/ *v.* šiti

shade /šejd/ *n.* hladovina, sjena; sjenilo, širm; *v.* zasjeniti

shadow /'šaedou/ *n.* sjena

shady /'šejdi/ *adj.* sjenovit

shake, shook, shaken /šejk, šuk, šejkn/ *v.* drmati, tresti, titrati; klimati glavom; *n.* drmanje

shaky /'šejki/ *adj.* klimav, drmav

shall /šael/ *v.* treba da, morati

shallow /'šaelou/ *adj.* plitak; *n.* plićak

shame /šejm/ *n.* stid, sramota; *v.* posramiti

shape /šejp/ *n.* oblik, lik, kalup, uzorak; *v.* oblikovati

share /še,r/ *v.* dijeliti, imati udjela; *n.* udio, dionica

shark /ša:k/ *n.* ajkula, morski pas

sharp /ša:p/ *adj.* oštar, nabrušen, našiljen; lukav

shave, shaved, shaven /šejv, šejvd, šejv,n/ *v.* brijati (se)

she /ši:/ *pron.* ona

sheep /ši:p/ *n.* ovca, ovce

sheer /ši,r/ *adj.* okomit; čist; puki; krajnji

sheet /ši:t/ *n.* čaršaf, čaršav, plahta; ploča; arak papira

shelf, shelves /šelf, šelvz/ *n.* polica, rafa, regal

shell /šel/ *n.* ljuštura, ljuska

shelter /'šelt,r/ *n.* sklonište, zaklon; *v.* skloniti se, zakloniti

shield /ši:ld/ *n.* štit; grb; zaštitna ograda; *v.* štititi, braniti

shift /šift/ *n.* smjena radnika; varka; *v.* mijenjati, preseliti(se)

shine, shone, shone /šajn, šo:n, šo:n/ *v.* sijati, blistati; *n.* sjaj, blistanje, glanc

shiny /'šajni/ *adj.* sjajan, blistav

ship /šip/ *n.* brod, ladja; *v.* ukrcati na brod

shirt /š,:rt/ *n.* košulja (muška)

shit /šit/ *n.* vulg. sranje, govno; *v.* srati, kenjati

shiver /'šiv,r/ *n.* groznica; treska, špliter; *v.* drhtati, tresti se

shock /šok/   *n.* udarac, slom (živčani);   *v.* sudariti(se), potresti
shoe /šu:/   *n.* cipela, kundura; okov; potkovica;   *v.* obuti
shoelace /'šu:lejs/   *n.* pertla, šnura, veza za cipele
shoot, shot /šu:t, šot/   *v.* pucati, ispaliti; nicati
shop /šop/   *n.* dućan, magaza; radionica, pogon
shopping /šoping/   *v.* kupovati
shore /šo:/   *n.* obala; žal
short /šo:t/   *adj.* kratak, kusav, knap; oskudan, nedovoljan
short-sighted /'šo:rt'sajtid/   *adj.* kratkovidan
shortage /'šo:tidž/   *n.* manjak, nestašica, deficit
shorts /'šo:rc/   *n.* kratke hlače, šorc
should /šud/   *v.* prošlo vrijeme od "shall"
shoulder /'šould,/   *n.* rame; ivica puta, bankina
shout /šaut/   *v.* povik, usklik
shove /šav/   *v.* gurati(se), odbiti(se)
shovel /šavl/   *n.* lopata;   *v.* lopatom tovariti, zgrtati
show, showed, shown /šou, šoud, šoun/ *v.* pokazati, prikazati, otkriti.
show   *n.* prikaz, predstava
shower /'šav,r/   *n.* tuš; pljusak
shrewd /šru:d/   *adj.* lukav, oštrouman, pametan
shriek /šri:k/   *n.* vrisak, zvižduk;   *v.* zviždati
shrimp /šrimp/   *n.* rak, skamp
shrink, shrank, shrunk /šrink, šraenk, šrank/ *v.* smanjiti(se), skupiti(se)
shrub /šrab/   *n.* grm, grmlje
shrug /šrag/   *n.* slijeganje ramenima;   *v.* slijegati ramenima
shut /šat/   *v.* zatvoriti; uhapsiti
shy /šaj/   *adj.* stidljiv; plašljiv; oprezan;   *v.* popla[iti
sick /sik/   *adj.* bolestan, hasta
sickness /'sikn,s/   *n.* bolest
side /sajd/   *n.* strana; obala;   *v.* (side with) stati na nečiju stranu
sidewalk /sajdvo:k/   *n.* trotoar
siege /si:dž/   *n.* opsada
sieve /si:v/   *n.* sito
sift /sift/   *v.* sijati; prorešetati

sigh /saj/   *n.* uzdah;   *v.* uzdisati, čeznuti za

sight /sajt/   *n.* pogled, vidik, prizor;   *v.* gledati, promatrati

sign /sajn/   *n.* znak, napis; potpis;   *v.* potpisati se

signature /'signič,r/   *n.* potpis; znak

significance /sig'nifik,ns/   *n.* značenje, smisao; važnost

significant /'signifik,nt/   *adj.* značajan; karakteristčan

silence /'sajl,ns/   *n.* tišina;   *v.* ućutkati

silent /sajl,nt/   *adj.* miran, šutljiv, ćutljiv

silk /silk/   *n.* svila

silly /'sili/   *n.* glupan, budala;   *adj.* glup

silver /'silv,r/   *n.* srebro

similar /'simil,r/   *adj.* sličan

simmer /'sim,r/   *v.* vriti, ključati

simple /'simpl/   *adj.* jednostavan, prost, kolajli; čist

simplify /'simplifaj/   *v.* pojednostaviti, olakšati

sin /sin/   *n.* grijeh, prestup, povreda;   *v.* griješiti

since /sins/   *adv.* od; odonda; otkako; budući da

sincere /sin'si,r/   *adj.* iskren, čestit; prav

sincerely /sin'si,li/   *adv.* iskreno

sing, sang, sung /sing, saeng, sang/   *v.* pjevati

singe /sindž/   *v.* opržiti, opeći

single /'singl/   *adj.* jednostruk, pojedinačan; neoženjen, neudata

sinister /'sinist,r/   *adj.* koban, zloslutan, ugursuz

sink, sank, sunk /sink, saenk, sank/   *v.* tonuti; malaksati;   *n.* sink, sudoper, lavabo

sip /sip/   *n.* gutljaj, šluk, srkanje;   *v.* gucnuti, srknuti

sir /s,:r/   *n.* gospodin, efendija

sister /sist,r/   *n.* sestra

sister-in-law /'sist,r in,lo/   *n.* svastika, snaja, zaova, šurjakinja

sit, sat, sat /sit, saet, saet/   *v.* sjedititi, sjesti; zasjedati

site /sajt/   *n.* mjesto; položaj

sitting-room /'siting,ru:m/   *n.* dnevna soba, salon, voncimer

situation /,situ'ejšin/   *n.* situacija; položaj, služba

six /siks/   *num.* šest

size /sajz/   *n.* veličina, broj; obujam, format

skate /skejt/   *v.* klizati se;   *n.* klizaljka, sličura
skeleton /'skelitn/   *n.* kostur, skelet; okvir; skica
ski /ski/   *v.* skijati se, smučati;   *n.* skija
skill /'skil/   *n.* vještina, sposobnost, spretnost
skim /skim/   *v.* skidati kajmak/vrhnje
skin /skin/   *n.* koža, krzno, ljuska;   *v.* oguliti kožu
skinny /'skini/   *adj.* mršav
skip /skip/   *v.* preskočiti;   *n.* preskok
skirt /'sk,:rt/   *n.* suknja
skull /skal/   *n.* lobanja, lubanja
skunk /skank/   *n.* tvor; hulja, podlac, hinja
sky /skaj/   *n.* nebo
skylight /'skaj,lajt/   *n.* prozor na krovu
skyscraper /'skaj,skrejp,r/   *n.* neboder, oblakoder
slab /slaeb/   *n.* debeo komad (kamena, drveta, hljeba), tabak
slack /slaek/   *adj.* labav, nenategnut, loker
slam /slaem/   *v.* zalupiti, tresnuti;   *n.* tresak
slang /slaeng/   *n.* sleng, neknjiževni izraz
slap /slaep/   *v.* udariti, pljusnuti;   *n.* pljuska, šamar
slaughter /'slo:t,r/   *n.* pokolj, klanje
Slav /sla:v/   *n.* Slaven
slave /slejv/   *n.* rob;   *v.* robovati
sled /sled/   *n.* sanke, saonice, saone;   *v.* sankati se
sleep, slept, slept /sli:p, slept, slept/   *v.* spavati
sleep-over /sli:pov,r/   *n.* spavanje kod nekoga
sleepy /'sli:pi/   *adj.* pospan
sleeve /sli:v/   *n.* rukav, arml
slender /'slend,r/   *adj.* vitak, mršav, šlank; nježan
slice /slajs/   *n.* kriška, komad, šnita, parče;   *v.* rezati na kriške
slide, slid, slid /slajd, slid, slid/   *v.* klizati se, sklizati se
slim /slim/   *adj.* vitak, tanak; lukav; mali
slimy /slajmi/   *adj.* muljevit; podao, pis; puzav
slip /slip/   *v.* okliznuti se, omaknuti se;   *n.* papir sa informacijama
slipper /'slip,r/   *n.* papuča
slippery /'slip,ri/   *adj.* klizav, sklizak

slit /slit/ *n.* rascjep, šlic; *v.* rasjeći, rasporiti

slope /sloup/ *n.* padina, nagib, strmina

slot /slot/ *n.* prorez, uzak otvor

slovenly /'slavnli/ *adj.* nemaran, neuredan, šlampav

slow /slou/ *adj.* spor, lagan, trom

sly /slaj/ *adj.* lukav, prepreden, podmukao

small /smo:l/ *adj.* malen, sitan, neznatan

smart /sma:rt/ *adj.* pametan, bistar, dovitljiv; moderan, šik

smash /smaeš/ *v.* zdrobiti, smrskati, zgnječiti

smear /smi,r/ *n.* mrlja, razmaz, fleka; *v.* zamrljati, razmazati

smell, smelt, smelled /smel, smelt, smeld/ *v.* miris, smrad, zadah; *v.* mirisati, zaudarati

smile /smajl/ *v.* smijati se, smiješiti se; *n.* osmjeh, smješak

smith /smit/ *n.* kovač

smoke /smouk/ *n.* dim; pušenje; *v.* pušiti, dimiti se

smoker /'smouk,r/ *n.* pušač

smooth /smu:t/ *adj.* gladak, ravan, glat ; *v.* gladiti, poravnati

smuggle /'smagl/ *v.* krijumčariti, šmuglati

smuggler /'smagl,r/ *n.* krijumčar

snack /snaek/ *n.* zalogaj; užina, brz obrok

snail /snejl/ *n.* puž

snake /snejk/ *n.* zmija; *v.* vijugati

snap /snaep/ *v.* snimiti, škljocnuti, ispaliti; ugriz; škljocaj

snapshot /snaepšot/ *n.* fotografski snimak; *v.* snimiti

sneak /sni:k/ *n.* podlac, tužibaba; *v.* biti podmukao, odšuljati se

sneakers /'sni:k,rs/ *n.* teniske, tene

sneeze /sni:z/ *v.* kihati; *n.* kihanje, kijavica

sniff /snif/ *v.* njuškati; *n.* njuškanje

snore /sno:r/ *v.* hrkati; *n.* hrkanje

snout /snaut/ *n.* njuška, gubica, rilo

snow /snou/ *n.* snijeg; *v.* sniježiti

so /sou/ *adv.* tako; dakle, helem, elem

soak /souk/ *v.* namakati, kvasiti; *n.* namakanje

soap /soup/ *n.* sapun; *v.* nasapunjati

soar /so:r/ *v.* lebdjeti; vinuti se

sober /'soub,r/ *adj.* trijezan, staložen; *v.* otrijezniti se, smiriti se
soccer /'sok,r/ *n.* nogomet, futbal
sociable /'souš,bl/ *adj.* društven, socijalan
society /so'saj,ti/ *n.* društvo
sock /sok/ *n.* sokna, čarapa (kratka)
soft /soft/ *adj.* mekan, nježan, gladak; tih
soft drink /soft drink/ *n.* bezalkoholni napitak
soil /sojl/ *n.* tlo, zemlja, domovina; *v.* uprljati
soldier /'souldž,r/ *n.* vojnik, soldat, asker
sole /soul/ *n.* djon; taban; dno; *v.* podjoniti
solemn /'sol,m/ *adj.* svečan, važan, dostojanstven
solid /solid/ *adj.* čvrst; trajan; masivan
solitary /'solit,ri/ *adj.* usamljen
solitude /'solitju:d/ *n.* samoća, usamljenost
solve /solv/ *v.* razriješiti (problem)
some /sam/ *adj.* neki, nekakav, nešto
somebody /'samb,di/ *adj.* neko
somehow /'samhau/ *adv.* nakako
someone /'samuan/ *n.* neko
something /'samting/ *n.* nešto
sometime /'samtajm/ *adj.* raniji, prijašnji
sometimes /'samtajms/ *adv.* ponekada
somewhere /'samve:r/ *adv.* negdje
son /san/ *n.* sin
son-in-law /san,inlo/ *n.* zet
song /song/ *n.* pjesma
soon /su:n/ *adv.* uskoro
soothe /su:t/ *v.* umiriti, ublažiti
soothing /'su:ting/ *adj.* umirujuši
sophisticated /s,'fistikejtid/ *adj.* mudar, iskusan, unaprijedjen
sore /so:r/ *adj.* ranjav, bolan, osjetljiv
sorrow /'sorou/ *n.* žalost, jad, čemer; *v.* tugovati, žaliti
sorry /'so:ri/ *adj.* žalostan, zabrinut
sort /so:rt/ *n.* vrsta, sorta; *v.* razvrstati, sortirati
soul /soul/ *n.* duša

sound /saund/   *n.* zvuk, glas; sonda;   *adj.* zdrav;   *v.* zvučati
soup /su:p/   *n.* supa, juha, čorba
sour /'sau,r/   *adj.* kiseo; mrzovoljan; ogorčen;   *v.* ukiseliti se
source /so:rs/   *n.* izvor, vrelo
south /saut/   *n.* jug;   *adj.* južni;   *adv.* južno
sow, sowed, sown /sou, soud, soun/   *v.* sijati, posijati
space /spejs/   *n.* prostor; razmak; svemir
spacious /'spejš,s/   *adj.* prostran
spade /spejd/   *n.* lopata
spare /spe,r/   *v.* štedjeti, šparati;   *adj.* rezervni
spark /spa:rk/   *n.* iskra, varnica;   *v.* iskriti
sparrow /'spaerou/   *n.* vrabac
spasm /'spaez,m/   *n.* grč
speak, spoke, spoken /spi:k, spouk, spouk,n/   *v.* govoriti
speaker /'spi:k,r/   *n.* govornik
specialize /'spe[,lajz/   *v.* specijalizirati se
specimen /'spesimin/   *n.* primjerak, uzorak
spectacles /'spekt,kls/   *n.* naočare
spectator /'spektejt,r/   *n.* gledalac
speech /spi:č/   *n.* govor
speed, sped, sped /spi:d, sped, sped/   *v.* žuriti se
speed /spi:d/   *n.* brzina, žurba
spell /spel/   *v.* sricati, izgovarati
spelling /'speling/   *n.* pravopis
spend, spent /spend, spent/   *v.* trošiti (novac, vrijeme)
sphere /sfi,r/   *n.* kugla
spice /spajs/   *n.* mirodjija, začin;   *v.* začiniti
spicy /'spajsi/   *adj.* začinjen, pikantan; nepristojan
spider /spajder/   *n.* pauk
spill, spilled, spilt /spil, spild, spilt/   *v.* proliti, prosuti
spin, spun, spun /spin, span, span/   *v.* okretati, vrtiti
spinach /'spinič/   *n.* špinat, spanać
spine /spajn/   *n.* kičma, kralježnica; trn
spirit /'spirit/   *n.* duh, duša; raspoloženje
spiritual /'spiriču,l/   *adj.* duhovni, duševni

spit, spat, spat /spit, spaet, spaet/   *v.* pljuvati; nabosti
spite /spajt/   *n.* pakost; prkos, inat
spiteful /spajtful/   *adj.* pakostan, zloban
splash /splaš/   *v.* prskati, štrcati, špricati
splendid /'splendid/   *adj.* sjajan, divan
splinter /'splint,r/   *n.* krhotina, iver, špliter
split, split, split /split,split,split/ *v.* rascijepiti, raspući;   *n.*   pukotina
spoil, spoilt, spoiled /spojl, spojlt, spojld/   *v.* pokvariti; razmaziti
sponge /spandž/   *n.* spužva, sundjer;   *v.* očistiti spužvom
spontaneous /spon'tejn,s   *adj.* spontan, prirodan
spool /spu:l/   *n.* kalem, špula
spoon /spu:n/   *n.* kašika, žlica
spot /spot/   *n.* mrlja, fleka; mjesto; tačka;   *v.* zamrljati
spouse /spauz/   *n.* supružnik, bračni drug
spout /spaut/   *n.* njuška; kljun; mlaz   *v.* šiknuti, briznuti
sprain /sprejn/   *v.* iščašiti;   *n.* iščašenje
spread /spred/   *v.* raširiti, prostrijeti, prekriti
spring, sprang, sprung /spring, spraeng, sprang/ *v.* skočiti; uzletjeti;
spring /spring/   *n.* proljeće; izvor
sprinkle /'sprinkl/   *v.* prskati, škropiti
spy /spaj/   *n.* špijun, uhoda;   *v.* špijunirati, uhoditi
square /sve,r/   *n.* kvadrat; trg, mejdan, plac; *adj.* kvadratni; pošten
squash /skvoš/   *v.* zgnječiti;   *n.* kaša, vošni sok
squeeze /skvi:z/   *v.* stisnuti, gnječiti;   *n.* stisak
squirrel /'skv,:rel/   *n.* vjeverica
stab /staeb/   *v.* ubosti;   *n.* ubod
stable /'stejbl/   *adj.* stabilan, postojan;   *n.*   stabilnost, stalnost
stack /staek/   *n.* plast, stog; gomila
staff /sta:f/   *n.* osoblje, personal
stage /stejdž/   *n.* pozornica, scena, bina
stagnant /'staegn,nt/   *adj.* ustajao, koji stagnira
stain /stejn/   *n.* mrlja, fleka;   *v.* mrljati, flekati; obojiti
stair /ste,r/   *n.* stepenica, basamak
staircase /'ste,r,kejs/   *n.* stepenište, stubište, haustor
stake /stejk/   *n.* ulog, interes;   *v.* rizikovati, poduprijeti kolcem

stale /stejl/   *adj.* zagušljiv, ustajao, bajat
stand up /staend ap/   *v.* ustati
stand, stood, stood /staend, stud, stud/ *v.* stajati; izdržati;   *n.*
štand, tezga; stajalište
star /sta:r/   *n.* zvijezda
starch /sta:č/   *v.* uštirkati;   *n.* štirak
stare /ste,r/   *v.* buljiti, ukočeno gledati
start /sta:t/   *v.* krenuti, trgnuti se;   *n.* početak; polazak
starvation /sta:'vejš,n/   *n.* gladovanje, umiranje od gladi
starve /sta:rv/   *v.* gladovati
state /stejt/   *n.* država; stanje, prilike;   *v.* navesti, ustanoviti
statement /'stejtm,nt/   *n.* izjava, iskaz
station /'stejš,n/   *n.* stanica;   *v.* stacionirati
stationary /'stejš,n,ri/   *adj.* nepomićan, stabilan
stationery /'stejšn,ri/   *n.* pribor za pisanje
statue /'staet'ju:/   *n.* kip, statua
stay /stej/   *v.* boraviti; stajati; stanovati
steady /'stedi/   *adj.* stalan, čvrst, stabilan
steak /stejk/   *n.* šnicla, odrezak
steal, stole, stolen /sti:l, stoul, stoul,n/   *v.* krasti, ukrasti
steam /sti:m/   *n.* para, dunst;   *v.* pušiti se
steel /sti:l/   *n.* čelik;   *adj.* čeličan
steep /sti:p/   *adj.* strm;   *n.* strmina, ponor
steer /sti:r/   *v.* kormilariti
steering wheel /'sti,ring,vi:l/   *n.* volan
stem /stem/   *n.* stabljika, peteljka; deblo
step /step/   *n.* korak; stepenica;   *v.* koračati, stupati
stepmother / stepfather /'stemad,r/step,fa:d,r/   *n.* maćeha / očuh
stew /stju:/   *v.* dinstati, pirjati   *n.* meso (voće) skuhano u pari, kaša
stick /stik/   *n.* štap, prut, batina
sticky /'stiki/   *adj.* ljepljiv
stiff /stif/   *adj.* ukočen, krut
still /stil/   *adj.* miran; još uvijek
stimulate /'stimjul,jt/   *v.* poticati, stimulirati
sting /sting/   *n.* ubod, žaoka; štih   *v.* ubosti

stingy /'stindži/   *adj.* škrt, oskudan
stink, stank, stunk /stink, staenk, stank/ *v.* smrdjeti, zaudarati
stink /stink/   *n.* smrad
stir /st,:r/   *v.* mješati
stitch /stič/   *n.* štih; očica;   *v.* šiti
stock /stok/   *n.* panj, deblo; rod; zaliha; dionica;   *v.* nakrcati
stocking /'stoking/   *n.* čarapa
stomach /'stam,k/   *n.* stomak, želudac
stone /stoun/   *n.* kamen; košpica; zrno
stool /stu:l/   *n.* šamlica, hoklica
store /sto:r/   *n.* dućan (am.); skladište; depo, magaza
storm /sto:rm/   *n.* oluja; juriš;   *v.* bjesniti
story /'sto:ri/   *n.* pripovjetka, novela; sprat, kat
stove /stouv/   *n.* peć, šporet, furuna
straight /strejt/   *adv.* pravo, ravno; ad. prav, ravan
strain /strejn/   *v.* naprezati;   *n.* napor
strand /straend/   *n.* obala, žalo
strange /strejndž/   *adj.* stran, čudan
stranger /'strejndž,r/   *n.* stranac
strangle /'straengl/   *v.* zadaviti
strap /straep/   *n.* pojas, remen, kajš;   *v.* opasati se
straw /stro:/   *n.* slama, slamka
strawberry /'stro:beri/   *n.* jagoda
stray /strej/   *v.* zalutati; zastraniti
stream /stri:m/   *n.* struja; potok;   *v.* teći, curiti
street /stri:t/   *n.* ulica, sokak
strength /strent/   *n.* snaga, moć, kuvet
stress /stres/   *n.* pritisak, napetost, stres;   *v.* naglasiti
stretch /streč/   *n.* rastezanje, napetost;   *v.* rastegnuti
strike /strajk/   *v.* udariti, tući, štrajkovati;   *n.* štrajk
string /string/   *v.* konopac, vrpca, djerdan, šnjura;   *v.* nanizati
strings /strings/   *n. pl.* gudački instrumenti
strive, strove, striven /strajv, strouv, strivn/   *v.* težiti, truditi se, boriti se
stroke /strouk/   *n.* udarac; kap;   *v.* gladiti, milovati

stroll /stroul/   *v.* lutati, šetati;   *n.* šetnja
strong /strong/   *adj.* snažan, moćan, silan
structure /'strakč,r/   *n.* gradja, struktura; gradjevina
struggle /'stragl/   *v.* boriti se, otimati se;   *n.* borba, otimanje
stubborn /'stab,n/   *adj.* tvrdoglav, inadjija
study /stadi/   *n.* učenje; radna soba;   *v.* studirati
stuff /staf/   *v.* trpati, puniti, filovati;   *n.* gradja, stvar
stumble /'stambl/   *v.* spotaknuti se, posrnuti
stun /stan/   *v.* zapanjiti; zaglušiti (bukom)
stupid /'stju:pid/   *adj.* glup, budala
stupidity /'stu:piditi/   *n.* glupost, budalaština
sturdy /'st,:rdi/   *adj.* krupan, debeo; jak, snažan
stutter /'stat,r/   *v.* mucati
style /stajl/   *n.* stil, način života; moda
subdue /s,b'dju:/   *v.* podvrgnuti; obuzdati; ublažiti
subject /'sabdžikt/   *n.* predmet, sadržaj;   *adj.* podložan
subject /s,b'djekt/   *v.* podvrgnuti, izložiti
submarine /sabm,'ri:n/   *n.* podmornica
submit /s,b'mit/   *v.* podvrgnuti; pokoriti(se) predložiti
subscribe /s,b'skrajb/   *v.* pretplatiti(se); potpisati
subsidiary /s,b'sidj,ri/   *adj.* pomoćni, dopunski
subsidize /'sabsidajz/   *v.* pomagati (novčano), subvencionirati
substantial /sab'staenš,l/   *adj.* bitan, znatan
substitute /'sabstitju:t/   *v.* nadomjestiti, zamijeniti
subtle /'satl/   *adj.* fin, nježan
subtract /sab'traekt/   *v.* oduzeti
suburb /sab,:rb/   *n.* predgradje
subway /'sabvej/   *n.* podzemna željeznica
succeed /s,k'si:d/   *v.* slijediti; uspjeti, poći za rukom
successful /s,k'sesful/   *adj.* uspješan
such /sač/   *adj.* takav, taj
suck /sak/   *v.* sisati; upiti
sudden /'sadn/   *adj.* iznenadan, nagao
suddenly /'sadnli/   *adv.* iznenada, naglo
sue /sju:/   *v.* optužiti, tužiti sudu

suffer /'saf,r/   *v.* patiti, podnositi
sufficient /s,'fiš,nt/   *adj.* dovoljan
suffocate /'safokejt/   *v.* daviti (se), gušiti (se)
sugar /'šug,r/   *n.* šećer   *v.* zašećeriti
suggest /s,'djest/   *v.* predložiti, sugerisati
suggestion /s,'dješč,n/   *n.* prijedlog, sugestija
suicide /,su:i'sajd/   *n.* samoubistvo
suit /sju:t/   *n.* odijelo; parnica; molba;   *v.* prilagoditi, pristajati
suitable /sju:t,bl/   *adj.* odgovarajući, prikladan
suitcase /'su:tkejs/   *n.* kofer, kovčeg
sum /sam/   *n.* suma, svota, zbir
summary /'sam,ri/   *n.* rezime, kratak sadržaj
summer /'sam,r/   *n.* ljeto
summer resort /'sam,r ri'so:rt/   *n.* ljetovalište
summon /'sam,n/   *v.* pozvati, sazvati
sun /san/   *n.* sunce;   *v.* sunčati se
Sunday /'sandi/   *n.* nedelja
sunny /'sani/   *adj.* sunčan
sunrise /'san-rajz/   *n.* izlazak sunca
sunset /'san-set/   *n.* zalazak sunca
sunshine /'sanšajn/   *n.* sunčev sjaj
superb /sju:'p,:rb/   *adj.* sjajan, fantastičan, izvanredan
superficial /,su:p,rfiš,l/   *adj.* površan
superstition /su:per'stiš,n/   *n.* praznovjerje
supervise /'sup,rvajz/   *v.* nadzirati
supper /'sap,r/   *n.* večera
supplier /s,'plaj,r/   *n.* nabavljač, liferant
supply /s,'plaj/   *n.* nabavljati, snabdjevati, obskrbiti
support /s,'po:rt/   *v.* nositi, podupirati; izdržavati
suppose /s,'pouz/   *v.* smatrati, predpostavljati
suppress /s,'pres/   *v.* gušiti, ugušiti
supreme /s,'pri:m/   *adj.* nadmoćan
sure /šu,r/   *adj.* siguran, pouzdan
surface /'s,:rfis/   *n.* površina
surgery /'s,:rdž,ri/   *n.* hirurgija; operacija

surname /'s,:rnejm/   *n.* prezime; nadimak
surpass /s,:r'paes/   *v.* nadmašiti
surplus /'s,:rplas/   *n.* višak
surprise /s,r'prajz/   *n.* iznenadjenje;   *v.* iznenaditi
surrender /s,'rend,r/   *n.* predaja;   *v.* predat se
surround /s,'raund/   *v.* okrušiti, opkoliti
surroundings /s,'raundings/   *n. pl.* okolina, okoliš
survive /s,r'vajv/   *v.* preživjeti
suspect /s,s'pekt/   *v.* sumnjati, sumnjičiti, posumnjati
suspect /'saspekt/   *adj.* sumnjiv
suspense /s,s'pens/   *n.* neizvjesnost
suspicious /s,s'piš,s/   *adj.* sumnjičav, sumnjiv
sustain /s,s'tejn/   *v.* podnositi; izdržati; podupirati
swallow /'svolou/ *v.* progutati;   *n.* lastavica; ždrijelo; gutljaj
swamp /'svomp/   *n.* močvara
swan /svo:n/   *n.* labud
swear, swore, sworn /swe,r, swo:, swo:rn/   *v.* zaklinjati (se)
sweat /svet/   *v.* znojiti se;   *n.* znoj
sweatshirt /svetš,:rt/   *n.* trenerka (gornji dio)
sweep, swept, swept /svi:p, svept, svept/ *v.* mesti; pojuriti;
zamahnuti;   *n.* metenje; dohvat
sweet /svi:t/   *adj.* sladak; ugodan; ljubak
sweetheart /svi:tha:rt/   *n.* dragi, draga
swell, swelled, swollen /svel, sveld, 'svoul,n/   *v.* nateći,
nabreknuti swelling /sveling/   *n.* oteklina
swift /svift/   *adj.* brz, hitar, od čibuka
swim /svim/   *v.* plivati
swimming /sviming/   *n.* plivanje
swimming pool /'sviming,pu:l/   *n.* bazen za plivanje
swimsuit /'svimsju:t/   *n.* kupaći kostim
swine /svajn/   *n.* svinja
swing, swung, swung /sving, svang, svang/ *v.* njihati, ljuljati;
vitlati;   *n.* ljuljanje; zamah
switch /svič/   *n.* prekidač, šalter; šiba; skretnica;   *v.* prekinuti
sword /svo:d/   *n.* mač

T

tab /taeb/ *n.* etiketa
table /'tejbl/ *n.* sto, sofra; tabla; tabela
tablecloth /tejbl,klos/ *n.* stoljnjak
tablespoon /'tejbl-spu:n/ *n.* kašika, žlica
tablet /'taeblit/ *n.* tableta, pilula; pločica
tackle /'taekl/ *n.* pribor; kolotura; *v.* latiti se
tag /taeg/ *n.* privjesak, etiketa; *v.* staviti privjesak, nadovez
tail /tejl/ *n.* rep; povlaka
tailor /'tejl,r/ *n.* krojač, šnajder; *v.* krojiti, šiti (odijela)
take, took, taken /tejk, tuk, tejk,n/ *v.* uzeti; primiti; zgrabiti
tale /tejl/ *n.* pripovjetka, priča, bajka
talk /to:k/ *n.* razgovor; *v.* govoriti
talkative /to:kativ/ *adj.* razgovorljiv, pričljiv
tame /'tejm/ *v.* pripitomiti; *adj.* pitom
tan /taen/ *v.* pocrniti (od sunca); *adj.* preplanuo
tangerine /taendž,ri:n/ *n.* mandarina
tangible /'taendž,bl/ *adj.* opipljiv (fig.)
tangle /'taengl/ *n.* zbrka; *v.* zamrsiti
tank /taenk/ *n.* cisterna, tank; tenk
tap /taep/ *n.* pipa, slavina; *v.* tapkati, kuckati
tape /tejp/ *n.* pantljika, traka, vrpca, štrajfna
tape recorder /'tejp-ri,ko:rd,r/ *n.* magnetofon, kasetofon
tapestry /'taepistri/ *n.* tapiserija, goblen
target /'ta:git/ *n.* meta, nišan, cilj
tarnish /'ta:rniš/ *v.* potamniti, izgubiti sjaj
tart /ta:t/ *adj.* kiseo; *n.* torta
task /ta:sk/ *n.* zadatak, zadaća
taste /tejst/ *n.* ukus, okus, šmek; *v.* probati, kušati
tasteless /tejstles/ *adj.* neukusan
tasty /'tejsti/ *adj.* ukusan
tax /taeks/ *n.* porez; *v.* oporezovati
tea /ti:/ *n.* čaj

teach, taught, taught /tiːč, toːt, toːt/ *v.* podučavati, učiti nekoga
teacher /'tiːč,r/ *n.* učitelj, nastavnik
teapot /'tiːpot/ *n.* čajnik
tear, tore, torn /ti,r, toːr, toːrn/ *v.* derati, trgati, cjepati
tease /tiːz/ *v.* zadirkivati, bockati, gnjaviti
technique /tek'nik/ *n.* tehnika
technology /tehnolodži/ *n.* tehnologija
tedious /'tiːdies/ *adj.* dosadan, mučan
teenager /'tiː,nejdž,r/ *n.* tinejdjer
tell, told, told /tel, tould, tould/ *v.* reći, kazati, izjaviti, saopštiti
temper /'temp,r/ *n.* narav, ćud, karakter,tabijat; *v.*ublažiti, umanjiti
temple /'templ/ *n.* hram; sljepoočnica
temporary /'temp,r,ri/ *adj.* privremen
tempt /tempt/ *v.* iskušavati, mamiti
temptation /temp'tejšin/ *n.* iskušenje, napast
ten /ten/ *num.* deset
tenant /'ten,nt/ *n.* podstanar, stanar, kirajdjija
tend /tend/ *v.* smjerati, naginjati, težiti
tender /'tend,r/ *adj.* nježan, mek, osjetljiv; *n.* ponuda
tense /tens/ *adj.* napet, krut
tension /tenš,n/ *n.* napetost
tent /tent/ *n.* šator; tenda
term /t,:rm/ *n.* rok, trajanje
terminate /'t,:rminejt/ *v.* ograničiti, dokrajčiti, svršiti
terrible /'teribl/ *adj.* strašan, užasan
terrific /'terifik/ *adj.* izvanredan, strašan
terrify /'terifaj/ *v.* strašiti, prepadati
testify /'testifaj/ *v.* svjedočiti, dokazivati
testimony /'testimouni/ *n.* svjedočenje, iskaz
texture /'tekšč,r/ *n.* gradja, sastav, struktura
than /dzen/ *conj.* nego, od
than /dzen/ *adv.* tada, onda; zatim
thank /taenk/ *v.* zahvaliti
thank you /taenk juː/ *exp.* hvala
thanks /taenks/ *pl.* hvala

Thanksgiving Day /'taenksgiving dej/ *n.* svetkovina zahvalnosti (zadnji četvrtak u novembru)

that /daet/ *pron.* onaj, ona ono; da; za; da bi

thaw /to:u/ *v.* topiti, rastopiti

theater /'ti,t,r/ *n.* kino; pozorište, kazalište, teatar

theft /teft/ *n.* kradja

their /dze,r/ *pron.* njihov

theme /ti:m/ *n.* tema, predmet

there /dze,r/ *adv.* tamo

therefore /'dze,r,fo:r/ *adv.* zbog toga, dakle

they /dzej/ *pron.* oni

thick /tik/ *adj.* gust, debeo

thickness /'tiknis/ *n.* gustoća, gustina

thief /ti:f/ *n.* lopov, kradljivac, hrsus, tat

thigh /taj/ *n.* bedro, but

thin /tin/ *adj.* tanak; rijedak; mršav; *v.* prorijediti, slabiti

thing /ting/ *n.* stvar, predmet; biće, stvor

think, thought, thought /tink, 'to:t, 'to:t/ *v.* misliti, razmišljati

third /t,:rd/ *adj.* treći

thirsty /'t,:rsti/ *adj.* žedan

this /tis/ *pron.* ovaj, ova, ovo

thorn /to:rn/ *n.* trn

thorough /'t,rou/ *adj.* potpun, temeljit

thought /to:t/ *n.* misao

thoughtful /'to:tful/ *adj.* zamišljen

thousand /'tauz,nd/ *num.* hiljada, tisuća

thrash /traeš/ *v.* izmlatiti, istući; *n.* mlaćenje

thread /tred/ *n.* konac, nit

threat /tret/ *n.* prijetnja

threaten /tret,n/ *v.* prijetiti

three /tri:/ *num.* tri, trojka, trica

threshold /'traešould/ *n.* prag

thrifty /'trifti/ *adj.* štedljiv

thrill /tril/ *v.* obuzeti, prožeti; *n.* jeza

thrilling /triling/ *adj.* uzbudljiv

throat /trout/ *n.* grlo
throw, threw, thrown /trou, tru:, troun/ *v.* baciti
throw /trou/ *n.* bacanje, hitac, domet; rastojanje
thrust, thurst, thurst /trast, trast, trast/ *v.* ubosti; gurati
thumb /tam/ *n.* palac
thunder /'tand,r/ *n.* grmljavina; *v.* grmiti
thunderstorm /'tander-sto:m/ *n.* oluja sa grmljavinom
Thursday /'t,:rz-dej/ *n.* četvrtak
thus /tas/ *adv.* tako, prema tome, helem, elem
tick /tik/ *n.* krpelj; presvlaka, jastučnica; *v.* kuckati
ticket /'tikit/ *n.* ulaznica, karta; ceduljica; *v.* staviti oznaku
tickle /'tikl/ *v.* škakljati, golicati
tide /tajd/ *n.* vrijeme, doba; plima i osjeka
tidy /'tajdi/ *adj.* uredan, pristojan; *v.* pospremiti
tie /taj/ *n.* kravata; veza, vrpca; *v.* vezati kravatu, stegnuti
tiger /'tajg,r/ *n.* tigar
tight /tajt/ *adj.* tijesan, nepropustljiv; čvrst; napet
tights /tajts/ *n.* triko, štrumfhozne
tile /tail/ *n.* crijep; keramička pločica
tilt /tilt/ *v.* nagnuti (se); *n.* nagib, kosina
timber /'timb,r/ *n.* deblo; greda; drveće
time /tajm/ *n.* vrijeme, doba, vakat; puta
timid /'timid/ *adj.* bojažljiv, plašljiv
tin /tin/ *n.* lim, kalaj, kositar; konzerva; *v.* kalajisati
tingle /tingl/ *v.* zvoniti, brujati
tint /tint/ *v.* obojiti, šarati; *n.* nijansa, osjenjivanje
tiny /'tajni/ *adj.* sićušan
tip /tip/ *n.* vrh; napojnica, bakšiš; savjet
tipsy /'tipsi/ *adj.* pripit
tire /'taj,r/ *n.* guma na točku; *v.* umoriti se
tired /'taj,rd/ *adj.* umoran
tissue /'tišu:/ *n.* tkivo; tanka tkanina
title /tajtl/ *n.* naslov; titula; *v.* nasloviti, nazvati
to /tu:/ *prep.* ka, prema, na, za, sve, do
toast /toust/ *n.* prepećenac, tost; zdravica; *v.* pržiti

tobacco /t,'baekou/ *n.* duhan, duvan

today /t,'dej/ *adv.* danas

toddle /'todl/ *v.* gegati se

toddlers /'todl,rs/ *n.* djeca koja pužu

toe /tou/ *n.* prst na nozi

together /t,'gedz,r/ *adv.* zajedno; odjednom

token /'toukn/ *n.* žeton; znak; uspomena, dar

tolerate /'tol,rejt/ *v.* podnositi, tolerisati

toll /toul/ *n.* cestarina, putarina, mostarina; daća

tomato /t,'mejtou/ *n.* paradajz, rajčica

tomb /tu:m/ *n.* grobnica, grob, mezar

tomorrow /t,'mo:rou/ *n.* sutra

ton /tan/ *n.* tona

tone /toun/ *n.* glas, zvuk; način govora, ton; naglasak

tongue /tang/ *n.* jezik; govor

tonight /t,'najt/ *n.* večeras

too /tu:/ *adv.* takodje; previše

tool /tu:l/ *n.* alat, orudje, sredstvo

tooth, teeth /tu:s, ti:s/ *n.* zub, zubi

toothache /tu:sejk/ *n.* zubobolja

toothbrush /tu:sbraš/ *n.* četka za zube

top /top/ *n.* vrh, vrhunac, tepa, špic; gornji dio

torch /to:č/ *n.* baklja; djepna lampa, baterija

torment /'to:m,nt/ *n.* muka

torment /to:'ment/ *v.* mučiti

torture /to:rč,r/ *n.* mučenje; *v.* mučiti

toss /tos/ *v.* bacati u vis; prevrtati

touch /tač/ *n.* dodir; *v.* dodirnuti

tough /taf/ *adj.* težak, tegoban; žilav

tow /tou/ *v.* tegliti; *n.* tegljenje

towards /,'vo:dz/ *prep.* ka, prema za

towel /'tau,l/ *n.* peškir, ručnik

tower /'tau,r/ *n.* toranj, kula

town /taun/ *n.* grad, šeher

toy /toj/ *n.* igračka

trace /trejs/ *n.* trag; *v.* tragati, slijediti
track /traek/ *n.* staza, pruga; kolotečina; *v.* tragati
trade /trejd/ *n.* trgovina; zanat; *v.* trgovati; *adj.* trgovački
traffic /'traefik/ *n.* promet, saobraćaj; *v.* trgovati
trail /trejl/ *v.* vući (se); tragati; *n.* trag, rep
train /trejn/ *n.* voz, vlak; *v.* odgojiti, trenirati, izobraziti
traitor /'trejtor/ *n.* izdajica
tram /traem/ *n.* tramvaj
tramp /traemp/ *n.* skitnica
tranquil /'traenkvil/ *adj.* spokojan, miran
tranquility /traen'kviliti/ *n.* spokoj, mirnoća
transcend /traen'send/ *v.* nadmašiti, natkriliti
transfer /traens'f,:r/ *n.* prenos;   *v.*   prenijeti, premjestiti
transform /traens'fo:rm/ *v.* pretvoriti, preobraziti
translate /traens'lejt/ *v.* prevoditi, prevesti
translation /traens'lejš,n/ *n.* prevod, prijevod
transparent /traens'pae,r,nt/ *adj.* proziran, providan
transportation /,traenspo:r'tejš,n/ *n.* prevoz, transport
trap /traep/ *n.* zamka, klopka, busija, zasjeda; *v.* upasti u klopku
trash /traeš/ *n.* smeće; besmislica
travel /'traevl/ *v.* putovati; *n.* putovanje
traveler /'traevler/ *n.* putnik
tray /trej/ *n.* tacna, poslužavnik, tabla; tepsija
treacherous /'treč,r,s/ *adj.* izdajnički
treachery /'treč,ri/ *n.* izdaja
treason /'tri:zn/ *n.* izdaja
treasure /'trež,r/ *n.* blago; *v.* gomilati, skupljati
treat /tri:t/ *v.* postupati, tretirati; *n.* gošćenje, gozba
treaty /tri:ti/ *n.* ugovor
tree /tri:/ *n.* drvo
tremble /'trembl/ *v.* drhtati, titrati; *n.* drhtanje
tremendous /tri'mend,s/ *adj.* ogroman, silan, strahovit
trend /trend/ *n.* smjer, tok
trespass /'trespas/ *v.* kršiti (zakon.pravo); ometati posjed
trespass /'trespas/ *n.* zabranjen prolaz

trial /'traj,l/ *n.* proba, pokus; ispitivanje, proces
triangle /'trajaengl/ *n.* trokut, trougao
tribe /trajb *n.* pleme, rod
trick /trik/ *n.* trik, varka, lukavština; *v.* prvariti
tricky /triki/ *adj.* težak, pun zamki
trifle /'trajfl/ *n.* trica, sitnica, malenkost
trigger /'trig,r/ *n.* oroz puške, okidač; *v.* okinuti
trim /trim/ *v.* podrezati; dotjerati
trip /trip/ *n.* izlet, putovanje; *v.* skakutati, posrtati
triple /tripl/ *adj.* trostruk
triumph /'traj,mf/ *n.* pobjeda, uspjeh, trijumf
troop /tru:p/ *n.* trupa; mnoštvo; jato; krdo
trouble /'trabl/ *n.* nevolja, neprilika; *v.* zabrinjavati, mučiti
troublesome /'trabl,sam/ *adj.* neugodan, dosadan, zahmetli
trousers /'trauz,s/ *pl.* pantalone, hlače
trout /traut/ *n.* pastrmka, pastrva
truce /tru:s/ *n.* primirje
truck /trak/ *n.* kamion
true /tru:/ *n.* istina; *adj.* istinit, ispravan
trunk /trank/ *n.* deblo, balvan; trup
trust /trast/ *n.* povjerenje, pouzdanje, nada
truth /tru:s/ *n.* istina
try /traj/ *v.* pokušati, probati
tub /tab/ *n.* kada; bure, kaca, tekne
tube /tju:b/ *n.* cijev, tuba, rora
Tuesday /'tju:zdi/ *n.* utorak
tumble /'tambl/ *v.* prevrnuti (se),prebacivati (se)
tune /tju:n/ *n.* melodija
tunnel /'tanl/ *n.* tunel
turkey /'t,:rki/ *n.* ćurka, tuka, puran
turn /t,:n/ *n.* okret, zaokret; *v.* skrenuti; zavrnuti
turn off /t,:rn of/ *v.* zatvoriti
turn on /t,:rn on/ *v.* otvoriti
turtle /'t,:rtl/ *n.* kornjača
tweezers /'tvi:z,s/ *n.* klješta; pinceta

twelve /tvelv/ *num.* dvanaest
twenty /tventi/ *num.* dvadeset
twin /tvin/ *n.* blizanac, bliznac; dvostruk
twist /tvist/ *v.* okretati, zavijati; *n.* okretanje, uvijanje
two /tu:/ *num.* dva
type /tajp/ *n.* tip; uzorak; *v.* kucati na mašinu, tipkati
typewriter /'tajp,rajt,r/ *n.* pisaća mašina, šrajb mašina
typical /'tipik,l/ *adj.* tipičan, karakterističan
typist /'tajpist/ *n.* daktilograf

U

ugliness /'aglinis/ *n.* ružnoća
ugly /'agli/ *adj.* ružan, gadan, odvratan
ulcer /'als,r/ *n.* čir, zagnjojena rana
ultimate /'altimit/ *adj.* konačan, krajnji
umbrella /am'brela/ *n.* kišobran, šemsija; suncobran
unable /'an'ejbl/ *adj.* nesposoban, nemoćan
unanimous /ju'naenim,s/ *adj.* jednodušan, jednoglasan
unarmed /'an'a:rmd/ *adj.* nenaoružan
unbearable /an'baer,bl/ *adj.* nepodnošljiv, nesnosan
unbelievable /,anbi'li:v,bl/ *adj.* nevjerovatan
unbutton /'an'bat,n/ *v.* otkopčati (se), raskopčati (se)
uncle /'ankl/ *n.* ujak, dajdja; stric, amidja
uncommon /an'kom,n/ *adj.* neobičan, rijedak
uncover /an'kav,r/ *v.* otkriti; razotkriti
under /'and,r/ *prep.* ispod, pod, donji, podredjen
underdeveloped /,and,rdi'vel,pt/ *adj.* nerazvijen, zaostao
underdone /,and,r'dan/ *adj.* nekuvan, nedopečen
underestimate /'and,r'estimejt/ *v.* podcijeniti, loše procijeniti
undergo /,and,rgo/ *v.* pretrpjeti
undergraduate /,and,r'graedjuit/ *n.* student
underground /'and,r,graund/ *adj.* podzemni
underline /'and,rlajn/ *v.* podcrtati, podvući
undermine /,and,r'majn/ *v.* potkopati, oslabiti
underneath /,and,r'ni:s/ *adv.* dole, niže
undershirt /,and,r'š,:t/ *n.* podkošulja
understand,-stood,-stood /,and,r'staend, -stud, -stud/ *v.* razumjeti,
shvatiti, anlajisati
understate /,and,rstejt/ *v.* umanjiti, kazati manje
undertake /,and,r'tejk/ *v.* preduzeti, poduhvatiti se (nečega)
underwear /,and,rvae/ *n.* donje rublje, veš
undisciplined /an'disiplind/ *adj.* nedisciplinovan
undress /an'dres/ *adj.* neobućen, obnažen

uneasy /an'i:zi/ *adj.* nespokojan
unemployed /,anem'plojd/ *adj.* nezaposlen
unemployment /an'emplojm,nt/ *n.* nezaposlenost
uneven /'an'i:v,n/ *adj.* nejednak; hrapav; nepravedan
unexpected /'aniks'paektid/ *adj.* neočekivan
unfair /'an'fe,r/ *adj.* nepošten, nepravedan
unfaithful /'an'fejsful/ *adj.* netačan, neistinit
unfit /'an'fit/ *adj.* nepodesan
unfold /'an'fould/ *v.* raširiti, razmotati
unfortunate /an'fo:rčnit/ *adj.* nesretan, baksuz
unfriendly /'an'frendli/ *adj.* neprijateljski, neprijazan
unfurnished /'an'f,:rnišd/ *adj.* nenamješten
unhealthy /'an'helsi/ *adj.* nezdrav
uniform /'ju:nifo:rm/ *n.* uniforma, mondura; *adj.* jednoličan
union /'ju:nj,n/ *n.* savez, unija
unique /ju:'ni:k/ *adj.* jedinstven
unit /'ju:nit/ *n.* jedinica
unite /'ju:'najt/ *v.* ujediniti se
universe /ju:ni'v,:s/ *n.* svemir, kosmos
university /ju:ni'versiti/ *n.* univerzitet
unjust /'an'džast/ *adj.* nepravedan
unknown /an'noun/ *adj.* nepoznat, neznan
unless /an'les/ conj. osim da; ako ne
unlike /'an'lajk/ *adj.* različit, za razliku od
unlikely /'an'lajkli/ *adj.* malo vjerovatno, bezizgledno
unload /'an'loud/ *v.* istovariti, iskrcati
unlock /'an'lok/ *v.* otključati
unreal /'an'ri:l/ *adj.* nerealan, iluzoran, nestvaran
unreliable /'anri'laj,bl/ *adj.* nepouzdan, nesiguran
unstable /an'stejbl/ *adj.* nestabilan
untidy /an'tajdi/ *adj.* neuredan, aljkav, nečist
until /an'til/ *prep.* do; conj. dok, dokle
unusual /an'ju:žu,l/ *adj.* neobičan, rjedak
up /ap/ *adv.* gore, u vis, naviše; uspravno

up-to-date /'ap-tu-dejt/ *adj.* aktuelan
upbringing /'ap,bringing/ *n.* vaspitanje, odgoj
upon /e'pon/ *prep.* na; *adv.* na gore
upper /'ap,r/ *adj.* gornji, viši
upright /'ap'rajt/ *adj.* uspravan; *n.* pianino
uprising /ap'rajzing/ *n.* ustanak, buna; ustajanje
upset /ap'set/ *v.* prevrnuti; uzbuditi; *adj.* uzbudjen, uzrujan
upside-down /'apsajd'daun/ *adj.* obrnuto; u neredu, naizvrat
upstairs /'ap'ste,z/ *adv.* gore, na gornjem katu
urge /'e:dž/ *n.* žurba, hitnja
urge /'e:dž/ *v.* požurivati, goniti
urgent /'e:dž,nt/ *adj.* hitan; uporan
urine /'ju,rin/ *n.* mokraća, urin
use /ju:z/ *v.* upotrebljavati, koristiti
use /ju:s/ *n.* upotreba, primjena
useful /'ju:sful/ *adj.* koristan, upotrebljiv
useless /'ju:zlis/ *adj.* bezkoristan, neupotrebljiv
usher /'aš,r/ *n.* vratar; *v.* uvesti, najaviti
usual /'ju:žu,l/ *adj.* uobičajen, normalan
usually /'ju:žu,li/ *adv.* obično
utter /'at,r/ *adj.* izjaviti, izreći

V

vacancy /'vejk,nsi/ *n.* praznina, nepopunjeno radno mjesto
vacant /'vejk,nt/ *adj.* prazan, nezaposjednut
vacation /ve'kejš,n/ *n.* raspust, odmor, ferije
vaccinate /'vaeksinejt/ *v.* cijepiti, vaksinisati
vague /vejg/ *adj.* nejasan, mutan, neodredjen
vain /vejn/ *adj.* sujetan, uobražen, tašt
valiant /'vaelj,nt/ *adj.* hrabar
valid /'vaelid/ *adj.* osnovan, dokazan, valjan
valley /'vaeli/ *n.* dolina
valuable /'vaelju,bl/ *adj.* vrijedan, dragocjen
value /'vaelju:/ *n.* vrijednost
valve /vaelv/ *n.* ventil, zalisak
van /vaen/ *n.* zatvorena kola, vagon
vanish /'vaenish/ *v.* nestati, nestajati
variable /'vaeri,bl/ *adj.* promjenjiv
variety /v,'raj,ti/ *n.* raznolikost
various /'ve,rj,s/ *adj.* različit, raznolik
varnish /'va:rniš/ *n.* lak; *v.* lakirati
vary /'vaeri/ *v.* mijenjati, promijeniti
vase /vejz/ *n.* vazna, vaza
veal /vi:l/ *n.* teletina
vegetable /'vedžit,bl/ *n.* povrće
vehicle /'vi:kl/ *n.* vozilo; sredstvo
veil /vejl/ *n.* veo, šlajer
vein /vejn/ *n.* vena; sklonost
velocity /vi'lositi/ *n.* brzina
velvet /'velvit/ *n.* samt, baršun, kadifa
vent /vent/ *n.* otvor; *v.* dati oduška
venture /'venč,r/ *n.* rizik, stavljanje na kocku
verb /v,:rb/ *n.* glagol
verbal /v,:bl/ *adj.* usmen, verbalan
verdict /'v,:dikt/ *n.* presuda

verify /'verifaj/ *v.* potvrditi, ovjeriti
versatile /'v,:rs,tajl/ *adj.* mnogostran, okretan
vertical /'v,:rtik,l/ *adj.* okomit, vertikalan
very /'veri/ *adv.* vrlo
vessel /'vesl/ *n.* posuda; brod
vest /vest/ *n.* podkošulja, majica; prsluk
veto /'vitou/ *n.* veto, zabrana
vex /vaeks/ *v.* dosadjivati, mučiti
vibrate /vaj'brejt/ *v.* vibrirati, titrati
vice /vajs/ *n.* porok, mana
vicious /'viš,z/ *adj.* pokvaren, opak
victim /'viktim/ *n.* žrtva
victory /'vikt,ri/ *n.* pobjeda
view /vju:/ *v.* razgledati; *n.* vidik, pogled, prizor
vigorous /'vig,r,z/ *adj.* snažan
village /'vilidž/ *n.* selo
vindicate /'vindikejt/ *v.* pravdati, braniti
vine /vajn/ *n.* vino
violate /'vaj,lejt/ *v.* povrijediti, prekršiti
violence /'vaj,l,ns/ *n.* nasilje
violent /'vaj,l,nt/ *adj.* silovit, nasilan, žestok
violet /'vaj,lit/ *n.* ljubičica; *adj.* ljubičast
violin /,vaj,lin/ *n.* violina
virgin /'v,:rdžin/ *n.* djevica
virtue /'v,:rčju/ *n.* vrlina, krepost
visibility /vizi'biliti/ *n.* vidljivost
vision /'viž,n/ *n.* vidjenje, vizija, san
visit /'vizit/ *v.* posjetiti
visitor /'vizit,r/ *n.* posjetilac
vital /'vajtl/ *adj.* životni, vitalan
vivid /'vivid/ *adj.* živahan
vocabulary /vou'kaebjul,ri/ *n.* lista riječi
vocal /'vouk,l/ *n.* samoglasnik; *adj.* zvučan, glasan

vogue /voug/ *adj.* moderan
voice /vois/ *n.* glas
void /vojd/ *adj.* bez zakonske vrijednosti; poništen; prazan;
n. praznina
voluntary /'vol,nt,ri/ *adj.* dobrovoljan
vomit /'vomit/ *v.* povraćati, bljuvati
vote /vout/ *v.* glasati, izabrati; *n.* glasanje
vow /vau/ *v.* zakleti se, zavjetovati se
voyage /'vojidž/ *n.* putovanje; *v.* putovati
vulgar /'valg,r/ *adj.* prost, običan, vulgaran
vulnerable /'valn,r,bl/ *adj.* ranjiv

W

wade /vejd/ *v.* pregaziti; mučiti se; *n.* gaz; prelaz
wages /vejdžis/ *n.* plata, nadnica
wagon /vaeg,n/ *n.* vagon, teretna želj. kola
wail /vejl/ *v.* oplakivati, naricati; *n.* jadikovka, plač
waist /vejst/ *n.* struk, pas; pojas
wait /vejt/ *v.* čekati
waiter /'vejt,r/ *n.* konobar, kelner
waitress /'vejtres/ *n.* konobarica, kelnerica
wake /vejk/ *v.* probuditi se; bdjeti
wale /vejl/ *n.* masnica, modrica
walk /vo:k/ *v.* šetati; hodati; *n.* šetnja
wall /vo:l/ *n.* zid, duvar; stijena; *v.* ograditi, ozidati
wallet /'volit/ *n.* novčanik, budjelar; aktovka
wallow /volou/ *v.* valjati se, kotrljati se
walnut /'vo:ln,t/ *n.* orah
wander /'vond,r/ *v.* lutati, tumarati
wane /vejn/ *v.* nestajati, gasnuti
want /vo:nt/ *v.* željeti, trebati, tražiti; *n.* oskudica, potreba
war /vor/ *n.* rat
wardrobe /'vo:droub/ *n.* garderoba, ormar za odijela
warehouse /'ve,rhaus/ *n.* skladiište, magazin; ambar
warm /vo:m/ *adj.* topao; *v.* zagrijati (se)
warm up /vo:m'ap/ *v.* podgrijati
warn /vo:n/ *v.* upozoriti, opomenuti
warrant /vor,nt/ *n.* punomoć; potjernica; *v.* garantovati, jamčiti
warrior /'vori,r/ *n.* ratnik
wash /voš/ *v.* prati; izapirati
washing /'vo:šing/ *n.* pranje; veš za pranje
wasp /vosp/ *n.* osa
waste /vejst/ *adj.* neupotrebljiv, otpadni; *v.* rasipati, tračiti
wasteful /'vejstful/ *adj.* rasipan
watch /voč/ *v.* posmatrati, motriti; *n.* ručni sat; pažnja

water /vot,:/ *n.* voda; *v.* zaliti, politi; natopiti; nakvasiti
watermelon /'vo:t,r,mel,n/ *n.* lubenica, karpuza
wave /vejv/ *n.* val, talas; *v.* njihati se; mahati
wavy /'vejvi/ *adj.* valovit, talasast
wax /vaeks/ *n.* vosak; *v.* navoštiti, naviksati
way /vej/ *n.* put; pruga; način; sredstvo; stanje
we /vi:/ pron. mi
weak /vi:k/ *adj.* slab, nejak
weaken /vi:kn/ *v.* oslabiti
weakness /vi:knis/ *n.* slabost
wealth /vels/ *n.* bogatstvo; blagostanje; dobrobit, bonluk
wealthy /'velsi/ *adj.* bogat, imućan
weapon /'vep,n/ *n.* oružje
wear, wore, worn /ve,r, vo:r, vo:rn/ *v.* nositi, imati na sebi
weary /'vi,ri/ *adj.* umoran, zamoran
weather /'vedz,r/ *n.* vrijeme (atmosfersko)
weave, wove, woven /vi:v, vouv, vouvn/ *v.* plesti; tkati
web /veb/ *n.* paučina; paukova mreža; nec; tkivo
wedding /'veding/ *n.* vjenčanje
Wednesday /'venzdi/ *n.* srijeda
weed /vi:d/ *n.* korov, kukolj; *v.* pljeviti
week /vi:k/ *n.* sedmica, tjedan, hefta
weekend /'vi:kend/ *n.* vikend; kraj sedmice (subota i nedelja)
weep, wept /vi:p, vept/ *v.* plakati, oplakivati
weigh /vej/ *v.* vagati, mjeriti težinu
weight /vejt/ *n.* težina; teg, uteg, geviht
welcome /'velk,m/ *n.* dobrodošlica
well /vel/ *n.* izvor, vrelo, zdenac; okno *v.* izvirati
well, better, best /vel, bet,r, best/ *adj.* dobar, koji zadovoljava
west /vest/ *n.* zapad; *adj.* zapadni; *adv.* zapadno
wet /vet/ *adj.* mokar, vlažan
whale /vejl/ *n.* kit
what /vot/ *adj.* šta; koje; kako; koliko
whatever /'vot'ev,r/ *adj.* ma šta, ma koliko, koji god
whatsoever /'votso'ev,r/ *adj.* ma šta, ma koliko, koji god

wheat /vi:t/ *n.* pšenica, žito
wheel /vi:l/ *n.* točak, kolut, kotur; *v.* okretati
when /ven/ *adv.* kada, ćim, dok
whence /venc/ *adv.* odakle, prema tome
whenever /'venev,r/ *adv.* bilo kada
where /ve,/ *adv.* gdje, odakle, kuda
whether /'vedz,r/ *conj.* bilo da; da li
which /vič/ *pron.* koji, koja, koje
while /vajl/ *conj.* dok, dokle; *n.* trenutak, momenat
whip /vip/ *n.* bič, šipka, šiba, korbač, kandjija
whirl /v,:rl/ *v.* vrtjeti
whirlpool /w,:rpu:l/ *n.* vrtlog
whisk /visk/ *v.* tući snijeg; *n.* metlica; četka
whisper /'visp,r/ *v.* šaptati
whistle /'visl/ *v.* zviždati; fićukati; *n.* zvižduk
white /vajt/ *adj.* bijel, čist
who /hu:/ *pron.* ko, koji, koja, koje
whoever /hu:'ev,r/ *pron.* bilo ko
whole /houl/ *adj.* cijeli; potpun, čitav, sav
whom /hu:m/ *pron.* koga, koje
whose /hu:z/ *pron.* čiji, čija, čije
why /vaj/ *adv.* zašto; čemu
wicked /'vikid/ *adj.* zloćest, zao
wicker /'vik,r/ *n.* šiba, prut
wicker basket /'vik, bskit/ *n.* korpa od pruća, sepet
wide /vajd/ *adj.* širok, prostran
widow /'vidou/ *n.* udovica
widower /'vidouv,r/ *n.* udovac
width /vidz/ *n.* širina, prostranstvo
wife /vajf/ *n.* žena, supruga
wig /vig/ *n.* perika; ukor
wild /vajld/ *adj.* divlji; nenaseljen
wilderness /'vild,nis/ *n.* divljina
will /vil/ *n.* volja, amanet, testament; *v.* željeti, htjeti, namjeravati
willing /,viling/ *adj.* voljan, spreman

willow /'vilou/ *n.* vrba

win, won /vin, von/ *v.* dobiti, postići, pobijediti

wind /vind/ *n.* vjetar; nadimanje

wind /vajnd/ *v.* namotavati; zavrtati

window /'vindou/ *n.* prozor, pendjer

windy /vindi/ *adj.* vjetrovito

wine /vajn/ *n.* vino

wing /ving/ *n.* krilo; *v.* letjeti

winner /'vin,r/ *n.* pobjednik

winter /'vint,r/ *n.* zima

wipe /vajp/ *v.* obrisati; *n.* brisanje

wire /vaj,r/ *n.* žica; telegram; *v.* telegrafisati

wisdom /'vizd,m/ *n.* mudrost

wise /vajz/ *adj.* mudar, razborit

wish /viš/ *n.* želja; *v.* željeti

wit /vit/ *n.* duhovitost; dosjetka

witch /vič/ *n.* vještica, čarobnica

with /vidz/ *prep.* sa, s; pokraj; zbog

withdraw /viz'drou/ *v.* povući se

wither /'vidz,r/ *v.* venuti, usahnuti

within /vidz'in/ *adv.* unutar; iznutra

without /vidzaut/ *prep.* bez, izvan; *adv.* izvana

withstand /vidz'staend/ *v.* podnjeti, izdržati; odoljeti

witness /'vitnis/ *n.* svjedok; *v.* svjedočiti

witty /'viti/ *adj.* duhovit

wives /vajvz/ *n. pl.* žene; supruge

wizard /'viz,rd/ *n.* čarobnjak, vrač

woe /vou/ *n.* jad, tuga, nesreća, bol, dert

wolf /vulf/ *n.* vuk, kurjak

woman /'vum,n/ *n.* žena

womb /vu:m/ *n.* maternica

women /'vimin/ *n. pl.* žene

wonder /'vand,r/ *n.* čudo, čuđenje; *v.* pitati se, čuditi se

wonderful /'vand,ful/ *adj.* divan, izvanredan

wood /vu:d/ *n.* drvo; šuma

wool /vu:l/ *n.* vuna
word /v,:rd/ *n.* riječ; lozinka
work /w,:k/ *n.* rad, posao, zanimanje; *v.* raditi
worker /'v,:rk,r/ *n.* radnik
workshop /'w,:rkšop/ *n.* radionica
world /v,:rld/ *n.* svijet, zemaljska kugla, dunjaluk
worm /vo:rm/ *n.* crv
worry /v,:ri/ *n.* briga; *v.* brinuti se
worse /v,:s/ *adj.* gori, lošiji
worship /'v,:ršip/ *n.* obožavanje, poštovanje; *v.* obožavati, poštovati
worst /v,:rst/ *adj.* najgori, najlošiji
worth /v,:rs/ *n.* vrijednost; *adj.* vrijedan
worthless /'v,:rslis/ *adj.* nekoristan, bezvrijedan
worthwhile /v,:rsvajl/ *adj.* vrijedan, koji se isplati
wound /vu:nd/ *n.* rana; *v.* raniti
wrap /raep/ *v.* zamotati, zaviti
wrath /ro:dz/ *n.* bijes, ljutina, žestina
wreck /rek/ *n.* olupina; propast; *v.* pretrpjeti (skriviti) brodolom
wrestle /'resl/ *v.* hrvati se
wrinkle /'rinkl/ *n.* bora; *v.* naborati se
wrist /rist/ *n.* ručni zglob
write, wrote, written /rajt, rout, rit,n/ *v.* pisati, napisati
writer /'rajt,r/ *n.* pisac, književnik; pisar
writing /'rajting/ *n.* pisanje; pismo; rukopis
wrong /ro:ng/ *adj.* pogrešan; nepravedan; *v.* načiniti nepravdu

X

Xmas (Christmas) /'krism,s/ *n.* Božić
x-ray /'eks'rej/ *n.* x-zraci
xylophone /'zilefoun/ *n.* ksilofon

Y

yacht /jo:t/ *n.* jahta; *v.* voziti se na jahti
Yankee /'jaenki/ *n.* Jenki (Sjevernoamerikanac)
yard /ja:rd/ *n.* jard (0.914 metara)
yarn /ja:n/ *n.* predja; uže; *v.* pričati priče
yawn /jo:n/ *v.* zijevati; zjapiti; *n.* ždrijelo; provalija
year /j,:r/ *n.* godina, ljeto
yearn /j,:n/ *v.* čeznuti, žudjeti
yeast /ji:st/ *n.* kvasac; previranje
yell /jel/ *v.* vikati, vrištati
yellow /'jelou/ *n.* žut
yes /jes/ *adv.* da, jeste
yesterday /'jest,di/ *n.* jučer
yet /jet/ conj. još
yield /ji:ld/ *v.* dopustiti; donijeti plod/prihod
yolk /jouk/ *n.* žumance
you /ju:/ pron. ti, vi
young /jang/ *adj.* mlad; svjež; neiskusan
your /jo:/ pron. tvoj, vaš
youth /ju:s/ *n.* mladost
youthful /'ju:sful/ *adj.* mladalački

Z

zeal /ziːl/ *n.* žar, predanost, revnost
zealous /ˈzel,s/ *adj.* predan, revnostan
zero /ˈzirou/ *n.* nula, ništica
zest /zest/ *n.* slast; začin; nadražaj
zipper /ˈzip,r/ *n.* rajferšlus, ciferšlus, patentni zatvarač
zone /zoun/ *n.* područje, zona
zoo /zuː/ *n.* zoološki vrt

Abbreviations Used in U.S.A.
Kratice korištene u SAD

AAA	American Automobile Association—Auto-moto društvo
ABC	American Broadcast Corporation—Američka Radio Korp.
Acct.	Account—račun
A.D.	Anno Domini (lat.)—ljeta gospodnjeg, odredjene godine
AIDS	Sindrom smanjenja otpornosti organizma (SIDA)
AL	Alabama—Država unutar SAD
AK	Alaska—Država unutar SAD
a.m.	Ante Meridiem (lat.)— prije podne
Approx.	Approximately—približno, otprilike
AR	Arkanzas—Država unutar SAD
Ave	Avenue—avenija
AZ	Arizona —Država unutar SAD
BBC	British Broadcast Corporation—Britanska Radio Korporacija
Bldg	Building—zgrada
Blvd	Boulevard—bulevar
CA	California—Država unutar SAD
CAN	Canada
Cir	Circle—kružni tok
c/o	Care of—posredstvom treće osobe (kod nekoga, na adresi)
CNN	Cable Network News—televizijska stanica u SAD
CO	Colorado—Država unutar SAD
Co.	Company —kompanija, društvo
Corp.	Corporation—korporacija, firma, preduzeće
CT	Connecticut—Država unutar SAD
Ctr	Center —centar
C.V.	Curriculum Vitae (lat.)—rezime, pregled kretanja u službi
DE	Delaware—Država unutar SAD

Dept.	Department—odjeljenje, sektor, služba
DC	District of Columbia—Nezavisna oblast okolo Washingtona
Doz.	Dozen—tuce, dvanaest komada
Dr.	Drive—kolovoz, put
e.g.	Exempli Gratia (lat)—na primjer
Eq.	Equal—jednak
ESL	English as a Second Language—Kurs engleskog jezika za učenike kojima engleski nije maternji jezik
Esp.	Especially—naročito
Est.	Estate—imanje, posjed
etc.	Et cetera (lat.)—i t.d. (i tako dalje)
Ex.	Example—primjer
Expy.	Expressway—vrsta autoputa
Ext.	Extension—produžetak, dodatak
FL	Florida—Država unutar SAD
Ft.	Fort—tvrdjava, utvrda
GA	Georgia—Država unutar SAD
G.B.	Great Britain—Velika Britanija
HI	Hawaii—Država unutar SAD
Hts.	Heights—visoravan
Hwy.	Highway—cesta za automobile
IA	Iowa—Država unutar SAD
ID	Idaho—Država unutar SAD
i.e.	id est (lat.)—to jest
IL	Illinois—Država unutar SAD
IN	Indiana—Država unutar SAD
Inc.	Incorporated—inkorporiran, udružen; oznaka za firme sa ograničenom odgovornošću
Is.	Island—ostrvo
KS	Kansas—Država unutar SAD
KY	Kentucky—Država unutar SAD
LA	Lousiana—Država unutar SAD
Ln.	Lane—sporedni put (česta oznaka uz naziv ulice)
MA	Massachusetts—Država unutar SAD
ME	Maine—Država unutar SAD
MD	Maryland—Država unutar SAD
MI	Michigan—Država unutar SAD

MN	Minnesota—Država unutar SAD
MO	Missouri—Država unutar SAD
Mo.	Month—mjesec
Mos.	Months—mjeseci
MS	Mississippi—Država unutar SAD
MT	Montana—Država unutar SAD
Mt.	Mountain—planina
NC	North Carolina—Država unutar SAD
ND	North Dakota—Država unutar SAD
NE	Nebraska—Država unutar SAD
NH	New Hampshire—Država unutar SAD
NJ	New Jersey—Država unutar SAD
NM	New Mexico—Država unutar SAD
NV	Nevada—Država unutar SAD
NY	New York—Država unutar SAD
OH	Ohio—Država unutar SAD
OK	Oklahoma—Država unutar SAD
OR	Oregon—Država unutar SAD
PA	Pennsylvania—Država unutar SAD
Pl.	Place—mjesto (oznaka uz ime ulice, obično slijepe)
Pky.	Parkway—autoput
p.m.	Post Meridiem (lat.)—poslije podne
PR	Puerto Rico
Pvt.	Private—privatno
Rd.	Road—cesta
RI	Rhode Island—Država unutar SAD
SC	South Carolina—Država unutar SAD
SD	South Dakota—Država unutar SAD
Sq.	Square—trg
St.	Street—ulica
Ter.	Terrace—terase (oznaka na nekim ulicama ili područjima)
TN	Tennessee—Država unutar SAD
Tpke.	Turnpike—glavni autoput
TX	Texas—Država unutar SAD
UT	Utah—Država unutar SAD
VA	Virginia—Država unutar SAD

vs.	Versus—protiv
VT	Vermont—Država unutar SAD
WA	Washington—Država unutar SAD
WI	Wisconsin—Država unutar SAD
Wt.	Weight—težina
WV	West Virginia—Država unutar SAD
WY	Wyoming—Država unutar SAD

NUMERALS
BROJEVI

Cardinal Numbers		Prirodni brojevi
1	jedan	one
2	dva	two
3	tri	three
4	četiri	four
5	pet	five
6	šest	six
7	sedam	seven
8	osam	eight
9	devet	nine
10	deset	ten
11	jedanaest	eleven
12	dvanaest	twelve
13	trinaest	thirteen
14	četrnaest	fourteen
15	petnaest	fifteen
16	šesnaest	sixteen
17	sedamnaest	seventeen
18	osamnaest	eighteen
19	devetnaest	nineteen
20	dvadeset	twenty
21	dvadeset i jedan	twenty-one
29	dvadeset i devet	twenty-nine
30	trideset	thirty
31	trideset i jedan	thirty-one
39	trideset i devet	thirty-nine
40	četrdeset	forty
50	pedeset	fifty
60	šezdeset	sixty
70	sedamdeset	seventy
80	osamdeset	eighty
90	devedeset	ninety
100	stotinu	hundred

101	stotinu i jedan	one hundred and one
999	devet stotina dvedeset i devet	nine hundred ninety nine
1,000	hiljadu	one thousand
1,001	hiljadu i jedan	one thousand and one
9,999	devet hiljada devetsto devedeset i devet	nine thousand nine hundred ninety nine
99,999	devedeset devet hiljada devetsto devedeset i devet	ninety nine thousand nine hundred ninety nine

100,000	stotinu hiljada	hundred thousand
1,000,000	milion	million
1,000,000,000	milijarda	billion
1,000,000,000,000	trilion	trillion

Ordinal Numbers
Redni brojevi

1	prvi	first
2	drugi	second
3	treći	third
4	četvrti	fourth
5	peti	fifth
6	šesti	sixth
7	sedmi	seventh
8	osmi	eighth
9	deveti	ninth
10	deseti	tenth
11	jedanaesti	eleventh
12	dvanaesti	twelfth
13	trinaesti	thirteenth
14	četrnaesti	fourteenth
15	petnaesti	fifteenth
16	šesnaesti	sixteenth
17	sedamnaesti	seventeenth
18	osamnaesti	eighteenth
19	devetnaesti	nineteenth

20	dvadeseti	twentieth
21	dvadesetprvi	twenty-first
22	dvadesetdrugi	twenty-second
23	dvadesettreći	twenty-third
30	trideseti	thirtieth
31	tridesetprvi	thirty-first
40	četrdeseti	fortieth
41	četresetprvi	forty-first
50	pedeseti	fiftieth
51	pedesetprvi	fifty-first
60	šezdeseti	sixtieth
61	šezdesetprvi	sixty-first
70	sedamdeseti	seventieth
71	sedamdesetprvi	seventy-first
80	osamdeseti	eightieth
81	osamdesetprvi	eighty-first
90	devedeseti	ninetieth
100	stoti	hundredth
101	sto i prvi	hundred and first
200	dvjestoti	two hundredth
300	tristoti	three hundredth
1,000	hiljaditi	one thousandth
1,740	hiljadu sedamsto četrdeseti	seventeen hundred and forty
2,000	dvijehiljaditi	two thousandth
1,000,000	milioniti	billionth(Am.) millionth(Br.)

Other Numerical Values
Drugi brojni izrazi

jednostruko	single
dvostruko	double
trostruko	triple, threefold
četverostruko	fourfold, quadruple

peterostruko	fivefold
jedamput	once
dvaput	twice
triput, četiriput, pet puta	three, four, five times
dvaput toliko	twice as much
još jednom	once more
u prvom redu	firstly
u drugom redu	secondly

2x5=10 two times five equals ten (twice five is ten)
2+7=9 two plus seven equals nine
10-3=7 ten minus three equals seven
15÷3=5 fifteen divided by three equals five

1/2	one-half
1 1/2	one and one-half
1/2 hour	half an hour
2/3	two-thirds
1/4	one-fourth
3 4/5	three and four-fifths

0.7	point seven (seven-tenths)
2.6	two point six (two and six-tenths)

$265.75	two hundred sixty five dollars and 75 cents
$95.00	ninety-five dollars

American Measures
Američke mjere

1 inch (in; 1") = 2.54 cm
1 foot (ft; 1') = 12" = 30.48 cm
1 yard (yd.) = 3 feet = 91.44 cm
1 mile (ml) = 5280 ft. = 1609.32 m = 1.60932 km

1 ounce (oz.) = 28.35 g
1 pound (lb.) = 16 ounces = 453.59 g
1 ton = 2000 lbs = 907.184 kg

1 gallon (gal.) = 4 qts = 4.543 l
1 pint = 0.473 l
1 quart = 2 pints = 0.946 l

1 acre = 0.405 hectares (ha)

1 Fahrenheit (°F) = 32 + 9/5 °C
1 Centigrade (°C) = 5/9 °F - 32

1 dozen (doz.) = 12 kom.
1 gross = 12 dozen = 144 kom.
1 score = 20 kom.

MORE SLAVIC AND BALTIC
DICTIONARIES FROM HIPPOCRENE

Bulgarian-English/English-Bulgarian
Practical Dictionary
0331   ISBN 0-87052-145-4 $8.95 pb

Byelorussian-English/English-Byelorussian
Concise Dictionary
1050   ISBN 0-87052-114-4 $9.95 pb

Czech-English/English-Czech Concise Dictionary
0276   ISBN 0-87052-981-1 $9.95 pb

Estonian-English/English-Estonian
Concise Dictionary
1010   ISBN 0-87052-081-4 $11.95 pb

Latvian-English/English-Latvian Dictionary
0194   ISBN 0-7818-0059-5 $14.95 pb

Lithuanian-English/English-Lithuanian
Concise Dictionary
0489   ISBN 0-7818-0151-6 $11.95 pb

Russian-English/English-Russian
Standard Dictionary
0440   ISBN 0-7818-0083-8 $16.95 pb

English-Russian Standard Dictionary
1025   ISBN 0-87052-100-4 $11.95 pb

Russian-English Standard Dictionary
0578   ISBN 0-87052-964-1 $11.95 pb

Russian-English/English-Russian
Concise Dictionary
0262   ISBN 0-7818-0132-X $11.95 pb

Slovak-English/English-Slovak Concise Dictionary
1052   ISBN 0-87052-115-2 $8.95 pb

Ukrainian-English/English Ukrainian
Practical Dictionary
1055   ISBN 0-87052-116-0 $8.95 pb

Ukrainian-English/English-Ukrainian
Standard Dictionary
0006   ISBN 0-7818-0189-3 $16.95 pb

All prices subject to change.

HIPPOCRENE HANDY DICTIONARIES

Common phrases are conveniently listed through key words. Pronunciation follows each entry and a reference section reviews all major grammar points. *Handy Extras* are extra helpful—offering even more words and phrases.

ARABIC
$8.95 • 0-87052-960-9

CHINESE
$8.95 • 0-87052-050-4

CZECH EXTRA
$8.95 • 0-7818-0138-9

DUTCH
$8.95 • 0-87052-049-0

FRENCH
$8.95 • 0-7818-0010-2

GERMAN
$8.95 • 0-7818-0014-5

GREEK
$8.95 • 0-87052-961-7

HUNGARIAN EXTRA
$8.95 • 0-7818-0164-8

ITALIAN
$8.95 • 0-7818-0011-0

JAPANESE
$8.95 • 0-87052-962-5

KOREAN
$8.95 • 0-7818-0082-X

PORTUGUESE
$8.95 • 0-87052-053-9

RUSSIAN
$8.95 • 0-7818-0013-7

SERBO-CROATIAN
$8.95 • 0-87052-051-2

SLOVAK EXTRA
$8.95 • 0-7818-0101-X

SPANISH
$8.95 • 0-7818-0012-9

SWEDISH
$8.95 • 0-87052-054-7

THAI
$8.95 • 0-87052-963-3

TURKISH
$8.95 • 0-87052-982-X